The Dizzy and Daffy Dean
Barnstorming Tour

The Dizzy and Daffy Dean Barnstorming Tour

Race, Media, and America's National Pastime

Phil S. Dixon

ROWMAN & LITTLEFIELD
Lanham • Boulder • New York • London

Published by Rowman & Littlefield
An imprint of The Rowman & Littlefield Publishing Group, Inc.
4501 Forbes Boulevard, Suite 200, Lanham, Maryland 20706
www.rowman.com

6 Tinworth Street, London, SE11 5AL, United Kingdom

British Library Cataloguing in Publication Information Available

Library of Congress Cataloging-in-Publication Data

Names: Dixon, Phil, author.
Title: The Dizzy and Daffy Dean barnstorming tour : race, media, and
   America's national pastime / Phil S. Dixon.
Description: Lanham : Rowman & Littlefield, [2019] | Includes bibliographical
   references and index.
Identifiers: LCCN 2019005903 (print) | LCCN 2019011310 (ebook) | ISBN
   9781538127407 (Electronic) | ISBN 9781538127391 (cloth : alk. paper)
Subjects: LCSH: Dean, Dizzy, 1910–1974. | Dean, Paul, 1913–1981. | Exhibition
   games—Press coverage—United States. | Negro leagues—History. | Racism
   in sports—United States—History—20th century.
Classification: LCC GV865.D4 (ebook) | LCC GV865.D4 D59 2019 (print) | DDC
   796.3570922 [B] —dc23
LC record available at https://lccn.loc.gov/2019005903

~

Contents

~

Preface

The St. Louis Cardinals' World Series win of 1934 was the conclusion to an unforgettable season for most of Dizzy and Daffy's teammates. They took their World Series shares and left for home to live a life of leisure, but the Deans kept playing. They were determined to cash in on their popularity by barnstorming. Record crowds at the World Series were evidence that their good fortunes would continue.

Attendance for all seven games of the 1934 World Series was 281,510, an increase of 118,434 over the 1933 total, the year that the New York Giants beat the Washington Senators and drew 163,076 for five games. The average attendance for each game of the '33 World Series was 32,615, compared to 40,216 in 1934. Ironically, the Cardinals had only drawn a home attendance of 334,863 for the entire 1934 season at Sportsman's Park. The Dean's barnstorming tour versus four African American teams would draw in the neighborhood of 125,000 fans—almost half of what the Cardinals had drawn in 80 games. The World Series included a host of highly advertised stars—some eventually became Hall of Fame inductees. Who would have predicted that their African American opponents would have any potential Hall of Fame players in the future?

Ten members of the Baseball Hall of Fame at Cooperstown, New York, performed in the 1934 World Series. The list, with their Hall of Fame induction years, includes Detroit's Mickey Cochrane (1947), Charlie Gehringer (1949), Hank Greenberg (1956), and Leon "Goose" Goslin (1968). The list of 1934 Cardinals enshrined in Cooperstown includes Frankie Frisch (1947), Dizzy Dean (1953), Dazzy Vance (1955), Joe "Ducky" Medwick (1968), Jesse

Haines (1970), and Leo Durocher (1994). If you add Bill Klem (1953), one of the umpires, the number would increase to 11. Branch Rickey, the Cardinals general manager in 1934, was inducted into the Hall of Fame in 1967. Dizzy's barnstorming tour featured two Hall of Fame players, himself and Joe Medwick—unless you count the men who are inducted into the Hall of Fame from the Negro major leagues.

An additional eight Hall of Fame inductees, nine if you include J. L. Wilkinson (2006), owner of the Kansas City Monarchs—athletes and an owner not even considered to be of major-league respect in 1934—saw action as Dizzy and Daffy's opposition. The list, with their Hall of Fame induction years, includes Satchel Paige (1971), Josh Gibson (1972), James "Cool Papa" Bell (1974), Judy Johnson (1975), Oscar Charleston (1976), Wilber "Bullet" Rogan (1998), Andy Cooper (2006), and Jud Wilson (2006). Historically, this presents many obvious questions as to the ability of these respective players when appropriate media is presented and equality of recognition genuinely added to their record. There were other Negro major league professionals who faced the Deans that the Hall of Fame has failed to recognize—but someday should. Players like John Donaldson and Vic Harris need to be honored. It is ironic that the official Hall of Fame website still contains discriminatory information when discussing these players.

As pitchers, were either of the Deans a more valuable Hall of Fame asset than Chet Brewer, Webster McDonald, Stuart "Country" Jones, or Charlie Beverly? The answer is an absolute yes! Was Mickey Cochrane a more able-bodied catcher than T. J. Young, Frank Duncan, or Bill Perkins? The answer is still the same yes. If segregation of their leagues and propagandizing of their baseball product had not prevailed, would Dizzy Dean or Mickey Cochrane have commanded higher salaries than Josh Gibson, Oscar Charleston, or Jud Wilson? Research shows Cochrane was purchased by the Detroit Tigers in 1933, from the Philadelphia Athletics, for something like $100,000 plus the contract of a reserve Tigers catcher. Cochrane was reportedly earning $25,000 a year during the '34 season. For leading his team from the second division to within a game of winning the World Series, the Tigers paid him an additional $10,000 in bonus money.[1] Managers Wilber "Bullet" Rogan, Webster McDonald, George Scales, and Oscar Charleston, who led his Pittsburgh Crawfords to a championship title that same season, didn't receive a fraction of the money Cochrane received. Based on capital alone, the whole of America remained convinced that men in the National League and American League, and even those in the white minor leagues, were superior ballplayers—but history has proven that wasn't true. Psychologically and emotionally it was a false narrative of major-league proportions, which this book shows.

~

Acknowledgments

Much of the grunt work for this publication was completed between 1989 and 2000. There are benefits to not having deadlines; this book undoubtedly benefited from this limit on freedom called a deadline. Between those years, many books were published with tidbits of information about Dizzy and Daffy's 1934 tour, but important details, interviews, and an overall understanding of how the institution of racism was executed in American media, along with a general lack of U.S. racial culture, was often missing from their text. In other cases, these writers were far too unprepared to corroborate the pain and suffering of African American males in a society where second-class citizenship proliferated. Most of these authors did not relate well to the mistreatment and daily denial of full participation in the American dream. These mistakes and oversights had tragic implications in telling the story of the Deans' barnstorming tour. For this reason, I decided the time had come to get this story told, to give a voice to the African American athletes who played against Dizzy and Daffy, while exposing the media. We also needed to hear more of the brother's own voices, not statements produced exclusively by writers in the media. We were careful not to make the writers' past mistakes our mistake. There were many who were not only ready, but also willing to help with the research.

This work was enhanced greatly by personal interviews and important friendships acquired through a lifetime in sports research. Leon Day; Newt Allen; Chet Brewer; Clint Thomas; James "Cool Papa" Bell; Bennie Charleston, Oscar Charleston's brother; and Mike "Red" Berry, a former Kansas City

Monarchs pitcher, contributed. T. J. Young's brother, Maurice—who played with the 1927 Monarchs, and their sister, Ann Ward— helped this publication to look and feel different than any other book written on the topic. As a unit, they provided stories about their teams, hometowns, and families, and articulated the isolation of living in a world of discrimination. As descendents of former slaves, many had come from communities where local politicians ignored their plight. Most lived in the "Black Belt" of the major cities, where raw sewage spread pathogens and generated toxic conditions that were as repulsive to see as they were to smell. In these communities, poverty and racial division were overt. There were talented individuals in these diverse places who couldn't realize their worth, especially in professional baseball. This, however, never stopped them from pursuing their passion in America's great national pastime. Together we tried to make sense of a period in history that was often backward and discriminatory. I can still hear the pride in their voices, guiding and encouraging me to continue my work.

Other stories in this publication were given by people who never played baseball but were as much a part of the game as any fan. Frank Duncan's widow, Bernice; Newt Allen's widow, Mary; Eddie Dwight's widow, Georgia; Newt Joseph's widow, Beatrice Joseph Garner; and Vic Harris's widow, Dorothy, embraced my work and nurtured me like a loving son. I was given similar treatment by the children and other family members of these former players.

Wilber "Bullet" Rogan's son Wilber Jr. (aka "Little Bullet") helped tremendously with his firsthand accounts of his father. I will never forget our many conversations in his South Kansas City home as he reminisced about traveling with his father as a Monarchs batboy. The same is true of Frank Duncan Jr., on his father, Frank Duncan Sr., and his mother, Julia Lee. Gladys Catron, J. L. Wilkinson's daughter, conversed with me often from her antique store in St. Joseph, Missouri. Harriett Wickstrom, the daughter of Tom Baird, reminisced with me often from her home in Kansas City, Kansas. She spoke well in her parents memory and added important details on Dizzy and Daffy verbally handed down by her dad. Floyd Baird, Tom Baird's brother, also embraced me and my work. Bill Beverly supplied valuable information on his relative, the great lefty Charlie Beverly. I am forever indebted to them all.

During the early 1980s, area semiprofessional teams had reunions at the Eagles Hall in Kansas City, Kansas. I was fortunate to speak with Andy Yurchak about his brother Leo during one of my visits. Leo was a Dean All-Star. Dorsey Moulder, who was unable to talk when I met him in his apartment off the Country Club Plaza in Kansas City, provided his interview in written notes. He was loaded with information about his time with Ray L. Doan's

House of David team; his minor-league play; and games played against the Monarchs, with and without the Deans.

For almost 40 years I remained on the hunt for information, which I often found in the library. Professionals in libraries and historical societies from Oklahoma City to Brooklyn, New York, provided newspaper sources and photographs so important to this project. They were my teammates in helping to portray this information as it appeared regionally. Thanks to David Cox, interlibrary loan team leader at the Kansas City Public Library, for acquiring many of the newspapers quoted in this text. Kathy Lafferty, copy services manager/reference at the Spencer Research Library in Lawrence, Kansas, provided photographs from the Tom Baird collection. I wish to thank the UCLA Library Special Collections for the beautiful picture of Satchel Paige, which came from the *Los Angeles Times* collection. Equally as important was Hadley Barrett's letter from Valerie Fabbro, associate general counsel of the Topps Company, who orchestrated my permission for use of one of the company's baseball cards. The same is true of Jeffrey Korman at the City of Baltimore Enoch Pratt Free Library; Usha Thampi, reference librarian at the Paterson Free Public Library; Bruce R. Bardarik, local history librarian at the Paterson Free Public Library; K. A. Rogers, reference librarian at the Public Library of Columbus and Franklin County; Joan L. Clark, head of main library at the Cleveland Public Library; and Laurel Sher, research and reference/ILLINET coordinator for the Interlibrary Loan Center and the Chicago Public Library. Special thanks always to the staff of the Wichita-Sedgwick County Historical Museum for their display on the Dockum's Drug Store sit-in. This is my thank you for your unstinting support. Historians and researchers also contributed mightily to this text.

Jay Sanford of Denver, Colorado, assisted with information on the 1934 Denver Post tournament. Historian Tim Rives of Kansas contributed documentation on Tom Baird. Mike Mastrangelo of Big Springs, Maryland, did research on the Deans' Baltimore visit. The Society for American Baseball Research (SABR) provided articles by Bill Nowlin on Julius Solters, Robert Kline on Gordon McNaughton, Bob Buege on Amos "Red" Thisted, Chris Rainey on Uke Clanton, Charles F. Fabers on Joe Medwick, Jacob Pomrenke on John "Lefty" Sullivan, Chris Rainey on Kenny Hogan, and L. Robert David's written history on slugger Nick Cullop. These articles supplied invaluable information for the development of this manuscript.

My wife, Dr. Kerry Dixon, continues to be my "Rock of Gibraltar" through many books, historical projects, and hundreds of presentations. I thank God for putting you in my life and making you the mother of our three beautiful children.

I am forever indebted to each and every contribution to this work. We have produced a historical document that covers a period in American society that should not be forgotten or misconstrued. The book has been a long time coming. Yet, with the help of a select few, we have finally met our deadline.

~

Introduction

The Dizzy and Daffy Dean tour of 1934 was, and probably still is, the greatest barnstorming tour of all time—it was certainly among the best-timed. It was unique for its baseball and certainly more monumental in its media than was ever portrayed in a number of prior publications. As a tour, it had the compelling potential to undo the authoritarian history of an American sporting institution, baseball. The scope of the tour's activities was condensed into two momentous weeks as the brothers smashed attendance records in Oklahoma, Wichita, Chicago, and Brooklyn. It is for these reasons that I decided to present the story in its entirety, showing both the glory of the games and the journalistic tactics, which were often disingenuous, that proliferated in a period of 14 to 15 days. Many books have dabbled in this topic; others have touched on it with one- or two-page summaries, and almost all misinterpreted the subject. Most of these publications give little attention to the tour's media or to Paul Dean or the All-Star teammates. Rarely do you hear the voices of their African American opponents. Most were thought to be silenced for all time.

As a longtime student of baseball history, I felt it important to revisit this momentous tour to examine the treatment it received with an introspective and enlightening look at its lasting legacy. My desire is to present a complete portrayal of the facts, media, and events surrounding the games as they occurred in the fall of 1934, while exposing much of the propaganda that was exhibited throughout to effectively show how discrimination—baseball's twisted sister—affected us then and still affects us now. The United States has a problem with its historical memory, as the events surrounding the

Deans' 1934 tour will clearly show. Public opinions haven't changed as much as we would like to believe, and certainly not when we care more for nostalgia than truth—more for fiction than facts.

During the past 20 years, writers have been motivated to research, write about, and record the history of Negro Leagues baseball. As a result, information about the Dean's barnstorming tour has appeared in numerous publications related to the African American baseball experience. Dizzy is almost always introduced into the text following the 1934 World Series. His brother Daffy is often missing from the conversation in spite of the significant role he played. These writers and publishers are seldom scrutinized for their omissions and lack of critical analysis. In many cases, their highly celebrated scholarship is misleading and at other times is outright fabrication. Their language is most colorful, but their research has been faulty, inconclusive, and lush with institutionalized racism. Their books and articles are often interfused with bigotry and cultural bias because they had neither the experience nor the ability to put this subject under critical analysis. Most critical are the ways authors have interpreted articles and other available data to complete their work.

This manuscript was started during that celebratory period when books on the Negro Leagues exploded. Unfortunately, I got busy with life and other writing activities, and shelved it for 20-plus years. In 2014, I embarked on a tour of 90 cities to improve race relations throughout the United States using baseball history. It was my way of bringing recognition to the Monarchs' world championship of 1924. I eventually traveled to more than 200 towns and cities where the Monarchs and other teams played. It allowed me to talk about Dizzy Dean and his interaction with the Monarchs. The response to Dizzy's stories was infectious. Everyone enjoyed hearing how Dean toured the country, barnstorming against African American teams, in opposition to American cultural norms. I began to view Dizzy as a sort of freedom fighter in an era when racial tensions, stressed and strained, were rarely mentioned in the media. History of the 1934 tour, as it appears in books and other publications, is largely inadequate and inconsistent. For those who wanted to know more, other than my own work, I could not recommend a definitive source to quench their curiosity. This encouraged me to resurrect my previously shelved treatment on the topic.

Dizzy Dean's record is unique among National League and American League players in that he pitched against the Kansas City Monarchs, Pittsburgh Crawfords, Philadelphia Stars, and New York Black Yankees on successive days, in a total of 14 games. Dizzy liked to brag and boast while playing fast and loose on the facts. His feat of playing four African American teams on consecutive days is a factual boast that no big-leaguer could match. Taking this into consideration, in the fall of 2016, I rescued my manuscript from my files and decided to use what I had learned and experienced on the topics of social inclusion, equality, and segregation in baseball. I wanted readers to hear Dizzy and Daffy's voices as they originally appeared, while allowing others to speak from my many interviews with Negro League players—almost all of whom are now deceased, but their stories live on.

It is impossible to cover the Dean's barnstorming tour without an educated understanding and appreciation for the social context in which the literature was originally written—especially when explaining the media's rhetorical strategies toward African American athletes. Furthermore, it is virtually impossible to write coherently on this topic without a proper discernment of African American culture and a vast realization of the legacy and doctrines of racism in the United States. Nor should it be written without an honest conversation about white privilege and its effects on U.S. social economics. I have learned that most anyone can gather articles, but not everyone can construe and analyze the information they collect. Such was the case with the Deans of the 1930s and their Depression-era barnstorming tour. *The Dizzy and Daffy Dean Barnstorming Tour: Race, Media, and America's National Pastime* is my response to all that was written during the tour and many historical situations and events that have occurred since that year.

This project benefited immensely from research provided in several books. *Ol' Diz*, by Vince Staten, published in 1992, and *Diz*, written by Robert Gregory, also published in 1992, were most helpful, as were Elden Auker's *Sleeper Cars and Flannel Uniforms* (2001) and *Branch Rickey* (2011), written by Jimmy Breslin. Equally as enlightening was Lee Lowenfish's *Branch Rickey: Baseballs Ferocious Gentleman*, published in 2009. I sought to read other books in an effort to see how each made reference to the tour.

Listed among the books that mention portions of the tour are *Pitchin' Man*, by Satchel Paige, as told to Hal Lebovitz, released in 1948; *Maybe I'll Pitch Forever*, also by Satchel Paige, as told to David Lipman, first published in 1962; *Voices from the Great Black Baseball Leagues*, by John Holway, first printed in 1975; *Satch, Dizzy, and Rapid Robert*, by Timothy M. Gay, published in 2010; Mark Ribowsky's *Don't Look Back*, published in 1994; Ribowsky's *A Complete History of the Negro Leagues, 1884 to 1955*, published in 1995; Bruce Chadwick's *When the Game Was Black and White*, printed in 1992; *Shades of Glory*, written by Lawrence B. Hogan and released in 2006; Tom Dunkel's *Color Blind*, printed in 2013; and Larry Tye's *Satchel*, published in 2009. I surveyed them all, painstakingly working my way from cover to cover, leaving no stone unturned.

The 1934 barnstorming tour was not, as many writers have long suggested, a tour that pitted Dizzy Dean against Leroy "Satchel" Paige. Much focus has been inappropriately placed on the Satchel versus Dizzy angle, which some have considered to be the tour's legacy. Such idealism is challenged with this work. Although Dizzy and Satchel were known commodities at the time, what occurred during this tour encompassed much more than the experiences of these two individuals alone. The desire to make this tour about two men eliminated the narrative of Dizzy and Paige's contemporaries—the Negro major league players, the other All-Stars, the media—and Dizzy's brother Daffy. Almost all of Dizzy's All-Star teammates are left out of these stories. There are almost one hundred All-Stars who had never had their names mentioned in any text. I want to also give them a voice.

Dizzy and Daffy's All-Stars were more than local sandlot players, contrary to how they are often portrayed. Indeed, some were local legends from regional sandlots, but others were league leaders with long and monumental careers in the minors, and some had lengthy careers in the National League and American League. They were a combination of ex-major leaguers on the way down, youngsters on the way up, and semiprofessional men who were usually among of the best ballplayers in that particular town or city. Their stories, in numerous cases, are collected and offered together in this text for the first time. For many, this is their initial introduction into the world of baseball lore. A number of these All-Stars were first-generation Americans, the children of immigrants from Europe. This did not go without recognition in the eyes of the African American players, who rarely had a voice and were always watching in anguish. "I was born in the United States of America. I'm an American, not a foreigner," advised George Giles, a star of the 1920s and 1930s. "For years, foreigners came here and had more opportunity than I had. It didn't seem right, but that was the American way of life."[1]

Giles had much to say, as did others from the Negro Leagues. You can finally read about them here, along with an evaluation of the comparative talents of the Kansas City Monarchs, Philadelphia Stars, New York Black Yankees, and Pittsburgh Crawfords. This information is presented in a way that will enhance readers' knowledge and understanding of the times in which they lived.

Obtaining images and photographs for this publication was most challenging because I desired to demonstrate through photographic images how a certain brand of inequity was achieved. African American athletes were rarely depicted in newspaper photographs. Thus, for this publication individual player scrapbooks were mined for images. We can now see the faces of the men and women history has forgotten.

Newspapers provided much of the historic foundation for this work. While supplying much of the detailed information needed to tell the story, these same publications demonstrate what it meant to have white privilege in the era of extreme segregation. As witnesses to actual events as they were occurring, reporters were charged with telling the truth—but they changed the narrative and rarely told the entire story. What readers got were lots of biased opinions, whitewashed facts, and little real information. This statement is especially true in the case of African American athletes, as the hotels in which they stayed, names, and modes of travel often went unrecorded. We don't know where teams stayed, we can't tell how they traveled, and, in other cases, we don't know who pitched or played the field. These writers were especially predictable when it came to proclaiming how well a player hit when facing the Deans.

African American players were seldom recognized for their achievements. Segregation was strictly adhered to, saturating American society and easily being seen in the newspapers and magazines of that time. Prejudice was incorporated into the laws of government, the philosophy of economics, and the diversity of religion, as well as in science, literature, poetry, art, film, and especially the minds and hearts of newspaper reporters. It was ever present. Reporters did not live in a colorblind society. As a result of their journalistic techniques, the 1920s and 1930s were ripe with racial pride and the delusion of factual history. Coverage of the Deans'[2] 1934 tour brought into focus the plight of baseball's bigotry in literature, while challenging little of the unfairness as it existed at that time.

These same writers and editors also failed to address such important topics as fairness or why segregation was doled out by the baseball owners. Instead, they chose to divest themselves from conversations about equal access to facilities and economic disparities as they related to African American athletes. By remaining silent, they supported an American culture that denied freedom to many of its citizens. Their reluctance to speak out against these social customs in professional baseball confirmed their racial bias within the sport. In this same period, Al Monroe, a black man writing for the Associated Negro Press, almost single-mindedly chose to attack the bias that the dailies rarely discussed. His declaration against the phrase "World Series" and segregation in professional baseball has stood the test of time. In an article that appeared in minority newspapers in late September 1934, Monroe proclaimed the following:

This Wednesday the Cards and Detroit start the world's series, which is supposed to name the world's champions. To some it does—to others it fails to prove who is who in baseball, and this writer stands out as a leader in the latter group. Truly I cannot see how any team can call itself champion of the world that hasn't batted against Satchel Paige, "School Boy" Jones, Bill Foster, and [Ted] Trent. And I am wondering if the Dean Brothers can gloat over their strikeout records and world's series wins over teams that failed to include Josh Gibson, Turkey Stearns, Jud Wilson, Oscar Charleston, and others in their lineup. Your reporter will continue to question that point.[2]

With the exception of Foster and Stearns, Dizzy and Daffy would soon meet every player named by Monroe. Both brothers would be tested nightly by what might be classed as baseball's silent majority. These were men with names unspeakable and faces unrecognizable to the average baseball fan of the time. They were the invisible stars of baseball, languishing outside an organization with unseen walls and hidden barriers well established to protect baseball's white elite. They were men of African American heritage who deserved more recognition and better pay for their entertainment value, something they never received. Most would never see their image in a daily newspaper; they weren't pictured on baseball cards and rarely played in American League and National League ballparks. They truly were the forgotten "stars" of baseball, as Dizzy and Daffy and the rest of America would soon discover.

In *The Dizzy and Daffy Dean Barnstorming Tour*, you will hear these voices as you've never heard them before. This publication is committed to telling their stories while decoding baseball's stormy past as it was written in an era of segregation. My account of these facts is written for the fans of this age and presented in a way that will enlighten us all.

CHAPTER 1

∿

Me 'n' Paul, Wilkinson, Baird, and Doan

Four well-dressed and attentive men sat around a table in a downtown St. Louis hotel. They conferred repeatedly while hammering out the finer details of their complex business transaction. Without heed, Jay "Dizzy" Dean and his younger brother, Paul, affectionately known as Daffy, stood, stretched, and extended a firm palm in the direction of baseball promoters Ray L. Doan, T. Y. Baird, and J. L. Wilkinson. Everyone smiled—they shook hands, laughed, and patted one another on the back. The climate veered from somber and serious to celebratory and cheerful. An impromptu celebration began a momentary elation.

In theory, the Deans had agreed to participate in the most celebrated baseball barnstorming tour the United States had ever seen. They were to play six games in the Midwest, double the number of games that Dizzy had played in 1933, against the Kansas City Monarchs. Everyone anticipated it would be a profitable venture. With two of the most iconic pitchers in baseball, it couldn't fail. How do we know of their abilities? We know because Dizzy provided this bit of information: "It ain't bragging if you can do it."

Is this fact or fiction? We can't be sure if it really played out this way—there is no public report of how the tour came to be. No one knows for sure since the men involved are no longer alive to tell the story. What you just read is my version of how that first meeting occurred and ended. We don't know who was in the room or where the meeting took place; however, the events that followed are far less speculative.

It could be said with certainty that each was seeking to cash in on the other's success and popularity, and everyone profited when the tour was increased from six games to 15 and moved from the West to the East. Yet, it was the underlining socioeconomic issues of race relations in the United States that made this tour more unique than anything ever arranged. By pairing Negro major-league players against the Deans, they struck gold during the U.S. Depression of the 1930s. In signing these agreements, Dizzy and Daffy had agreed on a whirlwind series of games against many of the best and brightest stars of the Negro Leagues. In return, everyone would make lots of money and enhance their brands, and Dizzy and Daffy would profit from their immense popularity with some of the best publicity ever given a pair ball-playing brothers. The brothers would also talk a lot. At times they would even rebuke some of the legendary literature that had propelled them to national stardom.

The barnstorming series would prove extremely profitable for Dizzy and Daffy. Their contracts called for a daily $1,000 guarantee, regardless of whether the game could be played. These contracts called for an additional $1,500 for actually playing the game, or a privilege of 50 percent of the gross gate receipts, for what was first publicized as six games. "Dean once confided that he made more on these tours with black men than he had winning the World Series—and the black men who made the cash register ring for Dean could reap similar rewards, pulling in as much as $1,200 themselves for two weeks' work."[1]

It was a solid financial plan, but the proposed tour would see its share of negative publicity. Some of the complaints were from men representing the National League and American League in baseball's highest positions, for example, the presidents of both leagues. It was the writers, however, who influenced the tour most often.

In articles, bylines, magazine stories, and radio interviews, reporters produced stories that reached a majority of Americans. Their influence was not to be taken lightly. These reporters, many of whom were meeting and dealing with Dizzy and Daffy for the first time, helped establish the brothers' legacy in ways previously unknown. These writers were determined to write about what they had seen, heard, or imagined, both positive and negative. How they viewed the brothers determined how we think of them today. Dizzy was giving them lots of ammunition, but some of the reporters still chose to embellish their stories with fabrications. Others positioned their articles to poke fun at the brothers. In each case, it exposed the writers' own personalities and political stances more than those of the Deans. There were others who didn't support the tour. They didn't care to see the brothers "tarnish" their legacy by playing African American opponents. This, too, was demonstrated time after time in how games were chronicled. One of the earliest fabrications was printed in a St. Louis newspaper, which Daffy later rebuked. The discussion was centered on a statement attributed to the brothers that they never uttered, which a writer penned prior to the start of the 1934 season.

Supposedly, the brothers had told Branch Rickey that they would combine for 45 victories during the 1934 season—20-plus wins for each brother. When asked by the interviewer to make a prediction for the 1935 season, the conversation went as follows: "Last spring you fellows promised 45 games between you," he reminded Dizzy. "You won 49—30 for Diz and 19 for Paul. Are you going to promise 50 victories this time?" Paul reportedly smiled "deprecatingly," as he responded, "Say, don't make us talk that way, will ya? That 45 games stuff was made up by one of the St. Louis newspapermen and got us in wrong with the other pitchers. I never said it, and I am not going to make any cracks about what we are going to do next season."[2]

The national media was there to report on every game. For most Americans, it was their initial introduction to an array of African American teams and players. They were hearing and learning of these men for the first time; however, full disclosure of what occurred in games seldom made it into print. Readers of the Deans' national media had the great misfortune of seeing these games through the distorted lens of reporters and photographers who were deeply influenced by negative stereotypes and elitist cultural bias. Their attitude toward African American men and women was often distorted, as was their portrayal of the Deans.

Dizzy and Daffy were portrayed in newspapers as a couple of backwoods hicks overwhelmed by their sudden success. The brothers had worked their way to the majors by way of the "Farm," a minor-league system designed by Branch Rickey, general manager and president of the St. Louis Cardinals. For Dizzy, it meant stopovers at St. Joseph, Missouri, in the Western League and Houston in the Texas League. Paul played three seasons before reaching the Cardinals, with tenures in Columbus of the American Association, Houston in the Texas League, and Springfield of the Western Association. Hank Greenberg recalled, "The Texas League was an outstanding minor league. If you were good enough in that league you could step right into the majors. Many players had done it. Dizzy Dean was one, and Paul Dean, Paul Derringer, and Ducky Medwick played against me there."[3] Upon reaching the majors the Deans faced new scrutiny.

Reporters poked fun at the Deans' lack of education and satirized their rapid flight to stardom. Some of the blame could be laid at Dizzy's feet for toying with reporters. From the start of his professional career, he gave conflicting names and birth date and birthplace information to reporters. The

Wichita Eagle jokingly noted that Dizzy "is the only celebrity alive to have been born in three different states at once and not be triplets."[4] James B. Reston wrote on the Associated Press wire:

> He [Dizzy] originally said he was born in Holdenville, Oklahoma, on January 16, 1910. Later he claimed it was Lucas, Arkansas, and gave his birthday as August 14, 1913, July 11, 1912, and then November 9, 1911. When it was pointed out that Daffy's birthday was August 14, 1913, he was asked if they were twins. "No, we're not twins," said the fibbing Dizzy, "but I think that date really is my birthday. Paul don't know when he wuz born. He wuz born in January 1910, I think."[5]

Later accused of lying about his birthday, Diz whispered, "I wuz helping the writers out. Them ain't lies; them's scoops."[6]

Other reporters compared the Deans to Amos 'n' Andy, a characterization—humorous and derogatory—made popular on national radio. It became more evident when Dizzy kept referring to himself and his younger brother as "Me 'n' Paul."

Actors Freeman Gosden and Charles Correll were creators of the *Amos 'n' Andy* program, which had captivated the nation since it first aired on March 19, 1928, over Chicago's WMAQ radio.[7] A newspaper column by Gosden and Correll was also published in daily newspapers. Even today, a later version made for television remains so stereotypically biased against African Americans that no television network will play the reruns. Gosden and Correll were both white, but on the radio they voiced so-called men of color. The duo had created a similar show named *Sam & Henry*, but they rose to entirely new heights with the *Amos 'n' Andy* concept. The story line was set in Chicago's urban community. Reportedly, Amos 'n' Andy were two black men who lived on State Street, which today is Martin L. King Boulevard, located in the heart of Chicago's South Side. Amos Jones, voiced by Gosden, and Andy Brown, voiced by Correll, were purportedly Southern farmers who had moved from outside of Atlanta to the city. It is important to note that the scripts said both men came to the city from the country and were hardworking, uncultured, and naïve. Amos and Andy were also self-assured and continuously looking for get-rich-quick schemes. Story lines were often about money. They spoke in dialect, a form of stereotypic talking that white America had negatively attached to African Americans while enjoying it as entertainment—such as they had minstrel shows from generations past. The radio show was a systematic programing of racism that ran in nightly serials and became one of the most popular radio shows of its time among white audiences in spite of the backlash it received from upstanding African American citizens throughout the United States.

There was no lack of sponsors for such nonsense. The *Amos 'n' Andy* radio show was nationally sponsored by such well-known American products as Pepsodent toothpaste and Campbell's Soup. The Deans were quickly identified as two white men cut from a similar cloth, and advertisers were equally as quick to profit from the brothers' celebrity for similar reasons.

Dizzy's success in the early 1930s thrust him into national prominence. Overnight, he and Daffy were transformed into real-life versions of the same caricatures that were portrayed as stereotypic characters on radio. Born in Lucas, Arkansas, Dizzy, like Amos, was beaming with confidence and always talked about money. Dizzy had a grade-school education and often talked in dialect. Likewise, he and Paul came from rural Arkansas to the city. Their father was a migrant sharecropper who found work where he could in Oklahoma and Arkansas—many times they were picking cotton right alongside people of color for 50 cents a day. Mama, Cash Eldred Monroe-Dean, had passed when Diz was three years old, a victim of tuberculosis, according to one report. True to the family tradition, his father, Albert, gave conflicting information about their past and another name for his mother to the Associated Press.

"I was born and reared in Phelps County, Mo," Albert was quoted as saying in the article. "And the Deans was quite a power thereabouts. Why, I guess there was around 300 of us Deans in Phelps County, an' whenever one of them ran for county office he was almost sure to be elected. My own pa was county sheriff there three or four terms." The article added, "Both Dizzy and Daffy were born in Lucas, Ark., in Logan County. It was here that Albert Dean met and wed Alma Nelson, a native of nearby Mansfield, Ark."[8] This, too, was a strange article, as Dizzy's mother's name was Cash, not Alma.[9]

Dizzy barely knew his mother. She died during the winter of 1917. He wasn't bred to be a scholar either. As a student, his education reportedly ended in the town of Chickalah, located in Yell County, Arkansas, where he struggled to get through the second grade. He told conflicting stories about his education. Diz later confessed in his original wit—"I didn't do so good in the first grade either." When filling out an application at the San Antonio Power Company in 1929, he advanced himself to a ninth-grade education.[10] Branch Rickey was known to have asked his own family "what a lawyer and educated man like himself was doing dealing with the likes of Dizzy Dean for a living."[11] For Cardinals' owner Sam Breadon, his reaction to the Deans' barnstorming was both taxing and strenuous.

Daffy was more of a straight man in the whole affair, but when he talked, he too was quoted in a colorful dialect. Reporters wrote with delight as they lampooned Dizzy and Daffy in the national media, thereby enhancing their popularity to an awaiting American public. These same newspapers took delight in belittling African Americans. Flashes of the reporters' prejudices appeared often during the Deans' legendary tour.

Dizzy and Daffy were a rarity in the 1930s. As two white country boys with baseball talent who seldom frowned on hobnobbing with African American ballplayers—they rather enjoyed mixing with men from the Negro major leagues, especially so in the fall of 1934—they were labeled an odd commodity. By mid-October 1934, the brothers Dean were stars beaming brighter than Babe Ruth. The Bambino's star status had gone into decline several years prior. Still, Ruth was larger than life, and it took two Deans to replace him on the national stage. Dizzy and Daffy together, based on their 1934 success, were more than logical contenders to reign as white baseball's next generation of legends. After the World Series, they were front-page copy in newspapers throughout the United States. They were revered to the point that St. Louis native Mrs. Clifford Wilson named one of her newborn boys Paul Dean Wilson.

In leading the St. Louis Cardinals in one of the most exciting pennant races in years, Dizzy and Daffy's arms had reinvigorated Major League Baseball of the 1930s as much as Babe Ruth's home runs had in the early 1920s. In the process, the Deans were transformed from country bumpkins to baseball idols, attracting media recognition that rivaled that of Ruth in articles—but not income.

The brothers' annual salary was well publicized, and so were their stubborn protests. They received lots of national attention for their mid-season strike against Cardinals management in an effort to increase their salaries. The strike had been successful in that Paul's salary was raised to $4,500 from the $3,000 for which he had originally signed. Dizzy, who was earning $7,500, received a $500 bonus from the Cardinals for winning the World Series; however, he was also fined $486 for missing an exhibition game in Battle Creek, Michigan, during his strike. When you subtract one from the other, Dizzy had $14 to show as profit for his holdout. This was only part of Diz's financial picture.

Paul Mickelson, Associated Press sportswriter, summarized the scope of what he considered to be "poor Dizzy's" financial woes in an article titled "Dizzy Dean, Most 'Underpaid' Star, to Earn $35,000 This Year."[12] His itemized accounting of the pitcher's earnings, in addition to his Cardinals salary, which was clearly stated in this October 3 article, grossly underestimated what Dizzy would earn as an interracial barnstormer. The anticipated figures included the following:

$1,000 for signing his player's contract
$4,000 to $5,000 for his World Series cut
$3,000 already earned under an agreement with a St. Louis firm for doing some advertising over [the] radio
$2,000 earned in exhibitions
$12,000 to $20,000 to be earned in vaudeville after the series

After Dizzy's brilliant six-hit, 11–0 triumph in Game 7 of the 1934 World Series, most of the animosity concerning the strike was forgotten and the might of the media took over. Recognition and fame would spread the Deans' name all over the nation. It was a fitting crown to a remarkable season where the brothers' happy-go-lucky charisma had produced a 30–7 record for Dizzy and a 19–11 record for the younger Dean in his National League rookie campaign. They combined for 49 wins, the most in a season by brothers in the long history of National and American League play. In the World Series—the first ever broadcast via national radio—Dizzy and Daffy each won a pair of games in the four-out-of-seven Series. All of the Cardinals' World Series victories belonged to them. The final Cardinals' victory, which Dizzy pitched, ended in the most lopsided Series shutout margin since Christy Mathewson blanked the Philadelphia Athletics, 9–0, in 1905. Dizzy was now in elite company—a class that included only four other National League pitchers—or maybe he wasn't.

Only four other National League pitchers had recorded 30-win seasons. Christy Mathewson of the New York Giants had done it four times—1903, 1904, 1905, and 1908. Joe McGinnity, also of the Giants, achieved the feat in 1903 and 1904, the same years as Mathewson. Grover Cleveland Alexander of the Phillies logged 30 for three consecutive years, with 31, 33, and 30 wins, respectively, from 1915 to 1917. It is, as Herbert Simons, a *Baseball Digest* writer once noted, "highly debatable whether he [Dizzy] actually won all of the 30 games with which he was credited."[13] There are others who still say Dizzy didn't crack the 30-win mark.

Two wins, numbers 12 and 13 of his amazing season, came under immense suspicion, and both were played at Sportsman's Park in St. Louis. In a June 23 game against the Dodgers, the Bums from Brooklyn were leading all the way, 4–0. In the sixth, the Cardinals scored five times to take a 5–4 lead. Dizzy came on in relief of lefty Bill Hallahan in the seventh inning with the Cardinals ahead by one run. He pitched shutout ball for the next three innings to preserve the win. Hallahan should have gotten the win because the Cardinals were in the lead when Dizzy entered the game, but an appeal on high to the National League office blessed Dizzy with the victory. If that wasn't bad enough, Dean should have been kicked out of the game or lashed with a heavy fine for what he did to the umpire.

When Charley Moran, the umpire, called one of Dean's pitches to Hack Wilson a ball instead of a strike, Dizzy called time and approached the arbiter. Roy Stockton, a veteran sportswriter for the St. Louis Post-Dispatch, noted that Dean grabbed the ump and, putting one hand on Charley's stomach and using the other to bend him over, made a remark about not being able to see the plate. The other questionable win occurred that same month.[14]

Against the New York Giants on June 27, Dean was taken out in the top of the ninth with the score tied, 7–7, with a pair of runners on base and two outs. Jim Mooney came on to retire the final batter, Mel Ott. In the Cardinals' home ninth, Bill Delaney homered off Adolfo Luque, and St. Louis won, 8–7. The official scorer, Mike Haley, awarded the win to Dean. An official scorer who would credit Dean with this win should have been banned from the press box. Hallahan ended the season with eight wins, and Mooney got three in an effort to push Dizzy to 30.[15] What happened after the World Series caught almost everyone by surprise. Apparently, no one knew what was to come next—even the Cardinals were blindsided.

As winners of a World Series, Dizzy and Daffy agreed to be tested on other levels. Unlike many players from their league, they were willing to take a chance. The testing would come from ballplayers, sportswriters, and their African American opposition—men the Deans had never seen up front or in person. Dizzy had absolute confidence in the brothers' ability to dominate the opposition. There would be plenty of night baseball, lots of questions about money—not how much the Negro teams were making, no one seemed to care about that—and a steady stream of propaganda surrounding major- and minor-league records. It was obvious that the newspapers cared deeply about the Deans' earnings and achievements, while totally ignoring the earnings and accomplishments of African Americans on the opposite side of the diamond. For some in the minority media, it was a moment they had long awaited. "The participation of our teams in wheels with the opposite race whenever possible," advised the Cleveland Call and Post, "is a major step towards breaking down this wall of prejudice."[16]

A year earlier, Wilkinson and his partner, T. Y. Baird, had sought ways to profit from the Deans' popularity. The Monarchs owners based their original barnstorming tour on the theory that fans off the beaten track were willing to pay large sums to see Dizzy. St. Louis was the westernmost major-league franchise, and it had a supportive fan base in Missouri, Kansas, Iowa, Nebraska, Arkansas, and Oklahoma, states west of the Mississippi River. Their hunch was on the money. Dizzy was hired to pitch in three games against the Kansas City Monarchs in 1933. Diz, paired with the Monarchs, drew 6,000 people to tiny Oxford, Nebraska, followed by 8,000 in Kansas City and another big crowd in Concordia, Kansas. Diz learned by experience that these Monarchs weren't a docile group of hitters and fielders of the inferior type. They never considered themselves inferior, Dizzy soon discovered, regardless of how hard the press worked to make it so. Monarchs co-owner J. L. Wilkinson was a clever genius when it came to promotions, and he had a long history with barnstorming tours and overcoming the oppression in American sports.

As the trailblazing owner of the Bloomer Girls, the All-Nations, and the Negro National League's Kansas City Monarchs, James Leslie Wilkinson, also called "Wilkie" by his close associates, was a marketing wizard and creative giant. He was born in Iowa, a place where his creative genius in marketing, publicity, and human relations originally started. He introduced many innovations to baseball and was among the first to create a mixed-race, mixed-nationality team, naming it the All-Nations. Wilkinson was also instrumental in allowing women to play baseball with men and brought about touring by bus, playing nighttime baseball, and wearing uniforms with letters as opposed to numbers on the back. It was Wilkinson who gave Satchel Paige a last chance in professional baseball and Jackie Robinson his first. Wilkinson owned teams from 1908 to 1946, and showed a profit every year he put a team on tour.

Wilkie was the son of a college president and a former college athlete himself. While attending Highland Park College in Des Moines, Iowa, he pitched semiprofessionally for a variety of regional teams under the alias Joe Green. Leaving college before he had graduated, Wilkinson played professionally with Marshalltown in the Iowa League and later in the Southwestern circuit, where he batted in the low .200s. He left professional ball to sign with a team sponsored by the Hopkins Brothers Sporting Goods store in Des Moines. One day the team's manager vanished with the gate receipts and stranded the team at Fort Dodge, Iowa. J. L.'s teammates voted him the new manager, deciding that he would be a better manager than player.

Wilkinson also had a great feel for what the fans wanted. He understood that baseball fans in Iowa, Nebraska, North Dakota, Minnesota, and other points in the Midwest would pay to see a team of mixed-race players long before it was popular, which is why he created the All-Nations with partner J. E. Gall. He operated out of Des Moines with a small sponsorship from the Hopkins Brothers Sporting Goods stores. Their concept was considered radical at the time. His teams were frequently forced to travel in their own private Pullman car. Yet, he never stopped looking for the best athletes his wallet could afford.

One of his first feats was to lure lefty John Donaldson from the all-black Tennessee Rats, who he later promoted as baseball's greatest "colored pitcher." Aside from Donaldson, he kept "Carrie Nation," a female who he billed as baseball's "greatest female" player, from his old Bloomer Girl days. The remainder of the All-Nations team was a mixture of Chinese, Japanese, Cubans, Indians, and whites playing behind Donaldson and legendary Cuban Jose Mendez, who was hired in 1914.

In 1915, following new sponsorship, the team relocated to Kansas City, Missouri. Gall later ran away with the money, leaving Wilkinson to go it alone until he formed a partnership with Tom "T. Y." Baird in early 1919, before the founding of the new Negro National League. Their first-year team, the Kansas City Monarchs, was joined by seven others to form an eight-team circuit. Seldom told is the story of how Wilkinson and Baird became the only non–African American owners in the new league.

With the formation of the Negro National League in 1920, Wilkinson was not the league's first choice for ownership. Dr. Howard M. Smith, a physician in the children's hygiene division of the city health department and one of Kansas City's leading African American political figures, had first dibs on the new team. Smith was well connected with the Elks Lodge, the Chi Delta Mu medical fraternity, and the Kansas City Medical Association. The new league was imminent, so Wilkinson took steps to get the new franchise before Smith. In the fall of 1919, Wilkinson staged a series of games in Kansas City and invited Andrew "Rube" Foster, the future league president, to bring his American Giants to town. It proved to be successful. Next, Wilkinson signed a partnership agreement with Tom Baird for the business organization and management side of the baseball team, to be known as the Kansas City Monarchs Base Ball Club. The agreement was dated December 1919. Wilkinson also had the lease on Association Park, an obstacle that was impossible for Smith to overcome. When the new league organized on February 14, 1920, Wilkinson and Baird were in; Smith was out in Kansas City.

Wilkinson was loved by his players. George Giles referred to his team's owner as a "prince of a man." In an interview, Giles went on to state, "Wilkinson was a man; Baird was a businessman."[17] Paying tribute to his players, Wilkinson advised, "There aren't as many Negro ballplayers as there are white, but when a colored boy is a good athlete, a good baseball player, he's very apt to be mighty good. That's why he rated his club major-league caliber."[18] As an owner, Wilkinson had other accomplishments to celebrate.

Wilkinson is considered the father of modern nighttime baseball. Baird told the story often. "Night football was new and proving very popular with the fans," he recalled. "We took our Negro ballplayers to nearby Lawrence, Kansas, home of the Haskell Institute Indians [School], one evening in the fall of 1929, and for several hours they had the players hitting fungoes flies, ground balls, and line drives."[19] They quickly discovered it wasn't too difficult to follow the ball. As Baird remembered, they decided "then and there that the Monarchs were going to play night baseball." Baird continued, "We worked all that winter on devising a portable lighting unit."[20]

During the Depression years of the 1930s under the leadership of Wilkinson and Baird, the Monarchs toured coast to coast, meeting and almost always beating their opponents. In Kansas, Missouri, Nebraska, and Iowa, the Monarchs were in great demand. They toured in their own bus almost as soon as the first Doris buses rolled off the assembly line in 1926. The bus was an attraction wherever it was seen. It had reclining seats with high backs and air cushions, comfortable for travel and enabling the players to get some sleep.

During Wilkinson and Baird's original Dizzy Dean tour of 1933, there was no World Series win to celebrate. It was history that almost didn't happen because the Monarchs failed to organize until June 1932. "Wilkinson had said early in the season," advised one publication, "that he would wait for 1933 before attempting a comeback unless his players demanded his reorganizing." The Kansas City magnate continued, "Should the East fail to pay the men, then I shall return to the front and see that they make enough money to tide them over the winter."[21] By 1933, the Monarchs were back to full form, and Dizzy faced a formidable squad.

In 1934, the National League pennant race and World Series had changed Dizzy's prospects and popularity enormously. He wasn't traveling alone either. His brother, Daffy, and Dizzy's wife were traveling with him.

Wilkinson purposely scheduled games in territories traveled by the Monarchs during a 14-year span when they had experienced large guarantees, great ballparks, and big gates. They had already built up the crowds, and key promoters were identified. The tour went to cities where local fans believed the African American team to be almost unbeatable. Ray L. Doan, promoter of the House of David ballclub, who had toured against the Monarchs often, signed on to assist with contracts and act as Baird's assistant with publicity. Doan handled the publicity, along with his traveling secretary duties. The reporters, however, ignored Doan's press releases and wrote whatever they wished. One of the tour's first announcements appeared in an Associated Press article dated October 10, which reported, "The Deans, Dizzy and Paul, are going to keep right on pitching." Dizzy stated, "Shucks, Paul and me are just getting warmed up. I feel like I can throw baseballs all winter and then start right out on the 1935 season. So does Paul." Paul made it known, "I'm in great shape now."[22]

To fully appreciate baseball in the era before integration, you must take a serious look at the language and rhetorical strategies used by newspaper writers of the period, who, for various reasons, appeared to be on a celebrity high. Newspapers were one of the main sources in propagandizing this national agenda. These newspapers had taken a firm stance in several key areas of cultural conditioning. It was as if the writers had a playbook that was used by every newspaper in the nation. The type of language used by reporters for the most famous daily newspapers was written in such a way as to deny African American men, who they did not consider celebrities, their rightful respect in society.

For generations newspapers had told baseball fans how to think and feel about black Americans in their bylines and irresponsible articles. It was as obvious as night is from day that the mainstream media were proud of the National and American League affiliations, but seldom did they share this same respect and enthusiasm when writing about athletes of color and their segregated leagues.

During the 1920s, Kansas City's four daily newspapers clearly prohibited photographs of Monarchs baseball players in their publications. Instead, photographs of Babe Ruth, Ty Cobb, Lou Gehrig, Knute Rockne, Red Grange, Jack Dempsey, Gene Tunney, and others graced the sports pages. Only one photograph of a Kansas City Monarchs player appeared in a Kansas City, Missouri, daily newspaper between 1920 and 1938. A total of 24,753 editions of Kansas City's four daily newspapers passed on the opportunity to elevate Monarchs teams to a level of equality shown to the minor league Kansas City Blues. In keeping with the daily newspapers' twisted more-thrills-than-stills agenda, every aspect of impartiality went awry.

The editors of the daily press didn't see the economic power of the black community as an important resource and irregularly wrote about many of the most renowned teams in the United States. As a result, daily newspapers were often an enemy, instead of a friend, of professional baseball as played outside the major leagues, but the trickery, which masqueraded to look like support, confused many. A series of strategies were used, and many are still in force today. It might be said that these strategies worked so well that they continue to deny many their rightful place in baseball history. In the fall of 1934, these same newspapers were there to cover the Deans' every move. We know what they ate, where they stayed, how they dressed, and other personal details because it appeared in print.

Additionally, advertising for the Dean brothers' tour promised things you could not see in the major leagues, for instance, both brothers pitching in the same game or both Deans on the field for all nine innings. The Deans would also pitch at night. Nighttime baseball hadn't yet come to the major leagues, which also made this a rarity. The 1934 tour would take them to more cities, include more players, and be the longest barnstorming tour to date according to the number of days and geography, making it the father of all interracial baseball tours. Another twist was where the games would be played. Instead of major-league cities, the tour was slated to visit almost a dozen midsize Midwestern and eastern towns where minor-league or town-team baseball flourished. The tour would travel to 11 states: Oklahoma, Kansas, Missouri, Iowa, Illinois, Wisconsin, Pennsylvania, New York, Maryland, New Jersey, and Ohio. By playing African American teams, the social drama was increased. Almost all of the opponents were African American teams, except for one. Fans were promised they'd see the best of the big leagues playing against Negro baseball's brightest—a true rarity in 1934.

Because Negro League teams were almost always absent in the national media, their area of influence was often limited to a particular region. The Monarchs mostly covered the Midwestern states; their vast popularity seldom reached the east. The same was true for Edward Bolden's Philadelphia Stars, who seldom traveled west of Columbus, Ohio, or the New York Black Yankees, who regularly performed in territory controlled by Nat Strong's eastern syndicate. Gus Greenlee's Pittsburgh Crawfords had played in Lincoln, Omaha, and Sioux City, Iowa, in 1932, and were somewhat familiar to those reading the *Kansas City Call*, otherwise they too were exclusively known in eastern baseball circles. Others had read of Satchel Paige's wins in the 1934 Denver Post Series, although most had never seen him—not even in pictures. Except for a few rare exceptions, like the case of Paige, the Deans' opponents were not known individually, although many were equally as good. This lack of familiarity was said to be an advantage for the Deans. Their major-league notoriety, in the minds of most Americans, gave them preeminence and supremacy in public opinion. Unfortunately, it was mostly propaganda. In time, everyone would discover the Deans, and their major- and minor-league comrades had few advantages in the actual skills of playing baseball.

In addition to Dizzy and Daffy, members of the Deans' All-Stars included major- and minor-league stars. They were a motley collection of baseball talent from communities throughout the United States. How these men stacked up against players from the Negro major league was answered night after night as the tour challenged many long-held customs and beliefs in American society.

Interracial games had been going on for years; however, no major-league players had embarked on a jaunt as aggressive as the Deans. By taking on the nomadic ways of Negro major-league barnstorming teams, the Deans were taking on the nation's biased society. Their vantage point and level of observation were rarely discussed by the national media. What they saw was more than even they expected.

With the exception of Greenlee's Crawfords, who built a $100,000 stadium in Pittsburgh, the Deans soon discovered that blacks owned no parks, stadiums, or ball fields. They found that most of the teams were owned or booked by Caucasians or Jews. In addition to Ray L. Doan, who operated the House of David team and traveled the entire route with the Deans, there were other whites with controlling interest in minority baseball affairs. Wilkinson and Baird owned and operated the Kansas City Monarchs, Eddie Gottlieb was the promoter for the Philadelphia Stars, and the New York Black Yankees were booked by Nat Strong. These men controlled baseball outside the majors and minors, and no successful tour against African American teams could be executed without them. Strong, of New York, and others, like Gottlieb, Harry Passon, and Abe Saperstein in Chicago, had free rein to discriminate as they chose, while bounding up the talents and treasures of their African American customers. They set the stage for where the Deans would perform their colorful antics once the major-league season ended.

In a period of two weeks, Dizzy and Daffy played 15 games. The number of games would eventually top the 16 contests versus African American teams played by Babe Ruth during a number of years. This was not the original plan, but somewhere along the way more games were added to the tour. The original plan was outlined in an October telegram to Doan's wife.

In the October 10 telegram to Mrs. Doan, which turned into an article in Doan's hometown newspaper, the *Muscatine Journal and News Tribune*, it said the tour would last seven days. Reportedly, the tour was limited by a prior agreement with Fox Movietone and a scheduled vaudeville tour for the Deans. The first game was to be played in Oklahoma City, with the last game taking place in Chicago, where the article stated "they [the Deans] would leave Doan to take up the Movietone contract."[23] Originally, the Deans' only opponent was the Kansas City Monarchs. Exactly when the other African American teams were added to the schedule is not completely verified.

Media coverage of the Deans' African American opponents overflowed with inequality and neglect. Daily newspapers, in their slanted and biased coverage of the games, omitted and misspelled players' names and failed to record their achievements, while repeatedly using rhetorical strategies to downplay their success. Almost in unison, these newspapers failed to celebrate anything that was achieved versus the Deans. It was a calculated approach that would contribute to decades of continued segregation. When properly evaluated, it is an excellent study of how baseball's well-entrenched racism was exposed during the Deans' 1934 tour. These traditions were sel-dom confronted during the tour, although they were regularly articulated by the following methods:

1. There was to be little to no individual name recognition of African American athletes in the major daily newspapers.
2. African American teams and players did not receive recognition for their superior play against the Deans.
3. There were few photographic images of the African American players in the local dailies, and none were to be distributed nationally.
4. There was no mention of financial compensation totals for African American players or teams.
5. More attention was paid to the Deans' earnings than their opponents' play.
6. Credit was given to the Dean brothers' popularity when discussing drawing power in cities where they met African American opponents.
7. The majority of background data given in the articles was for Dizzy and Daffy, with minimal coverage of other players.

Customs and traditions in the cities where the Deans appeared are, by themselves, difficult to unravel. Most fans had heard of the Deans. The pennant, the number of pitching wins, and what they had achieved in the World Series were national stories. The same could not be said for any of their Negro major-league opponents, for whom no annual records of games won or lost were ever given.

The natural rivalry of the greatest pitchers in the majors against the poorly marketed talent of the Negro ranks should not have guaranteed success. This too was a misunderstanding. Many had witnessed locally the quality of play-ers in the Negro major leagues, but the nation's staunch prejudice didn't al-low them to be seen as equals. In the days that followed, more than 100,000 people—most of them white—poured into stadiums to see the games. Many wanted to see, touch, and feel the excitement of interracial play. It was verifica-tion of their longstanding beliefs about the inequality in professional baseball.

The decision to go on tour was clearly more Dizzy's than Daffy's. Paul never took ownership. The younger Dean was there for the ride and the money. By Dizzy's own recollections, the tour netted them between $10,000 and $12,000—big money in 1934. While no mention of the African American players' earnings ever appeared in print, it was obvious that this series meant far more than money. The interracial results would prove significant in race equality regardless of the intent, while shattering the concept of race superiority in baseball—but how quickly people forgot. In a two-week period, intentional or not, Dizzy and Daffy were about to defy baseball's long-held belief that the greatest professional players were in the National League and American League. They would soon prove this notion to be false in head-to-head competition—actual play.

Baseball's best talent was not exclusive to the all-white National and American Leagues—some of the greats were indeed African Americans performing in the Negro major leagues. The Deans would face men who played the game with a reckless abandon that transcended statistics. These men rarely calculated their averages, counted strikeouts, or tallied home run totals. Bill Finger of Cleveland's *Call and Post* may have said it best when he noted, "The participation of our teams in wheels with the opposite race whenever possible is a major step toward breaking down this wall of prejudice."[24] This is the backdrop for one of baseball's greatest and seldom-shared stories of the much-celebrated barnstorming tour that opened in the segregated South to a packed house on October 10, 1934, at Oklahoma City, Oklahoma.

⌒

CHAPTER 2

Oklahoma City, Oklahoma

The Whips That Lashed Detroit
Wednesday, October 10, 1934

Dizzy and Daffy's barnstorming tour following the World Series should have opened in Tulsa, Oklahoma, or maybe Oklahoma City or Wichita, Kansas. Who knew for sure. As late as October 10 and as early as October 8, the *Wichita Eagle* had advertised the tour's start in Kansas. Stadium officials there made plans for the largest crowd in Kansas baseball history. Additional bleachers were erected in the outfield, and heavy ropes to restrain the large crowd from pouring onto the field had been purchased. Much to their surprise, Oklahoma City promoters were haphazardly making a proposal to bring the Deans to their city. Jack Holland, owner of the local Texas League team, whose "specialty," according to the *Oklahoma News*, was "producing sad ballclubs little better than the pickup nines which perform at Sunday school picnics, when the fat fellows play the lean ones," and E. Jimmy Humphries, secretary of the Oklahoma Indians, were determined to outbid everyone for the tour's first game.[1] Ticket sales in Oklahoma City had been delayed until the end of the World Series and confirmation from the Deans, but the brothers were also scheduled for Tulsa, which wasn't as widely publicized. Dizzy finally confirmed by telegram a day or two prior that they would come to Oklahoma City first. "We'll be there, sure," he said in a telegram that was reprinted in the *Oklahoma News*. "We got to take today to dust these Tigers off, but that won't take long."[2]

Dizzy would not only send telegrams, but also he liked to send them collect, meaning the recipient paid. After a Cardinals victory in the World Series, Branch Rickey wired Dizzy congratulations and invited the brothers to be guests at a Friday night dinner party. Dizzy returned a telegram collect with the following response:

> Many, many thanks. This American League is a pushover. Breezed through today with nothing but my glove. If possible have Dad on airplane in time for game tomorrow. Wire time of arrival. Tell everybody hello. Henry Ford will be my guest in St. Louis Friday. Cooked a good meal for all of us—sandwiches and everything. Will Rogers and Joey Brown coming, too. Thanks again. Dizzy Dean.[3]

With Dizzy's most recent telegram in hand, Holland and Humphries won the bidding rights to have the tour begin in Oklahoma City. They sprang into action and opened for big business that same day. For customers who were doing the wait-and-see, Dizzy's written confirmation signaled it was time to purge their wallets and cookie jars. What occurred in Tulsa illustrated the calamity that was soon to follow.

On Tuesday, October 9, the *Tulsa Daily World* publicized an article under the headline, "Tulsa Date for Deans Canceled."[4] The article read, "Tulsa baseball fans won't get to see Paul and Dizzy Dean pitch after all, not yet at any rate." It went on to add that the "tentative date for Tulsa on Wednesday afternoon was canceled last night because the St. Louis Cardinal management objected stringently to the Deans working twice in one day on their barnstorming trip." The article also mentioned promoters Baird and Doan. "Tom Baird of Kansas City, associated with Ray Doan in promoting the Deans' trip, telephoned Steward last night that the Deans could not make the Tulsa visit because of the Cardinals' protests." Had the World Series not gone to a Game 7, the original plan was to bring the Deans to Tulsa on Tuesday and Oklahoma City the next night, Wednesday. When those arrangements fell through, the promoters wanted to schedule a day–night doubleheader in two cities, but the Cardinals balked at the arrangements. Tulsa was discarded, and Oklahoma City was guaranteed the tour's opening event.

Every seat at Oklahoma City's Texas League Park was suddenly up for grabs. By 9:30 a.m., inside Veazey's Drugs and Soda stores, a surge in customers was wreaking havoc as people engaged in a day-long effort to obtain passes.[5] Humphries, in charge of reservations made over the telephone at the team's office, never took a break. The phones wouldn't stop ringing. As if it came by total surprise, half-enthusiastic Texas League fans were unexpectedly going wild for baseball and the chance to see Dizzy and Daffy up close and in the flesh. National interest of anyone remotely drawn to baseball now shifted from the big-league cities of Detroit and St. Louis to the minor-league town of Oklahoma City, and to the Dean's new opponents, a team of Negro major leaguers called the Kansas City Monarchs.

Two days prior to the Dean's Oklahoma arrival, Texas League Park officials started hyping the big event while dressing their park for the celebrated barnstorming affair. They were planning for a noisy homecoming; they never expected a near-riot. Short notice of the game created all kinds of anxiety and commotion in Oklahoma City while tossing the Deans' itinerant schedule into momentary panic. The renowned barnstorming series was to open a day earlier than originally advertised—and in a different city. For Dizzy and Daffy, the earlier start meant little time for rest after the World Series.

As promised, Dizzy did in fact dust off the Tigers on October 9, in Game 7 of the 1934 World Series. Pitching in front of a crowd of 40,902, he struck out five Detroit batters. The series was the first ever to be broadcast nationally on NBC Radio and CBS Radio. After the final game, Dizzy and his world champion Cardinals teammates traveled by train directly from Detroit's spacious Navin Field back to St. Louis, where they participated in a citywide parade. Less than 24 hours later, the triumphant brothers arrived at Oklahoma City's Municipal Airport on a 1:27 p.m. American Airlines flight for a game at the local stadium later that night. They were strategically moved like pieces on a chessboard from Detroit to St. Louis and then to Oklahoma City in the most modern accommodations possible—trains and airplanes. Major-league teams wouldn't adopt the airplane as a mode of travel until 1936, when the Boston Red Sox took to the air with league president William Harridge in tow. Even then, five players refused to fly and were left behind.[6] There were few of these luxuries for the Dean brothers' Oklahoma City opponents, the Kansas City Monarchs, who had the opulence of an uncomfortable four-hour bus trek across the sunbaked midwestern prairie from Kansas City.

Members of the Monarchs were resting up after defeating Thatcher's Colts, an African American team sponsored by a local mortuary, in a neatly played Sunday afternoon game on October 7. Rickety old Rock Island Park in Kansas City, Kansas, was the site of Kansas City's 10–3 win over the Colts.[7] The number of fans who watched couldn't begin to approach the number of onlookers who attended the final game of the World Series, and there was no radio broadcast either. Admission to the all–African American game was 40 cents, which was small peanuts compared to ticket prices paid to attend the all-white World Series games in Detroit and St. Louis.

Mike "Red" Berry, a recruit from Thatcher's Colts, worked against his former mates in a tryout with the Monarchs and faced Johnny Vivian, a crafty old veteran from Glasgow, Missouri, working for the opposition. Andy Cooper tossed the final few innings for the Monarchs. The game's highlight was Frank Duncan's seventh-inning drive over the left-field fence. It wasn't a festive affair; it wasn't well attended. It was just another exhibition in a long and exhaustive summer of barnstorming baseball. With African American fans as their primary supporters, one newspaper suggested, "This scattering of large groups of Negro citizens is responsible for our best teams having to make such long hops between games."[8]

Prior to the game's start, officials at the park, according to an account in the *Kansas City Kansan*, "brought in a radio and loud speakers," allowing the early birds to hear the World Series broadcast.[9] They delayed the start of the game until the conclusion of the World Series. A postgame article in the *Kansas City Call* made mention of owner J. L. Wilkinson's visit to St. Louis to watch Dizzy Dean. He was doing more than eyeballing the Deans and taking in the fun; he was negotiating intimate details to pair the brothers with his Monarchs after the World Series.

The brothers' visit created an atmosphere of carnival-like celebration. From the moment tickets became available, plans were being made to accommodate a record turnout—the largest crowd to ever attend a baseball game in the history of the state. A byline in the *Daily Oklahoman* advised, "The Deans, Paul and Dizzy, will be here tonight for a close-up at Texas League Park, so call off your weekly bridge or poker session and follow the crowd to the ball orchard."[10] The boys began talking the moment the plane doors opened, sharing phrases for which the pair had become nationally famous. Bus Ham, sports editor of the *Daily Oklahoman*, was there to exploit their every word.

The brothers arrived at the airport escorted by Democratic senator Elmer Thomas; promoter Ray L. Doan; and Dizzy's wife, Pat. A report carried over the newswire in the *Vidette-Messenger* of Indiana advised, "Most of the crowd at the airport failed to recognize the senator."[11] A reporter asked the politician, "What's the country coming to when a couple of baseball players get the attention and a U.S. Senator is almost ignored?" Given an opportunity to respond Thomas offered, "Oh, that's human nature."[12] He wasn't trying to politicize the activities of a few excited baseball fanatics.

When the brothers stepped off the airplane, the *Daily Oklahoman* reported that everyone was in awe of their appearance. The famed pitchers paused briefly to be photographed with Senator Thomas for the local newspapers. The politician was flanked on one side by Daffy and Dizzy on the other. A gentle wind threshed the iconic trio's hair about like wheat in an open field. No one was wearing a hat—they didn't need to, as it was much too pleasant of a fall day, especially so after the blazing hot summer of 1934, to need one. The temperatures in Oklahoma City had set records, making it the hottest summer in the city's history, with records dating back to 1891. Temperatures from June to August averaged an uncomfortable 85.9 degrees with a sweltering humidity. The brothers appeared somewhat coy as they left the airplane and inhaled the warmth of the Oklahoma fall breeze.

If the Deans had flown prior to this date, it wasn't explored in print. They were obviously uncomfortable with this mode of transportation. Their celebrity photo session was interrupted by what the newspaper classed as Paul's complaints. "I'm sick. It's that egg sandwich I ate," he said playfully. Dizzy reportedly jumped in to express his exhaustion by stating, "Whew, me? I'm tired [too]."[13] The senator, Doan, and Pat quickly "melted" into the background as Dizzy was being interviewed.

Dizzy talked boastfully about the World Series. "It's those Detroit fans that's dizzy," he suggested sarcastically. "They're wild and broke." When told that they challenged the assassination of King Alexander I of Yugoslavia for national headlines on Tuesday, October 9, Dizzy replied, "Oh, well. America must like its baseball."[14]

As the dynamic duo marched onward they signed their inscriptions on programs of indoctrination and white baseballs while Doan telephoned ahead for Daffy's breakfast. He requested a dish of vegetable soup, a beaker of milk, and oodles of crackers from the cafeteria at the Biltmore, where their elaborate hotel suites were secured. The boys signed everything thrown their way and continued to sign while fielding more questions. Paul was a bit timid at first; Dizzy was expressive as usual. Their chiseled chins were in constant motion, and they were seldom interrupted from the airport to the hotel.

When Paul was questioned about his zany nickname, he answered, "Nope, I don't care if they call me 'Daffy' as long as I get paid."[15] Dizzy glanced at Paul as if to say, please don't mention money, and quickly interrupted. "You better stop that stuff right now," said Diz. He didn't want the newspapers knowing that Paul didn't care much for the name Daffy. In addition, Dizzy was holding his money cards close to his chest and trying his best to keep their wealth out of the conversation. Paul continued, "Well, the players don't call me that, and the sportswriters say it won't last. They are not going to call me that much anymore. They say it don't suit a guy like me." How wrong he was. His nickname would soon become one of baseballs' most recognizable. The *Oklahoma News*, however, took a cue from Daffy and started calling him "Nutsy" during his Oklahoma visit.[16] Regarding his older brother, Paul added, "They call him Dizzy because he's always cutting up on the bench and kidding the youngsters."[17] The reality wasn't that Dizzy's nickname had been conjured up during his time in National League baseball. Its origin went farther back, back to his time in the army in 1926.

As a baseball pitcher in the U.S. Army, Jay Hanna Dean was pretty clever but not necessarily smart. Dean was known to have said, "The good Lord was good to me. He gave me a strong body, a good right arm, and a weak mind."[18] This mentality probably led to his downfall as a soldier. He knew he was a rank failure and routinely admitted he was something less than a good soldier in his Savior's eye. Dean came to the army on November 15, 1926, arriving at Fort Sam Houston, near San Antonio, Texas. Assigned to the 3rd Wagon Company, he had the great honor of shoveling mule dung out of the stables. He was so bad at it that they sent him to work in the mess hall as a cook when Sergeant William H. Barnett transferred the young lad to Sergeant James K. Brought of Battery C. It was Brought who schooled him on the finer points of cooking and baseball.

Dean had some big wins for the regiment's baseball team, although practice was limited. When he couldn't get to the field, he found other ways to keep his right arm limber. They made him the biscuitmaker and potato peeler of the unit, but instead of cooking, he rolled biscuits and cut potatoes into balls and tossed them at pots and pans hanging in the kitchen. One day as Brought was making his rounds, he saw Dean throwing the army's freshly peeled potatoes at garbage can lids. "You dizzy son of a bitch," was his natural response. The name Dizzy quickly stuck, and, by 1928, San Antonio newspapers were referring to the army's pitcher as "Dizzy Dean."

The morning's newspapers in Oklahoma City had already advised readers of the Deans' arrival. Ham, of the *Daily Oklahoman* wrote, "Don't expect Paul and Dizzy to bear down with all they have against the Kansas City Monarchs, the Negro champions of the world. The Deans are only barnstorming down this way, giving you a chance to see them as they scoop up loose change."[19] Ham's statement of moderation was quickly overruled by the elder Dean. "We're going to bear down in these exhibition games," announced Dizzy. "We're going to bear down just like in the [World] Series."[20] Most of the Deans' conversations to Oklahoma City newspapers were not written in dialect—something that was destined to worsen as the tour moved east—since how the brothers sounded to Oklahomans seemed reasonably normal to the ears of most residents. The culture and cuisine of Oklahoma was predominately Southern. The state, which borders Arkansas and Texas, was formerly a safe haven for country folk and Confederates who moved there after the Civil War to escape Reconstruction. It was a state steeped in Southern tradition and culture. When the impromptu interviews concluded, the Dean brothers' entourage was hustled to their overnight suites at the famed Biltmore Hotel.

Built on the southeast corner of Grand and Harvey, construction of the Biltmore was a massive Great Depression project. Civic leader Charles F. Colcord, along with the architectural firm Hawk and Parr, completed the 619-room, 33-story building in 1932. At its completion, it was heralded as Oklahoma's tallest building and featured modern amenities, with rooms offering free radio, circulating ice water, and ceiling fans with up-and-down drafts. There was no mention in the press as to where the African American Monarchs stayed, but you can bet it wasn't the Biltmore, where they would not have been treated as guests.

Jim Crow laws in Oklahoma and other states forced Monarchs players to find sleeping quarters elsewhere at such segregated hotels as the Vincennes in Chicago, the Powell Hotel in Dallas, the Patton Hotel in Omaha, the Crystal Hotel in Houston, and Kansas City's Streets Hotel—the best segregated hotels on the traveling circuit—or they kept rolling, riding, and sleeping overnight on the team bus, seldom touching a bed. Lodging wasn't a problem for the Deans, and neither were room rates. Advanced ticket sales had already guaranteed them a handsome payday. Their cut from the World Series, totals made public during their Oklahoma visit, increased their personal assets considerably.

Just before the start of the Oklahoma City game, it was announced nationally that 25 members of the St. Louis Cardinals would each receive $5,821.18 as equal shares of the World Series receipts after agreeing to donate $3,000 in handouts to clubhouse attendants. This assured a certain degree of financial success before Dizzy or Daffy played an inning of exhibition baseball. They were in the black. Whatever they made on the tour would be extra income.

It had been a hectic day. Even with the late 8:15 p.m. start, the Deans barely had time to shower and change from their street civvies into their baseball duds. At Texas League Park, there was a mad scramble on the field and at the box office, where record numbers of sports bugs bitten by the Deans' popularity clamored for seats. People started lining up as early as 4 p.m. in lines two columns wide that stretched into the street and wrapped around the corner. When the gates opened, thousands crammed into the ballpark weeping with pure joy. Before sundown, the 7,500-seat facility was full of humankind. It was a Wednesday night crowd that looked like a July 4th gathering. They were grabbing day-of-game general admission and grandstand seats priced at 65 cents for adults, 25 cents for children, and filling bleacher seats that were going for 40 cents each. The higher-priced reserve seats, priced at 90 cents, and box seats, which were commanding $1.00 each, disappeared like penny candy.

When the stadium's lights were turned on, every space where a person might be seated or standing had a body in it, but tickets sales never stopped. The crowd kept swelling as more standing room only passes were sold for spots down both foul lines and around the outfield. People pushed their way onto the playing surface for what space remained in hopes of getting autographs or a better glimpse of the nationally famous Deans. They were packed in just outside the playing surface. Only six law enforcement officers were on duty, and they quickly lost control of the proceedings. This was a far cry from the 60 marshals massed in solid lines guarding the doors at Detroit's Navin Field the day before. "The police, ordinarily feared like the plague," wrote Meredith Williams of the Oklahoma News, "waved their billy clubs with as much futility as Mr. Holland's young athletes swung their war clubs during the season, and this admittedly was the very quintessence of futility."[21] The Daily Oklahoman reported that officer's threats to move people back were "met with stiff resistance."[22] In the outfield, gate-crashers tore boards off the wooden fence and climbed through, while others snuck in by jumping over the wall. It was a chaotic scene.

At game time, park officials listed the attendance at 15,000, double the seating capacity of the ballpark, but they could only account for 11,976 tickets sold. Many more had maneuvered their way onto the grounds without paying. Park officials estimated that "2,000 more went in on passes or crashed the gates to bring the total to the record mark."[23] Gate-crashers and fence-climbers alike joined in with those who were waiting with pens and pencils in hand to see the men who had tamed the mighty American League Tigers. The Daily Oklahoman called it the "largest crowd in Oklahoma sports history outside of football games."[24] An article in the Cleveland Call and Post imagined, "Perhaps the 15,000 fans who jammed the park to see the game, during the frenzy of their excitement, even forgot that the opposing team was colored. It is therefore refreshing to see a Southern mob turning out to witness an interracial sporting event."[25] Kansas City selected a left-hander to do their bidding, but it wasn't Charlie Beverly, as previously advertised.

A late-season game, preferably an October postseason game in the South versus a contingent of major league All-Stars, was starting to become a season-ending ritual for Wilkinson and Baird's Kansas City Monarchs. One well-publicized game was played at Oklahoma City in the fall of 1933, when Charlie Beverly's pitching demolished a team of big-league All-Stars at Texas League Stadium. Included among the All-Stars were the Pirates' Paul Waner, Forest Jensen, Hollis Thurston, and Larry French, along with Glenn Wright of the Brooklyn Dodgers. Beverly tossed a two-hit game and struck out 14 to win by a 3–0 score. Beverly had also defeated Ray L. Doan's all-white House of David team at the same stadium a few weeks prior to Dizzy's visit. That game had been played on September 28, a day where the Kansas City pitcher logged another two-hit, 2–0 shutout.[26]

Charlie's complete game against Doan's House of David failed to get good follow-up in the Oklahoma City newspapers. Under the glare of electric lights, he beat Mildred Ella "Babe" Didrikson, who pitched one inning, and "Spike" Hunter, a winner against Kansas City in the final game of the 1934 *Denver Post* Tournament. Didrikson came to Oklahoma City with lots of advance publicity. Most renowned for having won two gold medals in track and field at the 1932 Olympics, few people knew of her baseball prowess. Early in the spring, while attending Doan's baseball camp in Hot Springs, Arkansas, Cardinals pitcher Burleigh Grimes, the last man officially permitted to throw a spitball in the major leagues, proclaimed something to the effect that had she been a boy, she would have been a top baseball prospect. And while she was born and raised in the South, she had little opposition to playing baseball with African Americans. "In Cleveland this summer we saw the spectacle of Babe Didrikson," wrote the *Cleveland Call and Post*, "a Texas white woman, playing baseball against colored men. She never thought of the lineup."[27]

If Didrikson, a woman, was a great prospect, Beverly was beyond explanation. Neither woman or man could match Beverly's performance. But as far as white Organized Baseball was concerned, African American ballplayers might as well be girls. The wisest of scouts stepped over them to hunt down a white .225 "slugger," who smoked, drank, lived like a heathen, chased wild women all hours of the day and night, and had 10,000-to-1 odds of ever joining a major-league team for more than a few games. It was high treason on the baseball diamond if ever such a term existed.

When speaking of his former teammate, Chet Brewer declared with certain frankness, "He [Beverly] was a fastball pitcher. He had a little hitch which threw the hitters off. He never had a curveball."[28] Another Monarch, George Giles, agreed, saying, "Beverly had no curveball, but he could throw hard."[29] Brewer, in conversation with Heinie Manush, a Caucasian member of the Baseball Hall of Fame at Cooperstown, New York, recalled the hitter saying, "I know he's throwing a fastball, and still I can't hit it."[30]

The *Oklahoma News* tagged Beverly as "one of the fastest hurlers in the game."[31] The newspaper wrote of how he was "pleasing to watch and [was] a favorite with the fans." The *Daily Oklahoman* thought it would be a natural crowd pleaser for Beverly to face the Deans in Oklahoma. They hadn't planned on the Monarchs having two outstanding left-handers. When the

Deans lurched into Texas League Park, lefty Andy Cooper was already there getting loose.

The combination of lefty Andy Cooper, right-hander Chet Brewer, and lefty Charlie Beverly formed a fearsome trio of hurlers that won often for the Kansas City Monarchs. They were undefeated in games played in Oklahoma City. Beverly had been a Monarchs workhorse since 1931, but John Wesley Donaldson, age 43, and Wilber Rogan, who was 41, took occasional turns on the mound when not playing in the outfield. They had joined the Monarchs in 1920. By comparison, Sam Jones, a hurler for the American League White Sox, at age 42, was the oldest player in the major leagues. Kansas City had retained two of these aging veterans from their celebrated past and were trading on their legacy as former world champions while recording more than 100 exhibition wins in 1934. Unfortunately, the team was not at its best when they returned to Oklahoma to face the Deans. One of their star players was ailing, and another was absent.

Carroll Ray "Dink" Mothell, a Monarch since 1924, was suffering from rotator cuff problems that would ultimately end his professional career. Chet Brewer would not be in the lineup either. He had signed on for another barnstorming tour that pitted mixed teams from the upper Midwest against Earl Mack's All-Stars. Manager Rogan took few chances with his remaining lineup. He reinforced his roster with several well-known stars from the ranks of the Negro major leagues as insurance. Ted Trent was added to solidify the pitching and Walter "Steel Arm" Davis to produce more hitting. An edition of Wichita's *Negro Star* noted, "The Monarch club has added Leroy Taylor and 'Steel Arm' Davis to its outfield, and at the time the club is impregnable in every department."[32] The articles made no mention of Ted Trent. Taylor never showed up for any of the games.

Dizzy's All-Stars, or Oklahoma All-Stars, as they were soon to be renamed, was a team stocked with veteran minor leaguers and one or two former major leaguers. Bruce Sloan, John Fitzpatrick, and Jess Welch were returnees from the previous year's All-Stars. John Fitzpatrick, who was often listed as Jack in the local newspapers, a catcher for Mission in the Pacific Coast League and a .278 hitter on the year, was hired to receive Dizzy and Daffy's slants.[33] Ed Hall, who had a banner season in 1933, when he led the Missouri Valley League with 151 RBIs and hit a lofty 23 home runs, signed on to play left field. Sloan, of the Oklahoma Indians, a .260 hitter during the Texas League season, consented to play center field.[34] The *Daily Oklahoman* didn't seem to care about the other minor celebrities on the Dean's haphazardly organized All-Stars, but their competing newspaper, the *Oklahoma News*, took a much greater interest in the remaining talent.

Writers at the rival *Oklahoma News* gave first and last names for many of Dizzy's All-Stars. Bernie "Spec" Peddicord, formerly of the Nebraska State League, played third, and his 1934 teammate Gene Nance was stationed at shortstop. Peddicord and Nance had played summer ball with Wilcox, an Oklahoma oil and gas company. Jess Welch, a former member of the Oklahoma City Indians, was stationed at second base. Cy Blanton, who was owned by the National League Pirates, was to follow the Deans to the mound. In uniform but not able to play was Curtis Rice, catcher for the Hugo sandlot champions. The newspapers labeled these ballplayers as "minor leaguers and sandlot stars"; however, they were far better than the newspapers' rank description. One of the so-called "sandlot" players was a first baseman named Uke Clanton, who hit from the left side and once played in the American League.

Sometimes called Ucal, Clanton had retired from professional play in 1930, after 10 years in the Southwest, Eastern, Three-I, Western, and Southern associations, and various other minor leagues. Clanton's major-league career was all of one game with the Cleveland Indians on September 21, 1922.[35] Postseason exhibitions weren't unique for him either. He once played for Walter Johnson's All-Stars—not many men could boast of having played with both the Johnson and Dean All-Star teams. In 1934, Clanton was acting manager/first baseman for the Shawnee, Oklahoma, Independents, one of Oklahoma's many town teams.

The newspaper's advance notices had also advertised the appearance of the Waner brothers, Paul and Lloyd, and Pepper Martin. "They had not arrived," reported the *Daily Oklahoman*, after tickets had been made available for sale. The *Oklahoma City Times* advised that Martin had "remain[ed] in St. Louis to undergo an operation on his left arm."[36] A later edition of the *Brooklyn Daily Eagle* said the injury required elbow surgery.[37] Even without the big-league star, there were enough men with identifiable local ties for the All-Stars to make a creditable lineup.

Lefty Andy Cooper and T. J. Young formed Kansas City's starting battery. Paul Dean and John Fitzpatrick were selected to start for the All-Stars. The brothers, decked out in their bright red-lettered, embossed Cardinals uniforms, with numbers 17 for Dizzy and 21 for Daffy, were more than obvious. Across the field, Manager Wilber "Bullet" Rogan readied his Monarchs for the important skirmish. He put forth his best lineup in the form of Newton Allen, Eddie Dwight, George Giles, Frank Duncan, Carroll Ray Mothell, and Newt Joseph. John Donaldson and Walter "Steel Arm" Davis were held in reserve. Rogan penciled himself into the left-field slot.

There are many words to describe Charles Wilbern Rogan; lackadaisical wasn't one of them. He had been a star pitcher and outfielder for Kansas

City since 1920, with time off for an illness in 1930–1931, and in 1932, for a season in Jamestown, North Dakota. Starting in 1926, he managed the Monarchs. Like many of the Negro major-league stars, he could pitch, run like the wind, and hit for power. In spite of his 5-foot-7 frame, he is credited with more than 400 home runs and almost as many victories as a pitcher. Rogan could be counted on for a home run, then shut out his opponents and practically win his own ballgame. Wilkerson always smiled warmly when discussing Rogan. "Yes, he's a great player," the Monarchs owner said, "the greatest in the league. He could make any major-league club and would be a star. Everywhere we go they want to see Rogan play."[38]

Like the much-touted Dizzy, he too was a former solider. Rogan served his nation honorably for nine years in the segregated 24th and 25th All-Colored Infantries. When standing next to 6-foot-2 Dizzy Dean, he might have looked like a midget, but "Bullet" was every bit Diz's equal when it came to tossing baseballs and making great hitters look feeble—especially in his pitching prime from 1911 to 1928. Rogan, a player who provided Ruthian size feats and thrills for fans outside of the National and American Leagues, was easily the most underpaid man in the universe. It was a paradox seldom taken into consideration by sportswriters of the major dailies.

Daffy's start was rocky. Rogan's Monarchs featured an attack of consistent base hits and numerous safeties. Paul bore down in the pinches and fanned three Kansas City batters. He left the game after a trio of innings, with the All-Stars protecting a 3–0 lead. Kansas City hit Paul's best pitches yet trailed in the scoring. The All-Stars' runs resulted from Hall's single into the crowd, which drove in three. The multitude of people had become unsettled and arduous to handle long before Dizzy's entrance. Their presence in the outfield complicated play considerably. Dizzy and Blanton tried to loosen up, but there wasn't much room for pitching along the sidelines without hitting a person. Both pitchers entered the game without proper prepping.

Law enforcement officials on duty at the ball field tried without success to brush back the massive crowd, but the fastidious customers refused to give an inch. The *Oklahoma News* reported,, "Someone drove an automobile around the diamond trying to force the delirious fans back from the foul lines." It produced a temporary hole that quickly filled after the car passed through. Baseballs were also disappearing. Any ball hit into the crowd was captured, held for ransom, or never returned, contrary to the tradition of returning foul balls at all minor-league parks. The *Oklahoma News* reported, "The dizziest gent on the ground[s] was not Dizzy, or even Nutsy, he was Ed Sheldon, who did the announcing at the ballpark."[39] Sheldon tried his best to control the fans.

"Come on now folks," Sheldon blared over the loudspeakers. "Get away from them [light] towers," he urged. "There are thousands of volts in them towers. I'm a warnin' ya."[40] When he pleaded with the crowd to open lanes so the pitchers could warm up, the result was laughable. Few people moved. Repeatedly ignored, he used his microphone to warn them that a "batted or pitched ball would break somebody's cranium."[41] His voice was also unable to disrupt the half-dozen or so mini skirmishes that broke out between fans. The *Daily Oklahoman* made note of a small boy who was "knocked flat" when he ran headfirst into a Blanton fastball as the pitcher attempted to loosen up near third base.[42] The reporter glazed over the boy's injury, but this youngster could have been killed. Blanton was known as a hard-throwing hurler who led both the Western and International Leagues in strikeouts, with 284 at St. Joseph in 1933, and 165 with Albany in 1934.[43] In 1933, Blanton used his speed to strike out 19 members of the Davenport, Mississippi, Valley League team in a postseason playoff game. Thank God the boy survived.

Sheldon fared much better when he asked Carl Hubbell, Oklahoma's World Series hero of 1933, to stand with a loudspeaker announcement. The big-league pitcher received an ovation and noisy cheers from the massive gathering. It was Sheldon's most favorable acknowledgment. Hubbell took a bow but was not suited up to play. This night belonged to Dizzy and Daffy— not King Carl. The *Oklahoma City Times* said the crowd "waxed hysterical" when Dizzy took the mound in the fourth inning.[44]

It was Dizzy's turn at an attempted slaying of Monarchs' batters. The applause was exhilarating as he ambled to the mound. There was plenty of hop on his fast one as he proceeded to strike out four batters and allowed no runs and a hit in his two innings of pitching. Dizzy was impressive—he looked like a winner of 30 games. The All-Stars scored another run during his tenure on the mound to gain a 4–0 advantage. Blanton, who had stumbled into the Monarchs on a prior occasion, replaced Dizzy in the sixth. Cy had faced the Kansas City team at St. Joseph, Missouri, in exhibition play on May 14, 1933. As a member of the minor league St. Joseph Saints, he struck out four, allowed two hits and a run in four innings, and was credited with a 5–4 win. On this night, as a member of the Deans' All-Stars, Blanton allowed no additional hits before the game abruptly ended in the last half of the sixth inning.

As the All-Stars came to bat in the bottom of the inning, park officials decided the safety of its local citizens was more important than baseball and halted the proceedings. The end of the game worked in tandem with the disappearance of the remaining baseballs. As the last of several dozen baseballs disappeared into the multitude of inhabitants, rather than pleading with the crackpots to return the balls, promoters dimmed the flood lights, effectively ending the game. The *Daily Oklahoman* described it as "sort of like running out of coconuts in the jungle."[45] Newt Allen, a Monarchs infielder, told author John Holway, years later, "We had to stop the ballgame, but the people were satisfied, they got to see Dizzy and Paul pitch."[46]

The final score was a 4–0 win for the Deans' All-Stars. For many, the score didn't seem to matter as much as the festivities. They were there to see Dizzy and Daffy, who had recently conquered the Tigers in the World Series. Added to their legacy was Kansas City's first loss in Oklahoma City. As the Deans fought to exit the field, hundreds of autograph seekers trailed behind them. Police quickly assembled to protect the brothers from aggressive souvenir hunters, prepared with fountain pens, programs, and the game's missing baseballs. It was a hectic ending to a memorable evening of baseball—if it could be classed as a baseball game at all. A spectator advised, "Any guy should be able to pitch with 7,000 infielders." The *Kansas City Call* phrased it differently by stating, "No team could beat a crowd of several thousand self-appointed fielders who every time a ball was hit swarmed on the field and pocketed the pellet as a souvenir."[47] Back at the Biltmore Hotel, Frances Corry of the *Oklahoma News* sought out the Deans for postgame interviews. He started with Pat Dean.

Corry sat patiently while Pat Dean shook hands and affably greeted the important people assembled in the hotel's dining room. She powdered her nose as reporters took lots of photographs while she aimlessly tossed her silver fox furs across her stately shoulders. When asked about the game, she said she thought the 15,000 fans at Texas League Park were "awful." Dizzy encouraged her to restate her opinion, at which time she changed her statement to, "It was wonderful to see that crowd. I saw the Tigers and Cardinals play that exhibition game in Battle Creek, and the crowd there was large, but it couldn't compare with the one in Oklahoma City."[48] Asked about her husband she said, "He's a great kid. He isn't dizzy, and he is very quiet. Of course he pops off and says what he thinks ever so often, but he's a great kid just the same. There's nothing dizzy about him that I can see—except the way he can make a batter feel when he's throwing the ball."[49]

Dizzy thought the showing was "great," while Paul "preferred getting the party on its way." The next day's report in the *Daily Oklahoman* was almost as bizarre as the game's conclusion.

The All-Stars may have won the game, but it was Rogan's Monarchs who showed extraordinary talent on the diamond—but you wouldn't know that by reading the local newspapers. The *Daily Oklahoman* wrote a series of haughty and well-articulated statements designed to circumvent Kansas City's on-field success. It must have been troubling for local reporters, who ignored batters in the Kansas City lineup, hitters who collected at least one hit each off the much-celebrated Dizzy and Daffy. Instead of saluting the Monarchs' effort, one newspaper conveyed, "Pitcher Paul Dean was nicked for eight hits. Most of them would have been easy outs under normal conditions."[50] They used the word "nicked" to imply that none of the Monarchs' hits were solid or forceful drives. The same could be implied for "easy outs."

In reality, Kansas City's eight hits off Daffy equaled the total achieved by the Detroit Tigers in nine innings when Paul defeated them in Game 3 of the World Series. Kansas City's ninth hit was obtained off the more famous of the brothers, Dizzy, and both the *Daily Oklahoman* and *Oklahoma City Times* strategically tagged it as a "scratch hit."[51] The word "scratch" led readers to assume this Monarchs' hit was obtained with some difficulty, although proof was insufficient in further reading of the article to support this claim. Each of these statements were intended to promote inferiority among Negro baseball players. By contrast, the *Daily Oklahoman* identified each of Deans' Oklahoma All-Stars' hits as "stinging singles," seemingly penning these words without the slightest blot on the writer's conscience.[52]

What Monarchs batters achieved was marginalized to almost nothing by reporters for Oklahoma City's daily newspapers. They watched as members of the Monarchs gave Dizzy and Daffy a grand reception to baseball as it was played outside of the majors and minors while invariably knocking the boys off their pedestals. The reporters at the game hadn't made much of Kansas City's performance, nor had they said anything about the African Americans in attendance at the game—practically ignoring both. There was no mention of fans pouring in from nearby "Sand Town," a community settled by freed slaves in about 1884, in the May Avenue and Reno section of Oklahoma City. Segregation in the stands and on the field was never mentioned.

Photographs of those in the Monarchs' lineup were also omitted. By contrast, images of Dizzy and Daffy appeared in Oklahoma City newspapers no less than nine times in pregame and postgame articles. African American ballplayers were not to be celebrated as equals in any shape or form, not even as hometown favorites.

Ham, at the *Daily Oklahoman*, embraced Dizzy and Daffy as native sons—something they were not—while Rogan, who was actually born in Oklahoma City on July 28, 1893, when it was still recognized as Indian Territory, went unrecognized. Rogan's mother was buried in Oklahoma City, but it was never mentioned. The compassionate, humane side of his life wasn't even newsworthy in America's prideful distortion of reality. There was no mention of Rogan's Oklahoma City connection prior to or after the game. The newspapers also failed to reveal that the Monarchs' T. J. Young and Walter Lee Joseph were also raised in the state of Oklahoma.

In closing, the *Daily Oklahoman* article listed Cy Blanton, Ed Hall, and John Fitzpatrick of the Deans' All-Stars with first and last name recognition. The *Oklahoma News* also mentioned many of the white players by first and last names—while omitting the first and last names of every Monarchs player. Lefty Beverly and "Lefty" Cooper had been the newspaper's only attempt to print the first names of any Monarchs players—and both so-called first names were nicknames.

These same newspapers reported that Kansas City, Chicago, Milwaukee, and Newark had been added to the itinerary, extending the tour to seven games. The Dean brothers' globe-trotting had hardly begun when the *Oklahoma News* took one final sarcastic swipe at the Monarchs by announcing the win had "maintained white supremacy," adding, "which is a good thing down here in the Democratic stronghold, even if it takes Dizzy and Nutsie [Daffy] to do it."[53] It served as yet another example of the closed mindset displayed by many in the mainstream media.

All three of Oklahoma City's daily newspapers reported the Deans as having left by airplane for Wichita to continue their tour. Packed away with their luggage was a chest full of cash earned from the Oklahoma appearance. Paul was quoted as saying their portion of the gate receipts, not including their take from concessions and parking, "equaled his entire year's salary with the Cardinals."[54] Dizzy, with his always robust personality, was surely laughing all the way to the bank.

One of the few minority-owned newspapers to overtly discuss the Oklahoma game was the *Cleveland Call and Post*, which made statements in direct opposition to the *Oklahoma News*. Their bold proclamation was printed under the title "Baseball in Oklahoma" and presented on page four, which was not the sports section. "The South cannot forever remain adamant in its most covered policy of persecution of the Negro," said the October 20 article. "Sooner or later the awakening masses of Southerners will break loose from their traditional moorings. Such a simple thing as a ballgame may be the provocative incident."[55]

With racist attitudes like the one printed in the *Oklahoma News*, it should come as no surprise that 18 more summers would pass before Bill Greason, a former Negro major-league pitcher, would hurdle the color barrier in Oklahoma City by joining the Texas League Indians in 1952.[56]

CHAPTER 3

~

Wichita, Kansas

Fast Talk and Slow Floaters
Thursday, October 11, 1934

After their huge success in Oklahoma City, Dizzy and Daffy cut a swath into Kansas. Traveling east made Wichita—the largest city in Kansas—the tour's next logical stop before reaching Kansas City. Upon their arrival in the central Kansas town they were guaranteed another $2,500 and an additional 50 percent of the gross receipts.[1]

The newspapers emphatically stated that "no rain checks [were] to be issued for the appearance of the Dean boys." With any luck at all, in two games they were about to exceed the amount each had received as their share of the World Series win—and numerous exhibitions were yet to be played. One local newspaper suggested, "If the tour has at least seven days to run and perhaps three weeks, and if they keep up the way they've started, [the Deans] may each make $50,000."[2] Tickets, which had gone on sale several days earlier, were moving at a brisk pace. Locally, the *Negro Star* newspaper advised, "The ardent baseball fans are fairly alive with rabid speculation and fervent anticipation over this coming event."[3]

An article in the *Negro Star* said, "The Deans have been under contracts to play in Wichita since way back in August." Many had planned for the brothers' appearance at the newly built Lawrence Stadium. As he would often do, Dizzy sent word ahead to announce their arrival. "I am gunning for the Monarchs," he declared to the Wichita Athletic Club in a telegram. He then suggested that "Detroit wasn't worrying him nearly as much as that one game against the Monarchs."[4]

Three or four days earlier, unreserved grandstand and bleacher tickets for the game had been made available for 75 cents each at Dockum's Drug Store, a local Rexall Drugs franchise and a place where segregation at the lunch counter was routinely practiced.[5] They quickly sold out. Only 500 box seats were originally reserved at the highest prices. Their rapid disappearance forced promoters to place an additional 300 reserved seats on sale to meet public demand.[6] Lawrence Stadium could accommodate 8,500 at capacity, and the event was guaranteed to be sold out. The Wichita Athletic Club, in charge of the stadium event, made preparations to sell an additional 4,000 tickets for standing room in the outfield if needed. A report in the *Wichita Beacon* advised, "Officials estimate that present accommodations could seat 8,500, and at least that many more would be allowed to stand in the field."[7] Well aware of the events in Oklahoma City the day before, Wichita officials were ready with added security to restrain the additional flow of spectators if a standing room area was needed so that a full nine-inning game could be played. Opportunities to see the two baseball idols up close were also increasing as Ray L. Doan added agreements for several new tour stops—and it didn't appear likely that the crowds would stop packing local parks anytime soon.

The brothers arrived in Kansas boasting and beaming with confidence— and for good reason. They were on a rollercoaster ride of success and ready to roll with this momentum for as long as possible. At this point in the tour, no one knew what to expect next. Would the crowds continue to grow? What would the brothers say? And how well would their African American opponents hit the famed twosome? There were few unanswered questions about the brothers' pay. They were being paid well for their services in Wichita, where their contract called for each to toss at least one inning, —but they offered to do more, which surprised promoters. Dizzy insisted he and Paul would pitch at least three innings each—more than half the game. N. B. Stauffer, organizer and member of the Wichita Athletic Club, appeared to be flabbergasted as he told reporters, "We were surprised at their promise to work at least half the game on the mound against the Monarchs."[8]

The Kansas City Monarchs' history in this central Kansas town was almost flawless. They were considered by many to be the best team to ever step onto a local ball field. They brought to Wichita pennant winners, World Series championship teams, and the novelty of nighttime baseball. Locally, they were practically uncontested in games won and lost. They arrived for the Dean exhibition sporting a Wichita record of 33 wins in 34 appearances dating back to 1923.[9] The wins had included victories against Grover Cleveland Alexander's House of David, Paul Waner's All-Stars, and every Wichita all-star team placed on the field, including Western League and factory opposition. Kansas City's only loss had come against Paul Waner's All-Stars on October 12, 1933, in one of the last games played at Wichita's historic Island Park. The contest had ended in an 11–6 final.[10] With the Deans' arrival in town, many were eager to lay down their hard-earned wages to see what Dizzy and Daffy might do to Kansas City's best hitters. The game attracted qualified players from throughout the area.

Ernie Holman, a .271 hitter in 156 games for the Southern Association's New Orleans Pelicans, was recruited. Fred Brickell, a career .281 hitter in parts of eight National League seasons with the Pirates and Phillies, also signed on. Fred had played in the 1927 World Series with the Pittsburgh Pirates. Pitcher Ira Smith, who split the 1934 summer between two teams, the Elmira Red Wings and Rochester Red Wings, where he appeared in a total of 69 games, also joined the squad. As a pitcher, Smith's 5–2 won–lost record for Elmira in the New York–Pennsylvania League and a 6–6 record for Rochester in the International League more than qualified him for professional play. He logged 15 long years in the minors without reaching the major leagues. Forrest "Woody" Jensen, who spent nine seasons in the National League with the Pirates, was another Dean recruit, as was A. C. "Mickey" Flynn, formerly of the Texas League and Western Association, managed the Wichita Civic Theater team to a Kansas semipro championship in 1933. Jensen would establish two records for the Pirates in 1936, most putouts, with 526, and most at-bats, with 696. In 1935, his National League batting average would be .324. Flynn, who caught the brothers during the All-Star affair, would grow whiskers and play for Doan's House of David team in 1936. The local *Negro Star* newspaper noted, "Four major leaguers were on the All-Star team,"[11] then listed the names of Jensen, both Deans, and Ralph Winegarner, one of the All-Stars' pitchers, while omitting the others.

Right-hander Ralph Lee Winegarner had been a student at Southwestern College in Winfield, Kansas, attending school on a sports scholarship but later dropping out and began working for Travel Air in Wichita. He was pitching for the company team in 1932, when it became Beech Aircraft Corporation, but major-league scouts eventually made him the property of the Cleveland Indians and later the St. Louis Browns. He had appeared in 22 big-league games prior to joining the Deans' Wichita All-Star squad. The Benton, Kansas, native played all or parts of five seasons in the American League. He was a good hitting pitcher, leading American League pinch-hitters with a .379 mark (11-for-29) in 1935. Monarchs starting right-hander Ted Trent was also a former college pitcher.

Theodore "Ted" Trent, or "Big Florida," as he was called in the Negro professional leagues, was born in Jacksonville, Florida, on December 17,

1905. He was a former college athlete at Bethune-Cookman before entering the professional ranks with the St. Louis Stars in 1927. If there was a soft spot in Kansas City's 1934 lineup, it was pitching, and Trent was there to fill the void. He and his batterymate, T. J. Young, had played together for a short time in 1932, when both were members of the Detroit Wolves. On loan from the Chicago American Giants, Trent was soon to show Wichita fans one of the best curveballs in baseball. He used this pitch to perfection, especially in exhibition games against white professional opponents, as when he struck out 13 in a St. Louis Stars 3–2 win against Max Carey's team of major- and minor-league All-Stars at St. Louis on October 4, 1930.[12] A year later, on October 17, 1931, Trent whiffed 15 of Joe Pirrone's All-Stars in a Winter League night game at White Sox Park in Los Angeles, winning 5–0. Monarchs first baseman George Giles, who had gone to Cuba with the great pitcher and was the first baseman in the Max Carey series in 1930, said, "Trent shot the major leaguers down like clay pigeons."[13] Off the field, Trent was known to take a nip after games, but it was the great plague of tuberculosis that ended his life in 1944. He would lay interned in an unmarked grave at Chicago's Burr Oak Cemetery for another 50 years.

T. J. Young was sort of a pioneer in Wichita, where he spent his winters. In his absence from the Monarchs during the early part of the 1933 season, he integrated the all-white Mulvane team in Wichita's Oil Belt League. It was only natural when the *Wichita Eagle* got busy drumming up promotions that they utilized what they said were "quotes" from Young, Kansas City's superb hitting catcher, who was back with the Monarchs, although much of what they wrote was fabricated.

In an article entitled "Monarchs Claim They Beat Dizzy," Young reportedly said, "We beat Dizzy last year at Kansas City, 5 to 1, and he pitched the entire game at that time. Of course Dizzy won 30 games this year and will be tougher to beat than ever."[14] It was certainly great press, but the score and other minor details were incorrectly quoted, if what he reportedly said had been stated by Young at all. Indeed, Dizzy was in the game, which his All-Stars lost to the Monarchs at Kansas City in 1933. The final score was 5–4, not 5–1, and Dean only hurled three innings—six innings short of a complete game. Lou Garland, a member of Kansas City's American Association Blues, was credited with the loss, not Dizzy, as Young had supposedly stated.[15] In other games from the three-game 1933 exhibition series against Kansas City, Dizzy pitched briefly at Concordia, Kansas, and Oxford, Nebraska, without tossing a complete game.[16] The local Wichita *Negro Star* was quick with another Young article. In this story, Young was both poignant and forthright.

"The colored baseball ballplayer is stirring up great enthusiasm among major league fans in the East," he stated proudly. "It won't be long before the colored player will crash the big leagues." With boldness, he said he could "select a colored team to beat either St. Louis, or Detroit, out of the World Series and wouldn't need to extend themselves." When asked if they would defeat the Deans, Young was quick to say, "If any ball team defeats Dizzy Dean in a night game, the players while they are at bat will have to keep the star dust out [sic] of their eyes."[17]

While the daily newspapers were manipulating the Monarchs' history, Dizzy was finding his own ways to relate to local fans. Dizzy had a knack for his own self-promotion, and teammate John "Pepper" Martin explained how he went about it. "Every time we're invited to some dinner and Dizzy has to speak," said Pepper, "he starts in by telling them this is the very spot where he was born or his wife was born or some relative." "He makes a hit right off the bat that way. Nobody would believe me. But they believe Dean." In Wichita, there was no need to change the script. Dizzy told reporters at the *Eagle*, "'It is like getting back home to be in Wichita.' He remembered well the time he broke into real baseball with the St. Joe club out at Island Park."[18]

There were added reasons why people paid to see this exhibition. Wichita baseball fans loved watching the all-black Kansas City team, resulting in some of the largest crowds in the city's history—attendance totals the Deans versus Monarchs game were expected to shatter.

Wilkinson and Baird were determined to set the all-time attendance record for a baseball game in Wichita. The opening of the new Lawrence Stadium in 1934 gave rise to the largest local crowds seen in years. Kansas City already owned the new stadium's record for the largest gathering of fans. In facing the Deans, they were about to surpass their own high-water mark set earlier in the summer. George Giles of Manhattan, Kansas, was there when they set the previous attendance record and was also a member of the team that beat Dizzy in 1933. Frank Duncan Jr. advised, "Giles hit Dizzy Dean like he was a softball pitcher."[19] At age 25, Giles was already a seasoned veteran.

Back in 1925, a 15-year-old George Franklin Giles had taken a $4.25 ride, the cost of a Union Pacific train ticket from Manhattan to Kansas City, with dreams of joining the Monarchs. A local white bank president, Evan Griffith, gave him the money to make the trip, and his grandmother, a cook at the Sigma Nu house on the campus of Kansas State University, consented by overruling his parents. "I thought I was going to make all the money," explained Giles. "I went up and told my grandmother that she wasn't going to have to work anymore. I caught the train to go to Kansas City that afternoon, and my grandmother died that night."[20]

Baseball was a segregated world, but the banker knew Giles was good enough to have that professional opportunity. About town Giles had been a batboy for the local segregated men's team.[21] By age 14, he was getting $15 a week playing in the area. He came to Kansas City and lodged at the segregated Paseo Street YMCA. Jose Mendez, the Monarchs manager at the time, took the lad under his nurturing wing and taught him how to shift at first base, but he didn't keep the youngster on his roster. Giles was released and sent to a traveling team called the Kansas City Royals. The next year, he played with Robert P. Gilkerson's Union Giants. He returned in 1927, for another crack at the Monarchs. This time he made the team and was paid a whopping $120 a month. He would receive his largest salary in 1935, when he took over field management for the Brooklyn Eagles, who paid him $450. He said it was "good money in those days, especially for black baseball players." Giles recalled that traveling accommodations for African American teams were "horrible," regardless of how much you earned.[22]

In towns on the barnstorming trail there were few places that could house the entire team. "Two had to stay in your house, two had to stay over there," he remembered. "They would feed us at the Baptist Church or we'd head to the grocery store because we couldn't go to town to eat. That's the way it was all over the country. Colorado was just as bad as Mississippi; New York was just as bad as Alabama."[23] There was virtually nothing the players could do about it either. They were trying to play baseball at the highest level; they were not trying to be the Rosa Parks of their generation. They took their travel in stride as they traversed the segregated United States, where hotels, restrooms, restaurants, water fountains, and even pay phones were off limits for them. They made friends of their enemies. Monarchs catcher Frank Duncan reportedly "knew the white farmers on the back roads."[24]

In 1929, Giles married and sprang the news on Wilkinson while asking for an increase in pay. Wilkinson told Giles he could "go down to Louisiana and get three ballplayers for what he was asking [in pay]."[25] Giles made a phone call, jumped Kansas City for Gilkerson's Union Giants, and got the money he requested. His teammates on the Monarchs said Wilkinson would never hire Giles back. When Wilkinson reorganized in 1932, the player he wanted at first base was Giles. He would call it quits in 1939, at age 30, not because he couldn't play, but because of the segregated lifestyle he was forced to endure. "You couldn't stay in hotels or shop in stores. Playing every day and traveling on busses. You get tired of that kind of life. You just got to try something else." Many years later, in an interview with the author, Giles said, "I want to be remembered as a good ballplayer. I played hard and clean, and I always hustled."[26] In Wichita, big crowds usually showed up to see Giles and his hustling teammates.

The record for the largest turnout to a Wichita baseball game was set in 1921, when Tulsa and Wichita drew a paid attendance of 8,900 at the old Island Park. A game between the House of David and Kansas City had drawn as many as 6,300 in 1933, at the same field.[27] The record for the largest Lawrence Stadium crowd was set in August 1934—during a Monarchs verses House of David game, which attracted a crowd of 9,000.[28] On this night, October 10, 1934, by the narrowest of margins, a new high-water mark was established. It was an immense crowd that fell well under the estimated 12,000 that club officials had originally planned for.[29]

An above-capacity crowd, which included "8,560 paid," crammed into Lawrence Field for the Dean's All-Stars versus Monarchs event. Bernie Williams of the *Negro Star* tagged it as the "largest crowd ever to attend a baseball game in Wichita."[30] The *Beacon* advised, "At least one-half of the mob was from out of town."[31] Hundreds of railbirds who couldn't afford to enter through the gates sat atop box cars beyond the left-field wall. For a second night, customers crowded in on the exhibition, handicapping infielders and outfielders in their attempts to retrieve foul balls. Hard-boiled fans formed lines that extended around every side of the field, in some places a half-dozen people deep. In the blur of people, probably the only recognizable face for Monarchs players was Flora Young, the Monarchs catcher's wife. They made their home in Wichita.

Dizzy began the exhibition on the mound and hurled three innings. He approached the game differently than the day before in hopes of retiring the great fastball hitters in the Monarchs lineup with trickery. He always said that he and Daffy just fogged it in and let the hitters take care of themselves. This was not how he approached Kansas City. The *Eagle* was well aware that he had tweaked his pitching style and noted, "The crowd realized he had a fast one, although he used it little."[32] He was relying on curves and slow floaters, declining to zip through his fast one. It was a good plan, but it did not work. He allowed one run and was tagged for three hits during his short tenure on the hill. Paul Hemphill and Ralph Winegarner pulled a clever fielding play to stop another score. Paul relieved his brother in the fourth and held Monarchs batters hitless for two innings. For the five innings they were on the mound Dizzy and Daffy did not yield a base on balls. This was the version of their performance presented by the daily newspapers. As one might assume, the *Negro Star* saw things differently.

In an article titled "Base Ball News," the writer observed,

The Deans displayed the reason why they are world champions. In the first three innings Dizzy used a change of pace. He would first use his deceptive curveball, then he would switch to his blinding fastball that was smoking hot when he swept across the plate. His control was miraculous.

He too admitted that "Paul pitched two innings and was more effective than Dizzy."[33]

The Dean brothers' contract had specified that both brothers pitch at least one inning—they were determined to do more—and no one resisted. When absent from the mound they were in the outfield. Combined, they gave fans five innings on the mound and two additional innings in the outfield. Daffy rotated himself out of the lineup in favor of Ira Smith in the sixth inning. Smith pitched three innings before yielding to Winegarner, who completed the affair. Few fans yelled for the brothers to return after they packed up their duds and retreated to their suites at the Allis Hotel. Most were satisfied having seen Dizzy and Daffy's cheerful faces. Trent was equally impressive for the Monarchs.

Trent pitched seven innings, and his curveball was breaking into the batter's zone. For history's sake, the *Wichita Beacon* and *Eagle* wrote of how the Deans chased curveballs. Neither of these papers listed Trent's total strikeouts; however, the weekly *Negro Star* did when it reported that Trent "fanned six All-Stars."[34] Local newspapers dared not show the imported Chicago pitcher at his best, while mainly focusing on the Dean's white All-Stars. Trent had the brothers Dean raking in every at-bat. "At bat Paul's batting was amusing to the crowd," submitted an *Eagle* reporter. "He let his bat fly at least five times in his one turn at the plate, broke a bat, and finally went out." Dizzy's batting was another feature. "Each time he had been bitten badly on two curves," the *Eagle* noted, "and looked like one of these washwoman-style hitters."[35]

Trent lost the outing when the All-Stars rallied in the third inning. Dizzy started the damage with a double that hugged the foul line, and before the inning was over, in yet another instance in which the local newspapers did not specify how the runs were scored, the All-Stars tallied four times. Williams wrote in the *Negro Star* that "he [Trent] surely did pitch a wonderful game." He then admitted, "Costly errors by his supporting cast ascribed his defeat."[36] Trent handed the game to teammate John Donaldson, a veteran who came on in relief.

John Wesley Donaldson of Glasgow, Missouri, was at one time called the "Negro Southpaw Wonder." Carroll Ray Mothell, who watched him regularly, had much to say about his teammate's superior play. "Donaldson was playing center field and pitcher," Mothell related. "He was a complete ballplayer. He could run, throw, hit, field, and pitch. He was fast and was just about as good an outfielder as you'd want to see."[37] It was also said he threw as hard as he hit, but by 1934 he was a shell of his former self. He had spent a lifetime in baseball, and the great southpaw was already grown and pitching when Dizzy was born in 1910. That same year, Donaldson, age 19, was already taking regular turns on the mound with his segregated hometown team in Glasgow. By the time Daffy was born in 1912, John was already a star with J. L. Wilkinson's All-Nations, traveling throughout the Upper Midwest in segregated Pullman cars and delighting fans with his marvelous strikeout record. One record Daffy might have found interesting was the number of strikeouts Donaldson recorded the year before the younger Dean was born.

In 1912, Donaldson recorded 21 strikeouts in games at Superior, Wisconsin, and Fort Dodge, Iowa. He whiffed 20 in Towner, North Dakota, and added two games of 19 strikeouts at Minneapolis, Minnesota, and LaMars, Iowa. He proceeded to turn back 18 men at Omaha, Nebraska; 16 at Melrose, Minnesota; 14 at Sioux Falls, South Dakota; and 13 more at Hibbing, Minnesota, for a grand total of 161 strikeouts in just nine games. This, however, was only a fraction of Donaldson's overall season. By contrast, Daffy recorded 150 National League strikeouts in 1934, but it took him 26 games to reach this total. While many may argue that Daffy or Dizzy was superior to Donaldson, they must be equally prepared to conclude that this African American pitcher clearly dominated his opposition in the era of Jim Crow—when racism obviously prohibited his upward mobility.

John Donaldson allowed four additional runs in the eighth as the All-Stars topped Kansas City in an 8–3 final. It is ironic that these two Monarchs pitchers, Trent from Florida and Donaldson from Missouri, are buried in the same Illinois cemetery. Trent is interred in section 5, lot 5, row 6, grave 91, and Donaldson in section 7, lot 1, row 4, grave 97, in Chicago's Burr Oak Cemetery. Donaldson and his wife Eleanor had moved to Chicago in 1930.

Kansas City played well but for a second consecutive night ended on the short end of the scoring and hits. The All-Stars finished with 11 hits; Kansas City got eight hits. Who did what at bat will forever remain a mystery—especially against Dizzy and Daffy. The *Wichita Eagle* and its rival, the *Beacon*, did not bother with a box score. Only brief summaries and line scores were printed. These same newspapers also failed to provide important scoring sequences for either team. They chose instead to subject readers to the negative aspects of how they thought Kansas City played.

Once again, the press opted to write their stereotypic version of the game, as was illustrated in the *Eagle*. Much consideration was given to the Dean's so-called physical exertion and the Monarchs' uncelebrated play. It was the typical reframe whenever the unexpected happened—which certainly happened in Wichita. When Dizzy failed to dominate Kansas City batters as expected, the newspapers claimed "exhaustion." The *Eagle* advised, "[Dizzy] showed the strain of his grueling performances in the closing days of the National League campaign and the World Series," then added, "[He] appeared worn and tired from the strain of the [World] Series."[38] Evidently the *Beacon* agreed when it noted: "Dizzy appeared worn and tired from the strain of the series but despite this fact he pitched his best most of the time."[39] The key word in both cases was "strain," as the newspapers promoted the ideology that neither pitched well and exhaustion was to blame.

Both brothers having failed in their efforts to whiff many of the Kansas City batters prompted the *Eagle* to reluctantly admit, "Neither was impressive on strikeouts; Paul seemed to have more steam on his pitches, as he has had more rest than the older of the pair."[40] There was no mention of how worn out members of the Monarchs might have been with their extensive barnstorming schedule and cumbersome travel restrictions in segregated America or how well they hit the Dean's pitching. Baseball's unwillingness to create convincing analysis of how it benefited from the prejudice and segregation of the 1930s would continue with little criticism.

When commenting on Kansas City's pitchers, Trent and Donaldson, the *Eagle* informed its readers that they had "functioned with only fair success." In stark contrast, the *Negro Star* said that Trent "surely did pitch a wonderful game." The *Eagle* labeled Kansas City's defense as "ragged." The *Wichita Beacon* echoed these sentiments and used terms like "loose" and "erratic" to describe Kansas City's defensive play. The *Negro Star* conferred to its readers that "many fans criticized the Monarchs for losing the ballgame to the Deans. But, however, the Monarchs are no more infallible than the New York Giants and Detroit Tigers, who with million-dollar aggregations failed completely against the Deans."[41] The *Eagle* did mention that both teams were "handicapped" by the massive mob of fans surrounding the field while providing no descriptive terms for the All-Stars' three miscues.

The unscrupulous custom of providing first and last names for members of the Dean's All-Stars and relatively nothing for Kansas City continued. Other than T. J. Young and pitchers Ted Trent and Lefty Donaldson, local newspapers failed to mention any of the Monarchs ballplayers by first or last name, and there were no photographs of them in any of the articles. They were the nameless and faceless in an affair against Dizzy and Daffy, baseball's most publicized stars, whose pictures appeared in local newspapers no less than five times leading up to and after the game. On their side of the ledger, Ernie Holman, Ira Smith, Ralph Winegarner, Fred Brickel, Forest Jensen, Mickey Flynn, Paul Hemphill, and Pete Schreffler—almost all of the All-

Stars—received first and last name mentions in both the *Eagle* and *Beacon*. On this day the only thing that mattered was Dizzy, Daffy, and their All-Stars teammates, which clearly demonstrated the local press' mockery in the fight against racism, something that was especially apparent at Dockum's Drug Store, where tickets to the game were sold.

On July 19, 1958, 24 years after the Dean brothers' visit, local students, members of the NAACP Youth Council, staged a sit-in at the same downtown Dockum's location, situated at the corner of Douglas and Broadway. The student-led operation was an effort to end historic segregation at the store's lunch counter, an effort the newspapers virtually ignored. For generations, African Americans had been refused services at the counter. They were not allowed to sit down or eat but could order from one end of the counter and carry outside to chow down in the blazing Kansas heat of summer or frosty cold in the winter. According to an account on the Kansas Historical Society's website, "Young [black] students began entering the drugstore every day and filling the stools at the counter."[42] Well behaved with good manners, they ordered soft drinks, but the store's management refused to serve them and demanded they leave. For weeks, students continued to break the custom of not sitting at the counters. In the chaos, they were cursed by white patrons and harassed by police, but they kept coming back. "Finally, on August 11, the owner relented, saying, 'Serve them—I'm losing too much money.' The victory was a win for equality in Kansas."[43] It was also the first successful youth-led sit-in, predating the February 1, 1960, sit-in at Greensboro, North Carolina, which received national attention, by two years.

As the hardball-playing Monarchs and brothers Dean exited the park, a local Kiwanis Club finished off a contingent from the Lions Club in a game of donkey ball, which as many as 2,000 onlookers hung around to watch. Reporters at the *Eagle* spoke well of their interaction with the Deans. "They proved personable, genial gents," one writer advised. "Dizzy, of course, has a swashbuckling sense of humor, but there is nothing even remotely arrogant about him. Paul shines in the reflected glory of his more publicized brother when it comes to interviews and is content to do so."[44]

Everyone associated with the Dean's traveling show separated and retreated to their segregated hotel rooms to prepare for an early morning drive to Kansas City, where another enthusiastic crowd fervently awaited their arrival. C. E. McBride in his buildup of the Deans' visit, told readers of the *Kansas City Star*, "The Deans will play a picked team against the Monarchs, the famed Negro club of this city, and that means a ballgame and not just a lot of exhibition throwing. When the Monarchs go out to battle, the other team must play ball and real ball or fall behind in the parade."[45]

CHAPTER 4

Kansas City, Missouri

Rubber Arms That Won't Wear Out
Friday, October 12, 1934

Dizzy and Daffy were riding a wave of success as their entourage motored toward Kansas City, Missouri, with a total of 20,536 paid admissions already secured. The area's prominent newspapers—the *Kansas City Kansan*, the *Kansas City Times*, the *Kansas City Star*, the *Kansas City Journal-Post*, and weekly editions of the minority-owned *Kansas City Call*—represented the neighboring cities of Kansas City, Kansas, and Kansas City, Missouri, and kept everyone well informed of the barnstormers' prior travel. Another enthusiastic crowd was predicted at the ballpark, which could comfortably seat 18,000. The game was front-page news in the *Call*, which published an eye-catching headline: "Deans on Mound against Monarchs Tonight."[1]

The Deans arrived mid-morning on October 12, and rested as best as they could before the 8:15 p.m. game. Their naps were cut short by a continuous string of interviews and personal appearances. By 4:00 p.m., they had donned their game attire and off they went to 24th Street and Brooklyn Avenue, where they were to appear at Muehlebach Field later that same night. The trip to the ball field was not direct. Their manager, Frankie Frisch, had invited them to speak at a local awards dinner where many regional baseball celebrities were to assemble in his honor.[2] As was customary during their travels, a whole new group of players was soon to become the Dean's All-Stars.

Fans were eager to see Dizzy and Daffy, and their soon-to-be-named All-Stars, but many were excited to see Manager Rogan's Monarchs as well. For years, Kansas City had been a Negro National League town. Because of the team's rigorous barnstorming schedule, the city was denied seeing the Monarchs regularly in 1934. As barnstormers, operating outside of the structure of a Negro major league, they rarely returned to Kansas City. Georgia Dwight, wife of Monarchs outfielder Eddie Dwight, recalled she had only seen her husband four or five times since April of that year.[3] This one game was a rare chance for her to unite with her husband before season's end and the fans only opportunity to see the Deans after the World Series.

There were a number of local activities planned for Dizzy and Daffy—but virtually nothing for the Monarchs. There was no public homecoming or celebration for Rogan's Monarchs—no parades, no banquets, no feature articles in the newspapers. On the city's South Side, there was a Cardinals celebration. Frisch was in Kansas City attending a benefit given by the South Central Business Association in his honor. Dizzy and Daffy were invited. More interviews, a speech or two, lots of baseball, and their All-Stars' first defeat would soon follow. A writer for the *Times* noted, "Right now Niagara [Falls] hasn't anything on these brothers when it comes to something a person wants to see."[4] Tickets for the game sold quickly. Promoters of the event were expecting almost every seat at Muehlebach Field to have a body in it. The *Kansan* informed its readers that it was "probable" that neither brother would pitch a full game. "Both are tired from their strenuous efforts in pitching the Cardinals to a National League pennant and world's championship," mused the article's author.[5]

Muehlebach Field had flung open its gates in July 1923. Since its inception it had served as the home field for the American Association Kansas City Blues and Negro National League Kansas City Monarchs. George Giles recalled, "We used to get passes to see Blues games when the Monarchs were not playing. Our team used to go out in groups and watch games."[6] They were ushered into segregated seating when watching the Blues—no integration was allowed. This was in stark contrast to Monarchs games at the same park, where anyone could sit where they pleased. Prior to the opening of the new ball field, Blues and Monarchs games had been played at Association Park on 22nd and Prospect, a diamond that both teams also shared.

Muehlebach Field, built by hotel owner/beer baron George Muehlebach, featured longer outfields, especially in right field, where an embankment known as the Brooklyn Bank was an obstacle in the deepest part of the field. That part of the field wasn't level—it was on a hill—but rarely did balls land in that area. Even in later years, after Kansas City became an American League town, I recalled a Kansas City Royals radio announcer saying only four men hit balls over the right-field wall onto Brooklyn Avenue, a list that featured, among others, Frank Howard, Don Mincher, and Mickey Mantle. He failed to mention that Negro major leaguer Willard

Brown had been hitting them over the same wall before integration of the major leagues.

Before the Deans touched the field Dizzy was busy assaulting the press with more arrogant statements about his abilities. Kansas City's *Journal-Post* wrote that Dizzy, with typical "modesty," announced, "We've just got rubber arms. I could pitch all day. My arm just don't get tired and won't wear out."[7] This was mild stuff compared to the statement he made before the 1933 game, when he announced, "If I've got a sore arm I'll only strike out five in the first three innings." After a moment of reflection, he said, "If the arm ain't sore we'll make it six." Dizzy was seldom particular about who wrote down his quotes or when. Prior to his 1934 Muehlebach Field visit, Dizzy insisted that no outfielders be secured for the remaining exhibition games. "Paul can play the outfield when I pitch, and we won't need any outfielders when he pitches."[8] The writer, although jotting down his comment for obvious media reasons, didn't take Dizzy seriously—not for a moment. Ray L. Doan, J. L. Wilkinson, and T.Y. Baird weren't taking him seriously either. A terrific supporting cast was being secured.

Some players were less than enthusiastic about playing with or against African Americans. This was seldom the case in Kansas City, where Casey Stengel led teams that had battled Monarchs teams on numerous occasions dating back to 1920. A preliminary announcement of the Dean's All-Stars appeared in an October 7 edition of the *Journal-Post*, which reaffirmed that the strongest possible lineup was being sought to aid Dizzy and Daffy. Bruce Connatser, Ed Clark, Jim Mosolf, James Horn, and "Hobo" Carson were mentioned as probable All-Stars.[9] The *Kansan* proclaimed that Harry Burns, a local semipro star of Kansas City, Kansas, and Leo Yurchak, a "local boy who played in the Arkansas League," would play third base.[10] On the day of the actual game, only Yurchak, Horn, and Mosolf remained from the previously advertised players, and only Horn, "Dutch" Siebold, and Dorsey Moulder returned from Dizzy's previous year's All-Stars.

James Frederick Mosolf had finished the 1934 season with the American Association Blues, batting .284 in 133 games. James Horn appeared in 20 games for the Blues in 1934, batting .217 in 60 official plate appearances. Dorsey Moulder, a journeyman minor-league infielder, was there to solidify the All-Stars lineup. He was no stranger to Monarchs pitching.

Infielder Dorsey Moulder, originally signed by the Kansas City Blues in 1931, had finished the 1934 season in the Western League at Des Moines, Iowa, where he batted .279 in 17 games. At one point in his career he showed great promise, as his 1932 signing with Waterloo, his 1933 opportunity in Des Moines, and his later 1935 option to Cedar Rapids illustrated. For most of 1934, he toured with Doan's colorful House of David Eastern squad. Moulder had batted against the Monarchs on several occasions. In August 1933, he had gone 2-for-4 off Chet Brewer in a 14–3 loss when Kansas City bested the Western League Des Moines Demons.[11] On September 20, 1934, at La Crosse, Wisconsin, Moulder, then a member of the House of David team, doubled twice and tripled in an 8–8 tie versus Rogan's Monarchs.[12]

Pitchers Morton "Mort" Cecil Cooper and Joe Emil Bowman, destined for long careers in the majors, were hired to hurl after Dizzy and Daffy's exit. Bowman had compiled a 5–4 record in 35 contests for manager Bill Terry's 1934 New York Giants, which the *Journal-Post* called a "successful year."[13] Joe's major-league career lasted 11 years and included play in both the National League and American League. He was said to be an admirer of Negro League players in a story that appeared in a 1934 edition of the *Brooklyn Daily Eagle*. The article stated, "He [Joe] is fond of talking about a Negro pitcher out in Kansas City who could throw the ball so fast even batters like the Waners couldn't see it." The article admitted, however, that "Bowman failed to remember the pitcher's name. It was something like Lorgan," he said, "or maybe Horgan," the writer concluded, "but Bowman says he was good."[14] Most everyone who read the article knew he was talking about Wilber "Bullet" Rogan, the longtime Monarchs pitching great. And yet, Bowman knew more than he was letting on. He knew Rogan as the man who had defeated him in a 1933 Major League All-Stars versus Monarchs appearance in Kansas City. Bowman, the pitcher of record on that night, was coming off a season during which he had compiled a 23–11 won–lost record for the Pacific Coast League Portland Beavers. The game had a dramatic finish.

On October 15, 1933, Bowman came on in relief of Ray Caldwell, once a star pitcher for the Cleveland Indians.[15] When Joe took the mound in the ninth inning the score was tied at 2–2. The *Kansas City Call* recalled the action, writing,

> Giles was safe when he hit to [Glen] Wright in deep short and beat the throw to first. Young hit to [Harry] Leibold, but both runners were safe when [Glen] Wright muffed the third baseman's toss at second. Giles and Young both took a big lead, and with the count three-and-two on Rogan, a hit-[and]-run play was put on. It worked! Rogan singled to center, and Giles slid home in the mud before [Jimmy] Gleason could get the ball home.

Bowman was listed in the box score as the losing pitcher. There was no denying the loss. The game was witnessed by 3,000 people.[16]

Dizzy's relief pitcher for the 1934 game was Morton Cecil Cooper. Cooper would have a long and illustrious career in the majors. And while he played only half as long as Rogan and achieved only a fraction of Rogan's overall feats, Cooper is better known because of his National League affiliation and nationwide publicity.

Cooper, also known as Mort, and his brother, Walker, were both born in nearby Atherton, Missouri. Both played in the majors. Mort saw action with two minor-league teams during the summer of 1934. At Elmira in the New York–Pennsylvania League, his pitching produced a respectable 10 wins and 12 losses in 29 games. He appeared in just three games for the American Association Columbus Red Birds and finished with a 0–1 record. Upon his return to Kansas City, he was hired as one of the Deans' All-Stars. Mort may have faltered against Kansas City's Monarchs as a member of the All-Stars, but his major-league career soared. He played 11 seasons, finishing with three years of 20-plus wins between 1942 and 1944, for the National League Cardinals. For the Dean brothers' series, Dutch Siebold, a former Kansas City Blues receiver, was there to handle the pitchers. Yurchak, one of the locally famous brothers from the Schneider Jewelers team, which competed in the 1934 *Denver Post* Tournament, completed the hard-hitting roster that faced the Monarchs.

A game at Muehlebach Field should have automatically given the Monarchs home-field advantage. Kansas City was their town. In 1934, however, few considered Kansas City their home court, as they rarely played there. Starting in 1931, the Monarchs had become a barnstorming team. They were continuously on the road, a vast difference compared to their pennant run in 1923, when they played a record 57 games in Kansas City. In 1934, the number of Monarchs home games dipped to three—and one of these games was played across the Missouri River in Kansas City, Kansas. The game against the Deans would be their fourth in metropolitan Kansas City for 1934—their third at Muehlebach Field. Even with the augmented demand for tickets, it hadn't felt like a homecoming, especially when you consider the coverage they received in the daily press. With little home-field advantage, Wilkinson and Baird's Monarchs rolled into town for game three of the Deans' All-Stars junket. Walter "Steel Arm" Davis further enhanced a rejuvenated Monarchs outfield for the Kansas City game.

There were four famous Negro major-league players who went by the nickname "Steel Arm." There was Steel Arm Dickey, Steel Arm Tyler, Steel Arm Taylor, and Steel Arm Davis. Two of the famous men nicknamed Steel Arm—Dickey and Davis—were murdered. Dickey's murder was the result of Southern injustice in 1923; Davis's death was a cold-blooded killing inside Chicago's well-known Indiana Inn on the city's South Side.

In late November 1941, it was said that Eugene "Red" Merrill walked into a tavern on Chicago's South Side. He struck up a conversation with a female acquaintance of Davis, and the ballplayer took offense. Steel Arm and a friend, James Banks, slapped Merrill around for speaking to the woman. The beaten man hurried from the bar and went home but returned with gun in hand and anger in his eyes. He came back looking for Davis and Banks. He fired his pistol, killing Davis and wounding Banks and another innocent bystander before escaping to Gary, Indiana, where he was later tracked down, captured, and tried for murder.[17] For Davis to have lost his life in such a senseless act—over a woman in a bar—is one of the sport's unfortunate tragedies. Late in his career Davis was bouncing from team to team like a ping-pong ball. He had just finished a season with Chicago's Palmer House Indians, the Illinois state champions, and earlier, in 1937, he was on the West Coast with the Yakima, Washington, Browns. Years before he had been a much-celebrated baseball player in Texas.

Davis was a highly respected hitter and fielder. He was an all-around talent, first as a pitcher, later as an outfielder, and eventually as a first baseman. He possessed a great throwing arm and was considered slick fielding in the infield. Early in the 1934 season, Davis was traded by the American Giants to the Nashville Elites. The *Chicago Defender* expressed doubt that "any of the new or old men replacing him can take the place of the big bat of 'Steel Arm' Davis." The writer added, "The passing of 'Steel Arm' Davis breaks up the wrecking crew that included 'Mule' Suttles, Davis, and Stearnes. Those three fellows coming up in rapid succession generally wrought terror in the hearts of opposing pitchers."[18]

A few days earlier, on October 7, 1934, Davis had been in Jamestown, North Dakota, performing against Earl Mack's Major League All-Stars. Steel Arm's whaling of the horsehide produced two home runs, a double, and five runs batted in off Mack's big-league pitchers. Tommy Thomas of the Washington Senators and "Doc" Cramer of the Philadelphia Athletics were victims of Davis's home run blast. There were no pictures of Davis in the *Jamestown Sun* newspaper, and only his nickname appeared in print; no real first name was presented in the 11–0 final.[19]

The series with Earl Mack's All-Stars ended on October 8, 1934, at Winnipeg, Canada, which allowed Davis time to travel to Kansas City for the Dean tour. It is difficult to know if Davis joined the Monarchs on the day before, as no box score exists for the Wichita contest.

The Dean brothers' stay at the Hotel Muehlebach was a well-hidden venture. Kansas City was a hide-and-seek stay, although tickets for the game were being sold at the same location. A story about Paul Dean was written from this "undisclosed location" after reporters tracked the brothers' movements. Evidently the younger Dean was alone when reporters converged on him. They questioned Paul about his romance and engagement to Betty Holt of Columbus, Ohio. Half asleep after being awakened from his short nap, and absent of Dizzy's interference, Paul stuttered and said, "I don't want to talk to nobody about that."[20] A day earlier, Paul had told a *Wichita Beacon* reporter, "I'd like to issue a general warning to all newspaper guys right now. Quit worrying me about when I'm gonna get married."[21] In a disjointed dialect, speech typically reserved by the mainstream media when quoting Negroes, Paul reportedly lamented, "My ahm sho' is tahed. I gotta get some sleep before pitching tonight."[22] Promoter Ray L. Doan came to Paul's rescue, ending the impromptu interrogation. In a statement given to a *Star* reporter, Doan said Paul was "burned up" about the interview and any statements about the Deans should come from Dizzy.[23] In a later article for the Associated Press, Paul admitted, "I ain't gonna get married for 10 years, and when I do, I'm gonna get me a gal down in Dixie."[24]

The three daily newspapers were busy recording anything Dizzy said. He had lots to say when the brothers stopped at the LaSalle Hotel for a spontaneous speech before the South Central Business Association dinner where Frankie Frisch, the "Fordham Flash," was being honored. Doan also fielded questions at this event.

Frisch's appearance at the South Central Business Association fund-raiser had been announced days earlier when the *Journal* released an article confirming his planned arrival. As manager of the world champion St. Louis Cardinals, Frisch was an honored guest at a dinner in celebration of a Missouri victory in the baseball classic. He arrived in Kansas City on the same afternoon as the Deans. The Business Association had also invited Dizzy and Daffy to the dinner, if only for a brief period. Other guests were Joe Bowman of the New York Giants, who was scheduled to play with the Deans' All-Stars later that evening; Mayor Bryce Smith; E. Lee Keyser, president of the Des Moines minor-league club; Johnny Kling, a business owner and former Chicago Cubs catcher; and major-league umpire Joe Rue. Other baseball figures in attendance were Casey Stengel, manager of the Brooklyn Dodgers; Joe Kuhel, first baseman for the Washington Senators; and Dutch Zwilling, a former Kansas City Blues manager and current minor-league manager.[25] Dinner was scheduled for 6:30 p.m., which led many to think the Deans would not show. Suddenly, out of nowhere, in marched the twosome. They were on a mission, as they made a hastily planned beeline toward the appetizers on the buffet.

Ray L. Doan, who was there with them, intercepted the media on the brothers' behalf. "Dizzy is only dizzy for a purpose. He is dizzy as he says, for business reasons—like Gracie Allen, who is dizzy because men like dizzy girls," proclaimed Doan. "I've been with him enough by now to know that Dizzy Dean is a whole lot smarter than he is given credit for being. He usually does and says the things which will reflect to his benefit."[26] Andy Anderson, sports editor of the *Houston Press*, who was writing a series of national articles on the Deans for United Press International, evidently agreed. "Dizzy Dean is not as dizzy as he would like to have folks believe," said Anderson. "Nor is he the braggart and swelled head that many sportswriters have indicated."[27]

The banquet room was taken hostage when both Deans stormed in dressed in Cardinals uniforms and brightly colored scarlet windbreakers. Only their cleats were missing. They stole the show from Frisch, wearing a boring gingerbread brown business suit. People watched in amazement as Dizzy ate a slice of apple pie, which he crammed into his mouth before standing to make this hasty speech:

> I suppose you want to hear about the series. Well, after the sixth game I was in the showers, and Frankie Frisch came up and asked me if I thought I could go in and work the last game. Frankie looked so worried I felt sorry for him. So I reached over and patted him on the shoulder and said, "You go home tonight and get a good night's sleep. Don't worry about the game. Dizzy is ready to pitch, and it will be just a breeze tomorrow." You all know how much of a breeze it turned out to be. Why, after we scored those seven runs in one inning, I just joked with those Detroit boys.[28]

Paul's brief statement followed. "I'm not qualified to make no speech," he said. "I'd rather be out in the box with a three-and-two count on the batter and the bases loaded."[29] Then he immediately took a seat. Frisch had plenty to say about his two pitchers, but one statement stood out. When asked to compare Dean with Detroit's "Schoolboy" Rowe, Frisch advised, "Well he's a pretty good pitcher, but he's not as good as Dizzy Dean or Carl Hubbell. As a matter of fact, the best pitcher the Tigers showed us was Tommy Bridges. He's a great pitcher." With that last statement, the Deans paused to be photographed with Frisch, excused themselves, and made their exit amid new details about the tour.[30] Before leaving, Dizzy remarked to Henry McElroy Jr. that "since he was going to take some money out of Kansas City, he might as well leave some here," and gave the son of the city manager $25 for Mercy Hospital."[31]

An article on October 11, in the *Star*, stressed that the Deans were signed for a series of fewer than a dozen exhibition games prior to the Cardinals winning the pennant, mentioning that these games were signed when it looked as though the Cards would finish second in the National League pennant race. The *Star* also mentioned how the Deans tried to void their barnstorming contracts. They soon found the contracts to be "ironclad," forcing them to go through with the original agreement. "When the Deans got into the World Series that changed things all around," stated the Oxford, Nebraska, *Standard*. It was further noted that promoters J. L. Wilkinson and Ray L. Doan were said to have "sweetened the ante considerably."[32]

Few were surprised when it turned out to be another profitable evening, as 14,000 people poured into the Brooklyn Avenue lot, a park with an 18,000-seat capacity when full. Ticket prices were increased from 65 cents for box seats to $1.10, which probably scared off some of the more frugal spenders. The vendors were making great money as well. According to the local newspapers, an adolescent hawker "interrupted" the pitchers as they signed autographs near the dugout. "Can you help us out?" the vendor asked politely. "Glad to, buddy," Dizzy answered, "What is it?" The hawker said, "All you got to do is stand up in front of the dugout so those men in that box can get a good look at you. They said they would buy everything I have if you would." Dizzy waved, and the sale was evidently made.[33] While Dizzy was busy appeasing the vendor, Daffy had taken the mound. A *Call* writer took note of Paul's planned appearance and offered, "Paul may not be able to stop those hefty hitters. The Monarchs can 'eat up' curveballs, and when it comes to solving those fast ones, they hold their own with the best teams in the country."[34]

It was about time for the game to begin, so the brothers hustled out to take a few cuts in the batter's box. "Dizzy drove the ball against the scoreboard in left field," and the fans applauded. He returned to the bench and asked, "Brother did you see that one?" When introduced to one of his new teammates, a big-leaguer, he had problems identifying him. It was Joe Bowman.

"Hello, Dizzy," he greeted the pitcher.

"Hello, there," returned Dizzy. "What kind of a year did you have?"

Bowman was puzzled. "I don't believe you remember me, do you?" he questioned.

"Sure I do," assured Dean. "You're from down South. I'll think of your name in a minute."

"You're wrong. But you ought to remember me. I know all of us Giants will remember you without any trouble."

Paul whispered to Dizzy.

"Bowman. Sure. Now I know you. I couldn't place you because you didn't have on a New York uniform. Say how did you fellows feel on that last day when Brooklyn took you down?"[35]

On the other side of the diamond, Andy Cooper, making his second start in three days, was taking warm-up tosses for the Monarchs. Displaying class in every aspect of pitching, Cooper held his own against the major- and minor-league stars. Kansas City struck first, scoring off Daffy in inning two.

T. J. Young tripled for the first extra-base blow of the night. As it turned out, this was the only hit Paul permitted. Davis's sacrifice fly to deep left field had the outfielders backing up and allowed Young to jog home with the game's first score. Daffy retired after two innings and turned the mound duties over to his older brother. The following day, the *Kansan* wrote of Young's triple and Davis's sacrifice by stating that Paul was "nicked" for a run.[36]

Dizzy relieved his brother in the third and also allowed a run. In that inning, Young doubled and scored on Bullet Rogan's single to center field. In his two innings, Dizzy allowed four hits and one run, and struggled to get batters out. He struck out a batter and made his exit. After the pitching change, it was a Cooper-versus-Cooper affair. The Monarchs pulverized Dizzy's replacement even worse. They hit Mort's best pitches to all corners of Muehlebach Field for 10 additional hits and five more runs. The most damaging was a bases-loaded, seventh-inning triple by George Giles. The loss, however, belonged to Daffy Dean because the All-Stars never dented the scoring column.

Those who had witnessed the Monarchs' 7–0 win watched the most explosive offensive display of the tour.[37] You could not read what the players thought of the win in the daily newspapers, where no such information appeared. For members of the Monarchs, their only voice was in the minority press. Young spoke elaborately about the game to a *Call* sports reporter in a postgame interview, stating, "I got a big kick out of hitting [Dizzy] Dean tonight. All my life it has been one of my ambitions to hit the best hurlers in the majors. So now I figure that maybe I'm not so bad with the bat. I also think we [the Monarchs] have a great bunch of hitters."[38]

Dizzy testified in the affirmative adding, "They are, on the whole, better hitters than the Detroit Tigers. We haven't been able to fool these Monarchs with our fast balls very much." Young had extra-base hits off both brothers.

Thomas Jefferson Young might have been inclined to call Oklahoma City; Okmulgee, Oklahoma; or even Wichita, Kansas, his hometown. Early in life he lived in them all. He had come to the Monarchs for a brief period in 1924, before joining them permanently in 1925, as the team's backup catcher. Frank Duncan was doing all the catching when he arrived; by 1934, Young was doing much more of the catching. It could be said that he was the better hitter and Duncan the better receiver. In Mankato, Kansas, during the 1933 season, Young hit for the cycle, scoring a home run, triple, double, and single in a Monarchs' 11–3 win. The tall fellow was known for his timely and often dramatic slugging. His first home run as a Monarch was a grand slam versus a minor-league team at Salina, Kansas, in 1925. He never fit the prototype of a National or American League catcher—he wasn't stout or slow. In 1931, he hit an inside-the-park home run at St. Joseph, Missouri, and circled the bases with amazing speed.

Chet Brewer, whose full name was Chester Arthur Brewer, and Young were bosom buddies. Wilkinson added Young to the roster and made him Brewer's personal catcher after an incident during the 1925 season. According to Brewer, the team was playing poker in some small town when he and Duncan got into an argument. "Duncan had one of the hottest tempers on the team," he proclaimed.[39] Frank pulled a knife and cut Brewer on his throwing arm, seriously injuring him. While he recovered, the Indianapolis ABCs, another league team, tried to acquire his services, but Wilkinson wouldn't trade his young prospect. The next year, Young was added to the roster to catch every game Brewer pitched. Chet, who carried the scar on his arm for the remainder of his life, was also a practical joker. He told this author about a bad joke he played on Young that made the catcher mighty angry.

Brewer laughed reflectively while thinking back on the beds they slept in. These beds were usually made for shorter people. The tall players, anyone more than six feet tall, like Brewer or Young, slid their feet between the bed rails to get more space when sleeping. One night, Chet gave T. J. the old "hot foot" routine. He recalled, "T. J. liked to tear the bed up trying to get his foot out of those rails. He was so angry, I stayed away from him all day," said Brewer.[40]

After the Monarchs' victory at Kansas City, you'd think the hometown newspapers would have given them their just reward—they did not. The *Kansan*, in a sniping summary of Dizzy and Daffy's visit, failed to mention Young's name. A writer at the *Times*, an eyewitness to Young's dominance over both Daffy and Dizzy, was unrepentant in his coverage of the game. What he wrote instead was a sheepish and unapologetic explanation of the days' results in an effort to preserve the reputations of both pitchers.

The *Times* noted, "Paul and Dizzy, playing in a lineup with Kansas City professionals and semiprofessionals, were unable to stop Young, the Monarchs' catcher."[41] The comment implied that the Deans might have fared better if backed by their St. Louis teammates. If their supporting cast had been partially to blame, much of the responsibility belonged to the famous brothers. Young's hits off Dizzy and Daffy had little to do with the All-Star team behind them. Additionally, there was no enlightened discussion regarding what Young might have achieved if he was able to play in the National or American League, which was a more logical approach than blaming others for Dizzy and Daffy's downfall. Reporters at the *Times* were unwilling to admit that Young was worthy of an opportunity in the American League or National League, but others were not.

Elden Auker, a Detroit Tigers pitcher, in his book *Sleeper Cars and Flannel Uniforms*, recalled playing against Young during this same period. The Detroit starter in Game 7 of the 1934 World Series once played with an Oxford, Nebraska, team under an assumed name, Eddie Leroy, to protect his college sports eligibility at Kansas State University. "Young hit a home run off me. There weren't any walls at the park, and the ball just kept going and going and going," he remembered. "He had some kind of power, and he had a great throwing arm, too. There is no doubt in my mind that if blacks had been allowed to play in the majors, he would have been an All-Star catcher."[42]

T. J.'s outing against the Deans was exceptional. The same could be said of his teammates. Eddie Dwight, Newt Joseph, George Giles twice, and Young three times scored all of Kansas City's runs. Each player in the Monarchs lineup, except for the ailing Carroll Ray Mothell, had at least one hit. Doubles by Young and Davis, triples by Young and Giles, and Newt Allen's stolen base said more about Kansas City's output than the newspapers cared to mention. There were six extra-base hits in the game, all belonging to the Monarchs, who racked up a total of 14 hits behind Andy Cooper, their future Hall of Fame pitcher, who issued hits sparingly.

Cooper pitched a complete-game shutout and allowed just four hits. He was meticulous as he rifled through the All-Stars lineup. Mosolf, who formerly played in the National League with Pittsburgh and Chicago, got a hit, and so did Bowman, Horn, and Yurchak—but none of the All-Stars obtained more than one. Cooper walked one batter and matched Dizzy's strikeout total of four in racking up the win. As a well-traveled and outspoken member of the African American community, Cooper was known to have said a few things about racism. In a 1934 edition of Wichita's *Negro Star* he offered, "I was in France during the World War; I have been to Cuba, Japan, China, India, and many islands in the Pacific. I find the Negro race to be the most wonderful of all races. But, I find the Negro to be suffering with an inferiority complex. The Negro is too ashamed of [being] 'black.'" On the topic of baseball, Cooper was nonapologetic as he stated, "Although the Negro has never crashed the major leagues, the Negro baseball player is one of the greatest of today."[43]

It is ironic that many of the African Americans on the teams Dizzy faced were world travelers, while many of his All-Stars had rarely left the states. Yet, one ethnicity of players was deemed inferior, while the other, less traveled and seemingly less educated on issues of race worldwide, was said to be superior.

After the game, local newspapers were crooning a familiar tune. In response to Cooper's masterpiece, the local *Times* newspaper proclaimed, "The Monarchs' ace was in rare form and never in danger." The term "rare" was meant to imply he was pitching with an invincibility that wasn't normal.[44] In reality, Cooper pitched this well often. There was nothing uncommon about his performance on that night. In fact, he was recognized as one of the Negro major league's top left-handers and, in 2006, joined baseball's elite as a Hall of Fame inductee at Cooperstown, New York.

It was evident that the "free press" in Kansas City had become a mouthpiece for prejudice and racial discrimination. The *Star's* coverage of the game wouldn't be much different from the rest of the country when it came to bias, and many of its advertisers followed suit. Chet Brewer recalled a time when he and his wife went shopping downtown with one of the newspaper's advertisers. He remembered, with uneasiness,

> I went down to Rothschild's, a big store there in Kansas City. My wife tried a hat on, and it didn't fit. A clerk had been watching, and when she tried to put it back on the shelf the attendant stepped in and said, "That's your hat now. You had it on. I can't sell it." She had to buy it whether it fit or not.[45]

There were unwritten customs and symbols of segregation throughout the city, and the daily newspapers were not exempt from displaying the exploitation. It was déjà vu when they reported on issues of integration, which could be seen in their coverage of the Dean brothers' visit. While the newspaper provided first and last names for the Deans' All-Stars, almost nothing in the way of first names for the Monarchs appeared in print. This wasn't outright rejection. It was a subtle neglect that buzzed past and sunk into the minds of its readers like a Satchel Paige 100-mile-per-hour fastball. Only three Monarchs were named in the numerous postgame reports. No one complained, and few outside of the African American community seemed to even take notice. Andy Cooper was the only Monarch to have his first name mentioned, by the *Times* and the *Kansan*. Young and Rogan's last names were mentioned in the *Times*, but nothing resembling a first name was printed. The *Journal-Post*, once a reliable Republican voice in Kansas City's African American community, not only omitted the printing of a box score, but also failed to mention any of the Monarchs by first or last name. This was the state of the baseball hierarchy in the Monarchs' hometown, which leads one to wonder how such a negative display of bigotry was played with the next generation.

During the Deans' Kansas City visit there was a convention of the National Scholastic Press Association. Nine boys, possible journalists from the next generation of writers, all of them editors involved with their high school newspapers, interviewed the Deans in the lobby of the Hotel Muehlebach at about 9:30 a.m. the morning before they motored to Des Moines for a game later that night. Dizzy fielded questions while Paul sat silently. Represented in the gathering were young boys from Muskogee, Oklahoma; Racine, Wisconsin; Peoria, Illinois; and Alliance, Nebraska.

"How do you account for the large score in the last World Series game?" asked one of the young interviewers.

"The boys were just hitting, that's all," Dizzy remarked. "I predicted that if the Series went to seven games I'd win with a shutout."

"Dizzy," asked one of the curious students, "are you a newswriter, too? I read some of your stories about the game."

"No," answered the Diz.

He stopped short of identifying Roy Stockton as his ghostwriter.[46]

When asked if he had signed any advertising contracts Dizzy was quick with an answer. "Sure. I've signed up for cigarettes and never smoked one in my life. I've also endorsed a lot of breakfast foods and some baseball bats. I've got a lot of contracts." Dizzy then terminated the interview session by saying, "We got to go eat."[47] It was an emotion teenage boys easily understood.

Shortly thereafter, members of the tour were on their way, escorted to the city limits by motorcycle patrolmen, headed for Des Moines, Iowa, where another immense crowd was expected. In parting, one ardent fan wrote to the weekly *Pittsburgh Courier* to express his feelings on the game just witnessed. "The greatest thrill I ever experienced," expressed the fan, "came to me when I saw catcher Young of the Kansas City Monarchs hit a scorching three-base drive off the great Dizzy Dean, World Series hero, in Kansas City the other night. The Monarchs won that game, 7 to 0, and what a game it was."[48] Such a statement never appeared in the mainstream media. It was a statement only an African American newspaper would print.

CHAPTER 5

~

Des Moines, Iowa

A Two-Man Team Becomes One and a Half
Saturday, October 13, 1934

Customers and fans of the Deans in and around Des Moines were dropping
big bucks in hopes of seeing the duo pitch when they reached Iowa. On October 12, the local newspapers reported that a police escort would greet the
Deans "25 miles outside the city limits and escort them to a local hotel."[1]
Listed at the bottom of the sports page was an ad for the game with prices
and a phone number—3-6010—to call for seat reservations at Western
League Park. Bleacher seats were bandied about for 60 cents and grandstand
seats 75 cents, while box seats were commanding $1.25 each, a pricey sum
in Depression-era dollars.

Boasting plenty of class, after a shutout win at Kansas City, the Monarchs were poised to repeat in Iowa's capital city— where they had never
lost a game. They were playing with a rhythm of domination and confidence. The tour's first mishap, an injury before the game to Daffy Dean's
shoulder, had Sam Breadon and Branch Rickey vexed back in St. Louis.
While shagging fly balls in the outfield during pregame workouts, Daffy
slipped and fell on his right shoulder. Concerned when the pain failed to
subside, he decided to limit his mound time in spite of the crowd's steady
demands for a longer appearance. Paul was worried that the night air might
chill his arm. Without Daffy, there was little doubt that the Monarchs
would continue their conquering spirit. The arm injury was soon to become
important news, and so were Frankie Frisch's comments before the game.
Both were scrutinized nationally. The legendary two-man team of Dizzy
and Daffy had become one.

When Cardinals manager Frisch, whose presence had been well publicized at the game in Kansas City the night before, was pressed for comments concerning Dizzy and Daffy, he told reporters that he had advised the Deans "not to make the exhibition tour."[2] Now that Daffy's arm was ailing, Frisch was off the hook for any long-term blame caused by the barnstorming brothers' injuries. His statement of nonsupport was noticeably an effort to free him from whatever criticism followed—and there would be plenty.

Nothing related to Frisch's hardcore stance had appeared in print when he and the Deans were together in Kansas City. Dizzy, somewhat confused, refuted the remark. "Frisch told us to clean up while we are hot," he said. "To get it while the getting's good."[3] Dizzy's statement was certainly logical, as he and Paul were cleaning up and the "getting" was without a doubt good. The first three games had drawn record profits. Ray L. Doan was dispensing large sums of money to the boys on a daily basis, and Dizzy's wife, Pat, who acted as the brothers' ad hoc bookkeeper/secretary and personal housemaid, carried a purse that was obviously bulging with booty.

Patricia Dean, formerly Patricia Nash, was described by James B. Reston of the Associated Press as a "plump, stubborn girl from Gulfport, Mississippi." It was said that she "didn't think Dizzy Dean's blunders were so funny, so he married her."[4] Some biographies said she was a department store sales clerk, while others said she was a bank teller. There was, however, no disputing her age. She was "eight years older," stated Lee Lowenfish in his book *Branch Rickey: Baseball's Ferocious Gentlemen*.[5] She told reporters she met Dizzy when he was pitching for Houston. When asked about their courtship she offered, "I had a date with him Monday night. We were engaged Tuesday night. We got our wedding license Wednesday night. And we were married Thursday night." In her most honest opinion she declared, "I guess when folk hear that, they'll think I'm dizzy, too."[6]

The date of their marriage was June 10, 1931—a date Dizzy wasn't allowed to confuse with any of his nonsense, but Paul was known to confuse the year.[7] During an interview in Wichita, Kansas, it was stated, "She says they have been married three years (Paul says it is four), [and Dizzy and I] never had a real argument. 'But we won't say we haven't had a few little ones,' she gingerly admitted."[8] Her presence was immediately felt in her husband's on-field performance.

That same year, 1931, he set the all-time single-season record for Texas League shutouts with 11. Dizzy stated his theory of matrimony, publicly pronouncing, "I think the major leagues ought to pass a rule that all players have to be married. Look at me, for example. Did I ever win a World Series before I was married? Look how serious I am about the game now. I never wuz that way before." He continued, "Ballplayers is funny about women, but I guess you gotta be funny about 'em."[9]

Pat remained married to Dizzy for 43 years. It was a till death do us part relationship. Buried deep within obituaries are the long-term marriages of their Negro major-league rivals. Eddie Dwight and Wilber "Bullet" Rogan, who were in that night's game, were happily married before Dizzy and had lengthy marriages. Dwight and his wife, Georgia Baker-Dwight, were married for 46 years, until his death. Rogan was married to Kathrine McWilliams-Rogan for 39 years, until her passing. Most of what was written about the Dean's marriage early on was penned by Reston, who would have an outstanding 50-plus-year career at the *New York Times*, where he was twice awarded a Pulitzer Prize. He was also given a host of other national awards, for example, the Presidential Medal of Freedom and 28 honorary degrees. His six-part 1934 story titled *These Incredible Deans* received a great response nationally on the Associated Press wire.[10] Yet, it was the local newspapers that provided information the national writers missed, for instance, the brothers' entrance into Des Moines. On the drive to Des Moines, Daffy lost his hat.

The barnstormers stopped off in Bethany, Missouri, for lunch. They visited Jack Lincoln's café. They didn't know it at the time, but Lincoln had bet on the Tigers to win the World Series. The local media said Dizzy and Daffy were "responsible for Lincoln's $2.50 loss."[11] Their celebrity status drew a crowd as word of their Bethany appearance became public. The entourage became jittery and rushed to leave. Daffy, in his haste to escape, left behind his hat, which Lincoln promptly seized as retribution.

Dizzy and Daffy's escort into Des Moines was arranged by E. Lee Keyser, president of the Des Moines Western League team. It was a dashing production fit for top Hollywood celebrities. Local law officers met the group on the interstate 25 miles outside of town, and a motorcade of police cars and colorful sedans escorted them to a city hotel with sirens blaring. Shortly thereafter, the Deans met their new teammates.[12]

There were lots of new athletes whose hands Dizzy and Daffy were compelled to shake—12 men total. In a complete renovation of the All-Stars' hurlers Lee "Mule" Brumley and R. C. Mack were there as relief pitchers for the famous brothers. Brumley had come to the All-Stars from the Third Battalion 80th Field Artillery team of Fort Des Moines. The fort, built at the junction of the Raccoon and Des Moines Rivers in 1843, would serve as an important Provisional Army Officer Training School for African Americans during World War I.

The names of the remaining All-Stars were peppered throughout articles leading up to the game. They were a mixture of semiprofessionals from three

Iowa teams. William Weigle, Glen Smith, and Whitey Young were from the Prager Beer state champion semiprofessionals. Louie Griffith, George Gingles, and Pete Tometich were members of the Slater, Iowa, Merchants, the same team Prager Beer had defeated on July 30, 1934, to win the state title. William "Bill" Muck of Colfax, Iowa, a former Western League catcher, was there to receive the brothers' pitches. "Lefty" Godwin and Keith Roy of Pointer Brews, another brewery team, formed the balance of the Deans' Capital City All-Stars.[13] For the first time in four games there wasn't a current or former big-leaguer among the All-Stars, which might explain why these men got media treatment reminiscent of that given to African Americans—little recognition—in the *Des Moines Register* and on local radio.

After a catnap Dizzy and Daffy headed over to 715 Locust Street in downtown Des Moines for an interview at KSO radio on the 5:30 p.m. broadcast.[14] The 500 watts of daytime power kept the city informed about the brothers' tour. The radio station was a *Register* and *Tribune* station. Newspaper tycoon Gardner "Mike" Cowles had purchased the station in 1931, to bundle it with his other enterprises, which included two local dailies, as well as the *Minneapolis Star* and later *Look* magazine.[15] The live radio interview was hosted by Lee Keyser. Keyser had been with the Deans the day before at the South Central Business Association dinner in Kansas City. He knew which questions to ask. Right away, Keyser inquired about a crucial play in the World Series.

Dizzy openly discussed the play, where he was plunked on the head and knocked out during Game 4. "It seems this doctor who fixed me up had $1,400 on Detroit," he stated. "[Doc] told me I'd better not pitch. [He] said injuries like mine would get worse in three or four days. Well, I pitched, and you folks know what happened."[16] Grantland Rice wrote of the near-tragedy in glowing color in a syndicated article. "The great Dizzy crumpled and fell like a marionette whose string had snapped," said Rice. "The blow that floored Dizzy would have knocked down two elephants. The wonder is that the entire top of his head was not shot away at such close range."

In keeping with the folklore that followed, Dizzy shared that a St. Louis newspaper's headline the next day said, "X-ray of Dizzy's Head Showed Nothing." In fact, none of the St. Louis newspapers—the *Globe-Democrat*, the *Post-Dispatch*, or the *Star-Times*—ever printed such a headline.[17] The National League wouldn't adopt batting helmets until 1941, and even then they were not mandatory.[18] This, however, was not the only time Diz had taken a serious blow to the head and lived to joke about it. A similar mishap occurred in a 1933 exhibition game at Oxford, Nebraska, where a park record of 6,800 customers turned out to see Dizzy and his Cardinals teammate, Pepper Martin, play against the Monarchs.

According to J. L. Wilkinson, who told the story to Pete Lightner of the *Wichita Eagle*, "Brewer, powerful Monarch right-hander, was pitching, and when Dizzy came to bat Brewer got one of his fast ones too close and beaned Dean. Dizzy 'dropped like [a] shot.'"[19] This occurred in the third inning, reported the local *Oxford Standard*, when "he was hit on the right arm by a thrown ball, which glanced to the body. He took the count."[20] "There was wild confusion," Wilkinson recalled. The local manager hurried to a phone and called for an ambulance. A mildly coherent Dizzy was carried to his team's bench, where cold towels were applied and whatever assistance that could be provided for the moment was given. Wilkinson and the Oxford manager were summoned to the front gate to meet the ambulance, which arrived about 10 minutes later. Wilkinson remembered, "When they went to get the body of Dizzy, there was no Dizzy to be found." They searched frantically, and finally someone said Dizzy had gotten to his feet and stumbled off. The teams were in the field, as the game was never stopped after Dizzy's injury. They kept playing as Wilkinson and his friend searched for the Cardinals pitcher. Wilkinson said they searched in the dressing rooms and box office, adding, "finally [they] wandered back into the park. Much to their surprise Dizzy came jogging to the bench from the outfield. His teammates said he had recovered and insisted on finishing the ballgame." According to the *Oxford Standard*, "He [Dizzy] was back in the game in the fourth inning, replacing Norman in left field. Laufler, pitcher for the St. Louis Cardinals, then took the mound for the rest of the game."[21]

During Dizzy's radio interview there was no mention of Frisch telling the brothers not to barnstorm. Keyser, the interviewer, doted on the brothers throughout the broadcast. It was a lively dialogue. Dizzy ended many of these interviews with the statement, "How am I doin' Edna?" It was a direct dig at the Detroit Tigers and a direct hit on Detroit's 22-year-old pitching ace, Lynwood "Schoolboy" Rowe. During the World Series, Rowe, on the radio and in newspapers, said that he and Edna Mae Skinner, an El Dorado, Arkansas, schoolmarm, were to be married after the World Series. Rowe ended the interviews with, "How am I doing Edna?" Bench jockey Leo Durocher of the Cardinals heard the broadcasts, as did other members of the St. Louis team. Durocher started the catcalls and laid into Schoolboy with repeated yells across the field, "How am I doing Edna?" He almost drove Rowe wild.[22] George Kirksey noted, "The Cards kept up a continual line of chatter from the bench when Rowe was on the mound with emphasis on, 'How am I doing, Edna, honey?'"[23]

It wasn't a good time for Rowe to respond to Dizzy's digs. Schoolboy's hands were full with issues related to racism. He had reportedly made "disparaging and offensive" remarks about African Americans and was trying to distance himself from the matter. Several newspapers carried the story. The statements were supposedly made in Philadelphia on August 29, during Rowe's effort to bring his winning streak to a record-breaking 17 straight, thus breaking the record of consecutive major-league wins held by Joe Wood, Walter Johnson, and Lefty Grove. Rowe, after winning the first game of a doubleheader, 12–7, returned to pitch the nightcap—two games in one day—in hopes of getting win number 17. The biggest crowd of the season, 33,718 paid, saw him leave after six and two-thirds innings in a 13–5 defeat. In a postgame interview it was claimed that Rowe attributed the loss to the presence of colored people in the grandstand, which distracted him from pitching.

At about 9:35 Monday night, October 8, after Rowe absorbed the defeat handed to him by Daffy Dean in the sixth game of the World Series, he came to the offices of Detroit's *Tribune-Independent*, a minority weekly newspaper, accompanied by Ray Whyte, president of the Eastern Chevrolet Company and an officer of the law in plainclothes. "Is the boss here?" the detective asked. When he was told no, "Rowe leaned forward and said, 'Ah'm Schoolboy Rowe.'"[24] He continued, "I came to see you regarding something I was supposed to have said concerning the colored people. I want the colored people to know that even though I'm from the South, I've never made the alleged discrediting statements to anyone regarding them and never will."[25] After he was repeatedly questioned, Rowe was asked if he would write his statement, which he did. It read, "To the colored people of Detroit: I wish to say to the colored people of Detroit, that I have never said one word to any paper concerning colored people of Detroit." The statement was signed Schoolboy Rowe. It was later reported that Rowe had received hundreds of letters from African American citizens inquiring if he had made the racist statement.

Back in Des Moines, Keyser was planning for a prosperous evening of activities. As owner of the Des Moines Western League team he stood to make a handsome profit for the Dean brothers' appearance. He was no stranger to promoting big events. Keyser was a recognized guru of the new innovation called night baseball, which hadn't yet reached National and American League parks on a permanent basis.

In 1930, Keyser and his Des Moines Demons played the first successful season of regular nighttime ball in an organized minor league—the Western. For this he became known as the "Father of Night Baseball," a title he routinely shared with Wilkinson of the Kansas City Monarchs. Keyser's past was checkered with lots of self-made Horatio Alger–styled endeavors. He never finished high school—he was too busy working from age 13, when he was hired at a railroad station in St. Louis and learned how to clerk. His love of clerking was overshadowed by his fascination with baseball. On weekends he began hocking hot dogs, peanuts, popcorn, and other concessions at local ballparks. Keyser connected with the St. Louis Terriers Federal League franchise and eventually became manager of concessions at Alexander Handlan's Federal League park. With money he saved, Keyser purchased a half interest in the Des Moines Western League team in 1920, which led to his historic day 10 years later, on May 2, 1930, when he introduced night baseball to the city with a lighting plant he installed for a reported $22,000.

In 1946, after years of team ownership in Des Moines, Keyser left Iowa to take a position as president of the Toledo, Ohio, Mud Hens in the American Association. He stayed in baseball for the remainder of his life and died at age 64. At the time of his death, in 1950, he was employed as secretary of the St. Louis Browns minor-league operation.

For Dizzy and Daffy's appearance there was plenty of advertising leading up to the October 13 game. On October 11, there was an article in the *Des Moines Tribune* that said, "Charlie Knight, secretary of the Des Moines Western League club," had the job of assembling a local team for the Deans.[26] Several local candidates' names were mentioned.

Western League Park, also called Holcomb Park, opened for business in 1914, on the corners of Sixth and Holcomb Avenues. The park, which originally hosted the minor league Booster's team, was now accommodating the minor league Demons, a third-place contender in the Western League circuit for the 1934 season. Seating capacity at the facility was 5,000. One of the park's largest crowds, which numbered in the neighborhood of 10,000 to 12,000, had attended the first night game in 1930. That night people filled the stands and formed a barrier 10 rows deep around the field. Unfortunately for Keyser, none of his Demons were there to support the Deans.

None of the local minor leaguers joined the Deans' All-Stars. Dorsey Moulder, a Demons infielder who united with the Deans in Kansas City, was the only Demons player to join the tour. But he wasn't in Des Moines on this night. The locals might have also benefited from Ossie Orwoll's .322 batting average, or Roy Hudson's .318, or even Fabian Gaffke's .311 Western League hitting. They certainly could have used Ralph Sams, an ace pitcher who finished with a 16–12 Western League record. Even without these marquee players Keyser expected the crowd to be somewhere near capacity. The final tally was disappointing. There were plenty of empty seats at game time. When Dizzy, Daffy, and the Monarchs took the field, only 3,500 people—the smallest crowd to date but a good size for a Saturday night in October in Des Moines—paid to see both brothers hurl a few innings.

Earlier in the day, the brothers were pictured together in the *Des Moines Tribune* under the headline "In Exhibition Contest Here Tonight."[27] An attached caption reminded readers of the brothers' World Series wins and their number of victories for the season. The same newspaper reprinted the "Nut Vendor" story from Kansas City and promoted the brothers' talk on the radio.[28] There were additional photographs of the brothers on page five of the *Des Moines Register*. Doyl Taylor noted, "It won't be altogether a new experience for Dizzy to pitch in Des Moines, for he was the victor over the Demons in several Western League games at the start of the 1930 Western League season." There were no photographs of the Monarchs, who the newspaper classed a "champion colored team." Taylor did, however, mention Chet Brewer and penned that he "beat the Demons in the Kansas City Monarchs' exhibition here last season."[29]

Before the game, the two brothers publicly debated that night's hurling assignment. "You pitch tonight, Diz. I'm tired. My arm's awful sore, but I'll play in the outfield," said Daffy.[30] Evidently Dizzy consented. Daffy started the game in left field, where he remained for five innings. Dizzy started for the All-Stars. After three innings, he made his exit. It was still a scoreless affair when he descended from the pitcher's mound, having surrendered one hit and struck out three. The hit that Dizzy allowed was called a "scratch hit over second" by Taylor. It was yet another of the all-too-common examples of the well-worn descriptions used to strategically minimize African American feats against the Deans.

Daffy didn't desire to pitch, but a steady stream of requests from the crowd forced him to at least try. In the sixth inning, he took the mound and pitched gingerly to one batter, Frank Duncan, who grounded out to the second baseman on the third pitch. Daffy was through after that. He exited the mound with pain in his right shoulder and never returned. What occurred after the brothers left the game remains somewhat of a mystery, as the reporting went from bad to worse. Intentional or otherwise, it blurred the results of the game for all time. The Monarchs hadn't received a square deal in the game's coverage, and the write-up of the proceedings made it perfectly clear who the reporters favored when Brumley came into the game as Paul's relief.

What the Monarchs achieved after the Dean brothers' exit was scarcely covered in the *Register's* recap of the game. Against Dizzy you can't tell who struck out or who got the one hit he issued. Monarchs batters went on to pound Brumley for four runs and six hits in two innings to successfully force the military hurler into retreat. Brumley was yanked from the mound, and when the battery became Mack and Muck, Kansas City continued its on-slaught, adding more runs and an additional five hits to bring the curtain down on Dizzy's All-Stars in a lopsided 9–0 win. Brumley got credit for the loss, not the Diz.

Information gleaned from the box score is most helpful—but not con-clusive. Kansas City ended the game with 12 hits. Edward Dwight, T. J. Young, Wilber Rogan, and Frank Duncan had multiple hits. Catcher Young and second baseman Mothell smacked doubles. Young reached base twice, increasing his hit totals to six in two games. This game was one of Duncan's best since starting the tour. Dwight also excelled—something he had been doing for a number of years without much national recognition.

Long before he became a grain inspector for the state of Kansas and even before his son Eddie Jr. became the first African American astronaut for NASA, Eddie Dwight Sr. was a Negro major-league star. He had a large fam-ily for a ballplayer, and his lack of sufficient income was responsible for his missing several years of play to support his growing brood. Right-handed all the way, fleet-footed "Eddie" Dwight used his speed in the leadoff position to ignite the potent Monarchs run offense of the late 1920s and early 1930s. His speed made him a nemesis of opposing pitchers and catchers throughout the United States and Canada. They feared having him on base. He excelled most often on the basepaths and was frequently billed as the "fastest base-runner on the club." His Monarchs advance publicity contained three words: "Dwight is fast." He ranked with the best stolen-base leaders in baseball his-tory and is often compared to James "Cool Papa" Bell as a daring and speedy baserunner in the era of segregated play.

Dwight, born in Dalton, Georgia, was the son of Lobe and Sarah Dwight. Speed was a family tradition. Georgia Dwight, Eddie's widow, said that Southern law enforcement officers ran Lobe out of town because he owed $2 on a mule, shooting at him as he ran while his children yelled, "Run, Daddy, run!" Lobe ended up in the Rattlebone Hollow section of segregated Kansas City, Kansas, where his family joined him in 1917. Young Eddie grew into a stocky, 5-foot-5 man, weighing 159 pounds as he entered high school. He excelled at athletics while attending segregated Sumner High School, where he excelled in football and track, and received his first recognition as a swift runner. When a friend, George Malone, took him across the river to Parade Parkway to join Floyd "Baby" Webb's teenage Kansas City Tigers, Eddie united with a team that featured "Chappie" Gray, Frank Duncan, Ruben Currie, and other future Negro major-league stars. Shortly thereafter, Dwight turned his attention to baseball on a full-time basis.[31]

After a season with the Royals, Dwight joined Walter Brown's Tennessee Rats, a barnstorming/minstrel entertainment squad based in Holden, Missouri. Eddie excelled and moved to the Negro major leagues in 1924, with the Indianapolis, Indiana, ABCs. The next year, Dwight tried out with Wilkinson's Kansas City Monarchs, but he was sent back to the ABCs for another season. In search of a prosperous team, he left the Negro major league to join Robert P. Gilkerson's Union Giants, a barnstorming team based in Spring Valley, Illinois, a team that also served as a minor-league operation for the Monarchs. Dwight spent two additional seasons with the Giants before joining the Monarchs in 1928. On the Monarchs team, he was joined by two other Kansas alumni—Wilber "Bullet" Rogan and Alfred "Army" Cooper. During the 1928 season, Dwight stole two or more bases against every catcher in the Negro major league.[32]

Eddie remained with the Monarchs through July 1929, helping the team to the first-half championship of the split season before a roster reduction forced him to rejoin Gilkerson's Union Giants. While traveling he met his wife, an Iowa native named Georgia Baker.[33] On October 5, 1929, they were married, and two weeks later Dwight was part of a Negro major league All-Star team that defeated future National League pitcher Joe Bowman in an interracial game at Kansas City's Union Pacific Park.[34]

When the Monarchs failed to organize at the start of the 1931 season, he left the professional ranks for a custodian's job at the Kansas City Board of Trade building. On weekends, Dwight played semiprofessionally around Kansas City while working nights cleaning offices. He also appeared in several games with the Indianapolis ABCs when they played the Monarchs in Kansas City. Dwight's teammate, Frank Duncan, also had a banner night at bat.

Frank Duncan, born on February 14, 1901, was one of that night's premier hitters. He had been a Monarchs regular since 1921. While is his early teens he, like Dwight, perfected his skills on the Parade Parkway with Webb's Kansas City Tigers.[35] The son of a coal and ice salesman, at the tender age of 19 he married Julia M. Lee, age 17.[36] Because of her young age, a brother, George W. Lee had to give his consent for the marriage. Julia Lee, a pianist and singer-songstress, recorded several number-one hits for Capitol Records under the name Julia Lee and Her Boy Friends. She was often booked to perform at white nightspots throughout the Midwest. Jim Crow customs forbade her husband from attending these events as a spectator. According to Milton Morris, a Kansas City jazz promoter, when Julia was appearing at a white club, "Frank had to carry a horn case and sit in the bandstand to see his wife perform, because Negroes were not allowed in the audience."[37] He was forced into playing the role of a roadie and told to sit in the bandstand, hidden away from the white patrons.

"I played up in St. Joe, Missouri, in 1920, at the Swift Packing House," Duncan recalled when discussing his start in professional baseball. "Easter Sunday 1920, the snow was that deep. Joe Green's Chicago Giants sent me $20 for a ticket to Chicago, so I jumped on a freight train and came on to Chicago, and I felt just like I was going to the New York Yankees."[38]

It is ironic that Duncan, born in Kansas City, started his professional career in Chicago with the Chicago Giants in 1921, when the Monarchs were seeking a catcher. He was passed over but later acquired in a two-for-one player swap with the Giants that same season. In addition to being one of the best catchers in the Negro major leagues, he was also a remarkable outfielder—and a team bus driver —when duty called.

Throughout the Dean brothers' tour Duncan was stationed in left field— he was a backup for Young and never caught a game. At Des Moines he went 2-for-3 in four plate appearances, stole a base, and was hit by a Mack pitch. The newspaper detailed Duncan's one at-bat against Daffy Dean—the only batter the Cardinals pitcher faced. In a rare full-name mention, the *Register* noted that Frank Duncan "grounded out to the second baseman on three pitches."[39] It should also be noted that Dizzy knew Duncan well. "I sure got a kick out of Duncan," said Dizzy. "He has a glove that makes the ball pop, and he tells them hitters, 'Boy, don't let that ball hit you, or it kills you.'"[40] In conversation Dizzy said to Duncan, "I'd love to take you to St. Louis with me," Frank recalled. "I said, 'I'd love to go too. Yeah, Dizzy Dean, my old partner.'"[41]

Meanwhile, lefty Charlie Beverly, the Monarchs' strikeout artist, was removing the spotlight from Dizzy and Daffy and shining it on himself. A brief comparison showed Dizzy as having pitched a one-hitter for three innings; Beverly tossed a five-hitter for nine. He pitched masterfully as he blazed through the lineup to obtain his team's second consecutive shutout win over the Deans' All-Stars. The *Register* hadn't bothered to mention the 15 strikeout victims who repeatedly waved at speedy fastballs thrown by the mighty Monarchs pitcher. In all of the gobbledygook written about the Deans, the newspapers totally left out Beverly's name. Failing to mention Beverly's name was trickery at the highest level—a war of word diplomacy that often left minority athletes without representation. All-Stars Weigle, Smith, and Griffith went 0-for-4 on the afternoon, and Muck and Whitey Young were both 0-for-3 as batters. As a team, the All-Stars had five hits. Lefty Godwin had two, and Dizzy Dean, Keith Roy, and R. C. Mack each had one. Doyle Taylor of the *Register*, an observer of the discriminated against Monarchs pitcher and a witness to his superb play, inscribed no words of praise. His jargon was standoffish toward the Monarchs, while adoring Dizzy and Daffy. The writer's perspective was hardly refreshing.

While praising Dizzy to the high heavens—as a hitter, fielder, and pitcher—Taylor's *Register* article said virtually nothing about any of the Monarchs. The article never mentioned the back-to-back shutouts, failed to detail any of the Monarchs' scoring sequences, and ignored Beverly's strike-outs. Most people have never heard of Charlie Beverly, and now we have one of the reasons why he is lesser known.

Charlie came from a baseball family. His brother, Green, played in the Texas–Oklahoma League, and nephews Tom Cooper, who caught for the Monarchs of the late 1940s, and William "Bill" Beverly, a pitcher in that same period for Houston and Birmingham in the Negro American League, were all family. Although he had been with Birmingham in the Negro National League during the 1925 season, Kansas City acquired Charlie from the Texas–Oklahoma–Louisiana League, where he had been a leading pitcher for the San Antonio Black Indians since 1928. He spent the following year, 1929, with the champion Houston Black Buffaloes and then burst onto the national scene with the Kansas City Monarchs in 1931. As a lefty, he had the pitching wisdom and ability of a Satchel Paige with none of the flash or personality.

Wilkinson found a good thing when he signed the pitcher. Unfortunately, he used Beverly too often. Just as Wilkinson had done to John Donaldson be-fore 1920, he allowed Beverly's arm to get damaged after only a few seasons of too many innings pitched. Unlike Paige and Donaldson, who made extraor-dinary recoveries, after Beverly's wing was injured, he rarely flew again—he never recovered. His remarkable career was virtually finished by 1936. Two years later, he attempted a comeback in what would be his last game as a Monarch, on April 10, 1938, at Houston, Texas. Beverly left baseball and eventually moved to San Francisco, where he found work as a longshoreman.

The Deans' stop in Des Moines, which was covered locally on the *Regis-ter's* front page and extended onto the sports section, failed to mention Mon-archs players by their full names. In the lengthy article that followed, only Duncan's full name appeared in the postgame write-up. In the articles prior to the game, Chet Brewer received first and last name recognition, probably because Des Moines was where he had grown up—but Brewer wasn't in town for the game.

Photographs of Dizzy and Daffy appeared in the *Register* on two occasions. They were also pictured in the *Tribune*. There were no printed images of the Monarchs before or after the game. Most revealing was the omission of Beverly's first or last name in the article after the game. He was only listed in the box score, where his 15 strikeouts were neatly tucked away with such details as hit by pitcher, balks, and walks. Beverly's lack of recognition was an egregious display of racism that made mockery inside the minds of ordinary baseball fans. It is a legacy that continues to subsist in baseball history, where a lack of recognition and equality of skills are met with continuous opposition.

Who scored runs for the Monarchs will also remain unknown. The run category was not a part of the box score, and nothing further appeared in the postgame text. This, too, was a backdoor slap, as it only affected Kansas City—the Dean brothers' All-Stars didn't even come close to scoring. Beverly and his teammates were branded as inferior by the media's culture of neglect, while Betty Holt, who was thought to be Paul's female friend, got major billing.

Holt's romance with Paul Dean was a story that wouldn't go away. In a United Press International wire report from Columbus, which was reprinted in the *Register*, Holt denied rumors of her engagement to Daffy. She admitted to knowing nothing about the bridal suite reserved for them in a Cleveland hotel. The article said the reservation was the work of an anonymous "practical joker."[42]

The Des Moines game was now history. The tour, however, was alive and well as it energetically moved on to its next destination. The Monarchs buzzed toward Chicago, passing through Ray L. Doan's hometown, Muscatine, Iowa, along the way. They traveled at night, sleeping on the bus, thereby hoping to avoid paying for another hotel stay—in an effort to increase the take-home pay of their players. Dizzy and Daffy had already escaped the crowd, disappearing like a home run hit into an Iowa cornfield. They were escorted from the ball field with a flamboyant display of police vehicles, sirens blaring, after the sixth inning. At the airport they boarded a flight for Chicago eager to cash in on the final days of the 1934 World's Fair. The tour's national media now shifted to Paul's injured shoulder, a story that was soon to dominate the press coverage, along with their take at the gate and a well-worn debate about major-league players barnstorming after the end of the National and American League seasons.

CHAPTER 6

~

Chicago, Illinois

High Pockets and a Heavy Purse
Sunday, October 14, 1934

Advertisements for the Chicago game had started as early as October 8, when William G. "Billy" Harley, manager of the Chicago Mills team, announced publicly that Dizzy and Daffy were signed to pitch against the Kansas City Monarchs.[1] Satchel Paige, whose name appeared for the first time since the tour's start, was advertised to arrive in Chicago to pitch some of the game for Kansas City. These two incentives, coupled with the World's Fair, caused tickets to move at a brisk pace. The Chicago World's Fair, which was scheduled to end on October 31, was a major contributor to the impulsive leap in ticket sales as thousands were unable to gain admittance to the diamond. Even with all of the advertisements two of the biggest-named recruits failed to show. The game started without Paige and George Caithamer, a popular 22-year-old catcher for the Chicago White Sox. Caithamer was advertised as the Deans' catcher, but he was nowhere in the vicinity of Mills Stadium at game time. No explanation was given for the absence of either player. They missed the Mills Stadium affair, a game that resulted in the highest scoring and largest crowds of the tour thus far.

The Deans' visit to Mills Stadium renewed local interest in Leroy "Satchel" Paige, who scribes at the *Chicago Tribune* tagged the "greatest colored" pitcher in the world, while repeatedly misspelling his name. They wrote "Page" instead of "Paige," which demonstrated how much they actually knew about this impending sepia star.[2] The *Tribune*'s article lamented on the struggle the Monarchs endured in attempting to hire the phenomenal pitcher who earned a national reputation for himself through his participation in the national *Denver Post* Tournament in Colorado and the East–West game played in Chicago. Like Jim Thorpe and Grover Cleveland Alexander before him, Satchel defied age and race. A similar article appeared that same day, October 13, in the *Chicago Herald and Examiner* with the same misspelling of the Crawfords pitcher's last name.[3] Wrong spelling or not, Alexander, a three-time 30-game winner in the National League, was quick to recognize Paige as a budding star.

Grover Cleveland Alexander and Ray L. Doan recruited Paige to pitch for the all-white House of David team in the 1934 *Post* Tournament, where Paige made three starts in five days and was laser sharp. He struck out 44 batters in 28 innings pitched. His control was almost perfect, as only one batter walked. Paige won an amazing 17-strikeout game against the Humble Oilers of Overton, Texas, and, in another outing, told his outfielders to take a knee as he retired the side. At one point, Paige logged 23 consecutive scoreless innings. He was getting batters out with nothing but a fastball. "Satchel had nothing but a fastball," said Ted Page. "Now why did I have to look for anything else but a fastball. He didn't have a curve or a changeup."[4] "Paige never was rated the fastest pitcher among the blacks who played or witnessed Negro ball in its two stages, before league play and after," an article stated. "Smoky Joe (Cyclone) Williams, John Donaldson, Cannonball Dick Redding, Rube Foster, and Wilber (Bullet) Rogan all were rated faster than Paige, but none, except the early Foster, could combine the perfect control that Paige possessed from his first day on the mound."[5]

Grover Cleveland's team of whiskers—promoted by Ray L. Doan with Paige's marvelous fastball—finished the tournament with a perfect 7–0 record to become the first team since 1922 to win the tournament championship without a defeat. Paige was equally superb in his East–West All-Star game appearance. The whiskered fellows collected $6,000 for the series, but it cost them $500 a game for Satchel.[6] Paige's demand was going up, and he was seeking the best buyers.

According to an article in the *Cleveland Call and Post*, penned for its June 2, 1934, edition, "Word has been received from Chicago that Leroy (Satchel) Paige is being detained on orders from the Pittsburgh police department. Paige is a member of the Pittsburgh Crawfords baseball team but was reported on his way to Bismarck, North Dakota." Satchel's version said, "Back in Pittsburgh Gus Greenlee must have really been burned up by all I was doing out West. Anyway, I started hearing he was after me for jumping out of that contract [in 1933] and going to Bismarck. He was trying to get the Negro leagues to ban me."[7]

The East–West All-Star Game was a fairly new concept in 1934. The game of African American stars was set in Chicago and began in 1933, with the West winning the inaugural game by an 11–7 score. The 1934 East–West game, played on September 1, was promoted as a battle between righty Satchel Paige and lefty Willie Foster. About 25,000 people attended the event expecting to see Paige and Foster in an acid test for baseball supremacy, but managers for their respective teams didn't start either pitcher. Stuart "Country" Jones and Ted Trent were chosen instead. Paige entered the contest in the sixth inning and promptly struck out five, allowing two hits in the remaining frames to gain a 1–0 win over the West. The *Cleveland Call and Post* wrote, "Probably some paleface sportwriter this season at last will journey to Comiskey Park and discover what we sepia fans have known for years, that Satchel Paige, Daltie Cooper, Stearnes, [are all] of major-league caliber."[8]

Based on Paige's added publicity and the Dean brothers' established success, 15,000 tickets went on sale at 9 a.m. at the Mills box office at Kilpatrick and Lake Streets. On October 11, Harley announced the "heavy demand" for tickets to the *Tribune*. By Saturday, October 13, every seat had been sold. In the *Tribune*'s October 14 edition, an article advised in no uncertain terms, "Since the announcement was made that the pair would visit Chicago there has been an unprecedented demand for tickets."[9] The sudden bump in sales was due to the Chicago World's Fair. Tourists from neighboring cities were in abundance, and almost all of the tickets went into the hands of out-of-towners. By game time, the supply of standing-room tickets was gone, and there was unrest outside Bill Harley's Mills Stadium by those who missed out. It was like a circus inside the old stadium, and members of the Kansas City Monarchs were the ones working for peanuts. The *Chicago Herald and Examiner* didn't sidestep the issue of race, as it surmised, "It will be interesting to note what the colored sluggers can do against the brothers, heroes of the World Series."[10] Listed below every *Herald and Examiner* article about the game were five words: "World's Fair Ends October 31."

The entire city was given over to World's Fair activities. Its effect touched the Negro Leagues when the Chicago American Giants ballpark, located at 31st and Wentworth Avenues, called Cole's Stadium in 1934, was turned into a dog racing track. Without a home field the American Giants were forced to play the majority of their games in Indianapolis, or on the road barnstorming. The Monarchs were frequent visitors to Chicago, but not to play the American Giants, as in years past; they were there to play Harley's Chicago Mills team at Mills Stadium.

Harley's Chicago Mills team was accustomed to playing the Monarchs and other African American opponents. As members of the independent Wisconsin–Illinois League their schedule was adjusted around teams like the Monarchs, Chicago American Giants, and Pittsburgh Crawfords. Harley had been a professional ballplayer himself. In 1913, the Columbus, Ohio, born Harley appeared briefly in the Federal League with Cleveland's Green Sox, a team that was managed by Hall of Fame pitcher Cy Young. Harley's Mills had squared off with the Monarchs in a series of doubleheaders starting in May, again in June, and twice in September.

On May 30, the Monarchs split a Wednesday night doubleheader with the Mills team, winning the first but losing the second to John "Lefty" Sullivan. They returned on June 3, to take both games behind the eight-hit pitching of Chet Brewer and, that evening, the eight-hit hurling of Charlie Beverly. In a doubleheader preceding the Deans' appearance, on September 16, Kansas City took both ends of the two-game set when Brewer captured the opener, winning 3–1 over Gordon McNaughton, and Andy Cooper, the pitcher of record in game two, defeated Lefty Sullivan in a 5–3 final. Harley knew which players to add to give the Monarchs a greater challenge. He started by adding a new first baseman from the National League. In an article dated October 14, and titled "Deans Pitch for Mills Today in Exhibition Game," the *Tribune* provided the name. Johnny McCarthy, who had made his major-league debut with the Dodgers on September 2, 1934. He was Manager Harley's choice to cover the initial sack.[11]

John Joseph McCarthy was a prototype major-league first baseman—big and slow. He stood more than six feet and had no speed to brag of. Born January 7, 1910, in Chicago, Illinois, he would steal a total of eight bases in 11 major-league seasons while participating in a total of 542 official games. In the minor leagues, McCarthy would steal just 10 bases in 966 games. His first big-league manager, Casey Stengel, was well acquainted with members of the hustling Monarchs. He was probably aware of the Monarchs first baseman, George Giles, who was destined to acquaint McCarthy with another style of first base play, offensively and defensively.

George Giles, born on May 2, 1909, was only a year older than McCarthy, although he had considerably more professional experience. On this day, Giles would outhit McCarthy two hits to one. McCarthy struck out once; Giles never fanned. In the field, McCarthy had a perfect day of fielding, as he gathered 10 putouts and one assist, and was flawless on errors. Giles finished with eight putouts and was also flawless in the field. It is ironic that both men would steal bases in the game, but Giles showed himself to be better with two stolen bases compared to one by McCarthy.

The rest of the All-Stars were Harley's regulars, and the lineup included an assortment of former major- and minor-league veterans. John Albert Stokes, who entered the American League in 1925, was a former Boston Red Sox catcher. George "Pickles" Gerken, a former Cleveland Indian of 1927 and 1928, was also in Harley's lineup, as were Doug McWeeny and Gordon McNaughton, former major-league pitchers. McWeeny's past record included 37 major-league wins with the White Sox, Dodgers, and Reds. And there were others.

Long-term minor leaguers Bernard "Benny" Helgeth and a Pacific Coast League shortstop named Danny Tapson, along with outfielder Dave Goodman, a .300 hitter in the Western League in 1934, were scheduled starters. Babe Goldwaite, a police officer and catcher from West Parks, joined in, as did Nick Polly, formerly of Lane Tech College. Polly, who would set an all-time American Association record for walks with 147 in 1944—10 years after his appearance with the Deans—would graduate to the Boston Red Sox for four games in 1945.[12] In 1937, Babe would appear in 10 games with the Brooklyn Dodgers. Polly was there, as were Art Conroy and Bert Atkinson, to comprise the heart of what was soon to be classed the Deans' All-Stars. The *Chicago Defender*, reprinting an article previously published in the *Tribune*, noted that everyone thought well of the new lineup, writing, "Man for man the Monarchs and Mills are about even in player strength, but with the Deans pitching for [manager] Billy Harley's club a shade must be handed the Mills."[13] McNaughton, one of Harley's star pitchers, was scheduled to follow the Deans on the mound. This guy was no Boy Scout.

Born on July 31, 1910, Gordon Joseph McNaughton was a former collegian at Loyola University of Chicago and Xavier University of Cincinnati. His mother, Catherine, was of Irish ancestry.[14] Gordon, a pitcher, was signed by the Boston Red Sox, with whom he made his major-league debut on August 13, 1932. His big-league tenure was a brief six games. In 1933, he reported to Boston's Reading club in the New York–Pennsylvania League but found minor-league ball too restrictive. He was coming off an 11–10 season in the East Dixie League when he rejoined Harley's Mills team in 1934. As a journeyman hurler he had been around the minors, and his pitching was improved—not a lot, mind you, but he was throwing stuff more than sufficient for semiprofessional baseball. Upon his return to Chicago, he worked as a postal clerk by day and moonlighted as a semiprofessional pitcher on evenings and weekends. History says he was a gadabout who often caroused after games. He obviously enjoyed his celebrity status and was never tied, for any length of time, to one woman. McNaughton's well-known reputation with women was crumbling in the early 1940s, and it ultimately led to his murder in 1942.

Gordon was shot to death by his married lover, a bleach-blonde exotic dancer named Eleanor Williams, on August 6, 1942, when she burst into his rented room at dawn at the New Lawrence Hotel in uptown Chicago. McNaughton was inside having an illicit affair with another blonde, Dorothy Moos, also married. In the trial that followed, it was said that Williams had abandoned her husband and a daughter to be with McNaughton three years prior. Her reason for murdering McNaughton was summarized in one sentence: "I loved him, but he tried to dust me off the way they do in baseball."[15] For her crime of passion Williams served a prison term at the state woman's institution in Dwight, Illinois.

Kansas City's starter was their right-handed ace, Chester Arthur Brewer. Lean and handsome, he stood at 6-foot-4, weighing 215 pounds in his prime, with a corking good fastball and curve, and amazing control. When shaking his hand, you would notice his hands were the size of a normal man's, not the massive hands of a Buck O'Neil. Clean living was Brewer's trade. He removed his hat and cap indoors and, in the presence of ladies, tipped his hat when complemented; preferred root beer over alcoholic beverages; had excellent table manners; and said yes sir to his elders and white folks. He didn't smoke or chew. His best attributes were endurance, control, and stamina. Born in Leavenworth, Kansas, in 1907, in the black district, Ward 6, he emerged as an international strikeout artist in a career that lasted from 1923 to 1953. He credited his stamina to his schoolboy days in Des Moines, Iowa, where he moved with his family and, as a third grader, started playing baseball. "I was the only pitcher we had in grade school, and if we played two or three games a week then I'd pitch them all," he said.[16] Unbeknownst to many was his boyhood injury. Brewer was essentially pitching with a handicap.

Early in life, Brewer lost two toes on his left foot—the important foot for a pitcher, the one he used to step toward home plate when pitching. The toes were severed when his foot was partially run over by a trolley in Leavenworth. After the accident, his father took a job in Des Moines, where Chet's uncle was living. In a 1985 interview, Brewer explained,

> I've always praised my father for that move because it was kind of like going to a new world. In Kansas it was so prejudiced, it was awful. Everything was all-white or all-black. You'd go downtown and you couldn't eat in a restaurant. I'd run errands for the older people—get me a nickel or a dime to go to the theater on Saturday to see the shoot-'em-ups. In Leavenworth you had to sit way up so high, way up where the projector was.[17]

Des Moines was different; Brewer didn't face the same kinds of discrimination in Iowa's capital city. "We lived in an integrated neighborhood, went to integrated [public] schools, and it was really like a different world. Going to Des Moines was like getting to heaven," he offered with a nervous chuckle.

Brewer overcame his earlier physical handicap and, by 1923, was a leading semiprofessional pitcher in Des Moines, although still in high school. He jumped at the opportunity to join Walter Brown's Tennessee Rats, a barnstorming team that traveled the Upper Midwest. Chet was 16 years old when he turned professional. Determined to continue playing in 1924, he signed on with Robert P. Gilkerson's Union Giants of Spring Valley, Illinois, another team that barnstormed the Upper Midwestern states. The next year, Gilkerson, who also acted as a scout for the Kansas City Monarchs, sent Chet packing to the Kansas City Monarchs of the Negro National League, where he played under the tutelage of the great Cuban-born manager Jose Mendez.

Brewer's first Monarchs win came in his debut on April 19. It was an exhibition game versus the YMCA club of Kansas City. While holding out for more pay from his Monarchs owners, he often returned to Leavenworth to work out with a lifelong friend, Melvin McRoy. "He had a mound and a home plate built in his back yard," McRoy said.

> After he'd gotten warmed up he'd throw 100 strikes knee-high on the inside part of the plate, then 100 knee-high on the outside part, all fastballs, then he'd do the same thing letter-high, then he'd start throwing curveballs. He'd break the curve in 100 times, then 100 of 'em out. His curve was so wide that you had to stand up to catch it. He'd nick it with the outside corner, and I'd catch it going down the first-base line.[18]

Clean living was another Brewer trademark, and it kept him in top form for another 25 years. He was exceptionally successful during the mid- to late 1930s, a period in which his name appeared in print often, especially when the Monarchs played the Homestead Grays.

On July 18, 1930, Cumberland Posey's Homestead Grays defeated the Kansas City Monarchs in the first-ever night game at Pittsburgh's Forbes Field. It was a 12-inning affair in which George Britt and Brewer battled to a 5–4 Grays victory in front of 12,000 screaming fans. Later that season, in Kansas City, the Grays' "Smokey Joe" Williams struck out 27, while Brewer fanned 19, in another 12-inning nighttime classic, this one also ending in a Monarchs loss. The final score was 1–0.

Brewer's arrival at the prestigious *Denver Post* Tournament in 1934, where he was matched up against the much-heralded Satchel Paige, drew another record crowd. He lost a 2–1 game to Paige but finished the tournament with 41 strikeouts in 30 innings—he walked five batters. It was Brewer, not Paige, who set the *Denver Post* Tournament single-game record of 19 strikeouts, a feat he achieved against the Greeley Advertisers. Brewer finished the tournament with a 2–2 record as Kansas City lost twice to Grover Cleveland Alexander's House of David. Brewer was a no-nonsense individual and, on occasion, would trade blows with his adversaries. He once fought Eddie Pick, a Massachusetts-born infielder, for calling him a nigger during a game on the California coast in 1929.[19]

Chet arrived in Chicago in time to rejoin the Monarchs for the 3:00 p.m. game against Dizzy and Daffy. He traveled from the Upper Midwest, where he was involved in a barnstorming series against Earl Mack's All-Stars, arriving in Chicago with little time to spare. Days earlier he had beaten the All-Stars with a brilliant four-hit shutout at Jamestown, North Dakota. In that contest, Brewer struck out Heinie Manush three times, a feat American League pitchers had accomplished just 23 times in 556 official plate appearances in the course of the entire 1934 season. Against a team that featured Jimmie Foxx, Mike "Pinkie" Higgins, Luke Sewell, Ralph Kress, Roger Cramer, and other highly publicized major-league ballplayers, Brewer breezed through their lineup with amazing ease, allowing only eight hits and a single run in 12 innings of exhibition play. It wasn't ironic or strange that the *Jamestown Sun* never mentioned Brewer's first name in the newspaper's account of the game, nor did the Associated Press release, which broadcast news of Chet's victory throughout the nation. Even without the publicity, he was ready to add yet another victory to his string of wins in Chicago.

As game time approached the turnstiles were bustling with business, and within a short while it became obvious that this would be the largest crowd to ever show up at Mills Stadium. Right up until game time fans converged on the park and crowded in wherever possible. The result was an enormous crowd of 20,000, taxing the capacity of the West Side grounds. Dizzy was amazed. He hadn't expected to see a crowd this large in a National League city. "How many cash customers do you all reckon this heah place holds?" asked Dizzy as he conversed with one of his temporary Mills teammates.[20] The answer was more than Kansas City and Des Moines combined.

Those that could not enter, noted the *Chicago Tribune*, numbered about 3,000. Railbirds, stated the newspaper, were on the L train tracks that ran along the side and above the park. They were taking full advantage of the free look. Inside Mills Stadium, lots of people were made to feel uncomfortable. Their view of the Deans was obstructed. Others frowned and grumbled as their feet were assaulted and toes repeatedly mashed. It should have been a miserable day; it wasn't for most. They were there to see the Deans work their magic, and they were not disappointed. During their visit, little of what the Deans thought of Chicago made it into print. Their visit was absent the media blitz seen in other cities, where almost anything said or done by the brothers was newsworthy.

Daffy's overnight recovery was somewhat of a modern medical miracle—like a blind man recovering his sight after years of darkness. The night prior his arm was so sore he struggled to raise it high enough to comb his hair. And yet, there he was on the mound, standing tall, ready to work, acting as if the shoulder pain in Des Moines was gone and totally forgotten. There were no complaints as he warmed up for the starting assignment. He was about to start his third game in five days.

Paul began the game by whiffing Newt Allen. The fans cheered.[21] It was short-lived because Eddie Dwight followed with a single and advanced to third on a Mills error, which subdued the audience considerably. As the speedy Dwight danced along the foul lines, Giles singled to score the runner and tally the game's first score. The run would go into the books as unearned. The speedy Dwight could have easily scored from second base had it been necessary. Paul returned to pitch the second inning. Kansas City showed momentary hope on Mothell's hit but failed to score. Daffy's exhibition was over by the third inning. Everyone was satisfied with his two innings—there were no complaints. Now it was Dizzy's turn to check the Monarchs.

Dizzy relieved his younger brother and allowed a one-out single to Giles—who obtained his second hit off a Dean on the same day—or was it an error? When shortstop Benny Helgeth juggled Giles's slow roller, allowing the runner to reach safely, it was thought to be unplayable for some scorers and clearly an error for others. The official scorer gave Giles a hit, but a *Tribune* reporter labeled it an error. T. J. Young followed with a double to deep center field, a hit that was not open to debate, scoring Giles. In the writer's haste, Giles's run was credited as unearned—maybe it was, maybe it wasn't. It may have helped Dizzy's exhibition numbers—but was it legitimate? Davis ended the third inning when Dizzy struck him out. In the fourth inning, Newt Joseph doubled off Dizzy. His drive bounced all the way to the wall. The inning ended, however, when Mothell and Allen were victimized by called third strikes. Dizzy left the game after a trio of innings with his All-Stars leading, 8–3. The *Star's* wire service went on record as saying, "Occasionally, they bore down when men were on base, but it was apparent they were saving whatever is left in their pitching arms for the remainder of their trip."[22] The

Deans' teammates had rallied for three in the third and two more runs in the fourth in an apparent battering of Monarchs pitcher Chet Brewer.

Brewer might have sued his teammates for nonsupport if such a rule was permitted. In just two and two-thirds innings, the Monarchs made four errors, resulting in six runs, three unearned. A report in the *Call* surmised, "While Chet Brewer, the Monarchs' moundsman, was strutting his stuff, his fielders were booting the ball all over the diamond. As a result of sloppy fielding, the bases were loaded, and a Texas leaguer into deep center, which Dwight got his hands on, but dropped, enabled three runners to cross home plate."[23] Brewer contributed greatly to his own demise by allowing four hits, two walks, and a wild pitch before Andy Cooper relieved him after two men were out in the third. Cooper exited the game after an inning, having extended his streak to 15 innings pitched in five days—more innings than Dizzy had thrown since the tour's start. No one was keeping count for Cooper, and his number of innings pitched went without acknowledgment. Essentially, he was pitching almost every game without the slightest mention of exhaustion or a sore arm by the media. Dizzy was a close second in innings pitched, having thrown 13 innings in the same five games. Ted Trent followed Cooper to the mound in an effort to extinguish the scoring after one man was out in the fourth. Trent's accomplishment also went without recognition.

In the four innings Trent pitched, six batters struck out, a total greater than Dizzy and Daffy combined on this same day. Trent struck out Atkinson and McCarthy in the fourth, George Gerkin and Sullivan in the fifth, Helgeth in the sixth, and Gerkin again in the seventh. Had it not been for the five-run seventh Trent might have fared better in the postgame write-up. Lefty Barney Brown entered the game after a man was out in the seventh and completed the contest for Kansas City.

Barney Brown, born in Hartsville, South Carolina, in 1907, was coming off a season where he had pitched for Jamestown, North Dakota, as part of that city's African American battery. At season's end he was selected to pitch for the Northern All-Stars against Earl Mack's All-Stars. A series of games was scheduled for Grand Forks, Valley City, Bismarck, Jamestown, and Winnipeg, Canada. Walter "Steel Arm" Davis and Chet Brewer, who participated in the Deans' tour, were also members of the All-Star squad that faced the major leaguers up North.

Brown was awarded the win at Valley City, where he allowed three hits in five innings, then returned to the mound for game one of a scheduled doubleheader at Winnipeg on October 10, 1934. In that game, Jimmie Foxx, holder of 44 American League home runs, who had donned catcher's gear that afternoon, added to his total. He homered off the Negro major-league hurler in his first at-bat. The next time the slugger stepped into the batter's box, Brown threw inside and darn near took the head off the major leaguer with a ball that was later tagged the "Winnipeg wild pitch."[24] The pitch knocked Foxx out cold. In the era when players batted without helmets, it was an automatic lights out. He was immediately taken to a local hospital for further examination, where he remained until he recovered from his injuries. The media went wild in its coverage of Foxx's injury.

The Associated Press was secretly leading the charge against exhibition games, and Foxx was their latest poster child. "Jimmy Foxx, first baseman of the Philadelphia Athletics and one of the best hitters in the game, may have been permanently injured," was the news they carried nationally, "when he was hit in the head in a game at Winnipeg a week ago."[25] The article went on to express that Foxx "was in no shape to play ball at Spokane yesterday but arrived there drowsy and wanted to sleep." Support of the statement could be easily found. "Jimmie Foxx being confined in a Winnipeg hospital as the results of being beaned," wrote Harry Grayson, "is just another illustration of why magnates object to players participating in postseason exhibition games."[26] At least one writer took issue with the Associated Press and others. "Reports that Jimmie Foxx will never play ball again are being taken with a grain of salt in this section," wrote Albert W. Kane. "Those who say that he is permanently injured have not consulted the doctors who handled his case. They are jumping at conclusions and trying to create a scare in the ranks of the followers of the Mackmen."[27] No one bothered to connect these stories when Brown took the mound to pitch the final few innings against the Deans' All-Stars—the writers never realized it was the same Brown who had almost fractured Foxx's cranium. The All-Stars had made a pitching change in the fifth, sending Lefty Sullivan to the mound.

Legend has proclaimed that John Sullivan, the son of an Irishman, was one hell of a pitcher. He'd been the property of the White Sox in 1919, but after four games he rejoined the local semiprofessionals, where he remained for another 20 years.[28] He had always been a thorn in the side for the Monarchs, who had faced him often. On July 4, 1925, while playing for the Chicago Pyotts team, champions of the Midwest League Sullivan battled the Monarchs to a 4 to 4 tie. In that game Sullivan fanned fifteen Monarchs.

The hullabaloo surrounding Sullivan said that he was bunted out of the American League. The knock on him was that he couldn't field bunts because he got dizzy when he bent over, resulting from a lifelong heart ailment that cut off the flow of oxygen to his brain when he doubled over. Evidently the Monarchs were well aware of this health issue, as Sullivan was quickly put to a test.

Giles dropped a bunt, which Sullivan struggled to field. It went into the books as a single. Young followed with another bunt. The pitcher picked up the ball but handed it to the third baseman, who earned an assist when he retired the runner at first base—it took three men to record the out. In the sixth, Rogan beat out another infield hit and Mothell also bunted, but no one scored, as Lefty bore down in the pinches. Sullivan left the game after two innings, allowing McWeeny to pitch the seventh and McNaughton the eighth and ninth innings.

The game ended in a 13–3 rout of the Monarchs. It was a wild affair with almost as many men on the field as there were in the grandstands. Seventeen men appeared in the Mills lineup—the most by any team on the tour. Twelve men saw action for the Monarchs—which included four pitchers. Twenty-nine men took the field that afternoon as the Deans' All-Stars out-hit the Monarchs, 12–8, in a game that was played, from start to finish, in less than two hours. At the conclusion Dizzy and Daffy were nowhere in sight.

After the fifth inning, the Deans made another one of their celebrated exits. Walking in front of the stands the crowd sent up one rousing cheer and assaulted them for autographs as they tried to exit. The brothers were leaving a paper trail of autographs and memorabilia across the United States, and they never complained about it—not once. It took a gallant effort by a squad of Chicago bluecoats to contain the fans as they pressed toward the exit to greet the two major-league stars. The next day's newspaper was laced with injustice. It was obvious that the Monarchs were being watched by ungracious eyes.

The *Herald and Examiner* failed to mention any of the African American players by first or last name, but it provided a box score. The newspaper made special mention of the $5,000 the Deans reportedly received for playing in the game and how money was "jingling in their pockets."[29] The same article made mention that the Deans "didn't say anything about being underpaid."[30] Details in the *Tribune*, although more complete, were equally as biased. Along with the Deans, local dailies revealed the names of Lefty Sullivan and Doug McWeeney, but they failed to mention a single Monarchs player by name except in the box score.

The *Chicago Defender* noted, "Twenty thousand fans didn't see so much of a baseball game, but 20,000 fans went away well pleased; they got their money's worth."[31] A *Tribune* writer assessed, "The crowd was more interested, of course, in the pitching of the Deans than the base hits, runs, or anything you care to mention."[32] Another report in Arch Ward's "Talking It Over" column informed readers that Billy Harley used "10 dozen baseballs" in the Sunday game between the Dean brothers and the Kansas City Monarchs.

Dizzy (left) photographing Daffy. If timing is important, Dizzy and Daffy's arrival was almost picture perfect. Their very presence in the 1930s provoked a clash between an older generation resisting change and a younger generation resisting tradition. *From the author's collection*

JOHN FITZPATRICK
coach PITTSBURGH PIRATES

John Arthur Fitzpatrick (1904–1990). Although John, also known as "Jack," never reached the majors as a player, he battled against the Monarchs as a member of two Hall of Fame–led All-Star teams, Paul and Lloyd Waner's All-Stars in 1933 and Dizzy Dean's All-Stars in 1934. *Topps® trading card, used courtesy of The Topps Company, Inc.*

Oklahoma City's Biltmore Hotel as it looked in 1934, when Dizzy and Daffy roomed there to start their barnstorming tour. Their opponents were forbidden from staying in the same hotels throughout the tour due to Jim Crow customs in the North. *From the author's collection*

Dizzy Dean, "Babe" Ruth cartoon (1934). Dizzy and Daffy had become baseball's newest and biggest attraction; Ruth, however, was still larger-than-life, which explained why it took both brothers to replace him on the national stage. *From the* Kansas City Kansan *newspaper, October 1934, author's collection*

Charles Wilbern "Bullet" Rogan (1893–1967), with wife, Kathryn, and son, Wilbur. As a soldier in the U.S. Army, Rogan served in the segregated 24th and 25th Infantry with honors from 1911 to 1919. *Courtesy of Wilbur Rogan, from the author's collection*

Jay "Dizzy" Dean. During an interview on an Oklahoma City radio station, Dizzy spoke favorably of his African American opponents, stating, "Don't expect me to strike out the Monarchs. They are really a major-league ballclub." *From the author's collection*

Nathan Thatcher's Colts. While the Deans were conquering the Tigers in the 1934 World Series, the Monarchs were beating Nathan Thatcher's Colts in Kansas City, Kansas, at tiny Rock Island Park. Within days, the Deans and Monarchs were in Oklahoma City to begin a schedule of six games in six days. *Courtesy of Fred Langford, from the author's collection*

Dizzy Dean and Patricia Nash "Pat" Dean. The *Philadelphia Evening Bulletin* noted, "His wife astounds players in the National League by insisting that he [Dizzy] take her on all road trips." *From the author's collection*

Theodore "Ted" Trent (1903–1944). Nicknamed "Highpockets" and "Big Florida," Ted pitched in two games against the Deans' All-Stars during the 1934 barnstorming tour, once at Wichita and a second time in Chicago. *Courtesy of Richard Byas, from the author's collection*

Jay "Dizzy" Dean, pitching. Dizzy boasted to the *Wichita Beacon*. "You can tell 'em we'll pitch at least half the game against the Monarchs and perhaps more. Paul may pitch more than me at Wichita, but we won't disappoint the cash customers." *From the author's collection*

Ralph Lee Winegarner (1909–1988). Ralph was no stranger to the Monarchs. He pitched six innings against them in a 6–2 losing effort with Paul and Lloyd Waner's All-Stars in 1932. He played parts of six seasons with the Cleveland Indians and St. Louis Browns. *Courtesy of Rock's Dugout Baseball Card Shop, Wichita, Kansas*

Paul "Daffy" Dean. While bragging to a *Wichita Eagle* reporter Paul said, "When I'm pitching I like to bear down, and you'll see me doing that even in the exhibition games. It's no fun to lob 'em over. Whizzing 'em past the suckers at the plate is my dish." *From the author's collection*

Bazz Owen Smaulding (1900–1962), far left, and George Franklin Giles (1909–1992), third from left. In a 1933 exhibition game against a contingent of major-league All-Stars at Wichita, Kansas, Giles had a perfect 5-for-5 game off pitcher Larry French of the Pirates. French had won 18 National League games that same season. *Courtesy of Maurice "Doolittle" Young, from the author's collection*

Mickey Flynn. Based on how well he handled the slants of Dizzy and Daffy at Wichita, Kansas, Flynn was recruited by Ray L. Doan for his House of David organization in 1935. *Courtesy of Rock's Dugout Baseball Card Shop, Wichita, Kansas*

Thomas Jefferson "T. J." Young (1902–1965). After getting extra-base hits off Dizzy and Daffy, T. J. told a *Kansas City Call* reporter, "All my life it has been one of my ambitions to hit the best hurlers in the majors. So now I figure that maybe I'm not so bad with the bat. I also think we [the Monarchs] have a great bunch of hitters." *Courtesy of Maurice "Doolittle" Young, from the author's collection*

Walter "Steel Arm" Davis (1891–1941), second from left, Clarence "Pops" Coleman (1884–??), third from left, and Edward Joseph Dwight (1905–1975), far right. Dwight batted .353 (6-for-17) in the 1934 *Denver Post* Tournament for the second-place Kansas City Monarchs and appeared in at least five of the games the Monarchs played against the Deans. *Courtesy of Georgia Dwight, from the author's collection*

Dorsey Moulder (1909–1987). Although the Kansas City native was originally signed by the American Association Kansas City Blues in 1931, he finished the 1934 season as a Western Leaguer at Des Moines, Iowa, where he batted .279 in 17 games. *Courtesy of Dorsey Moulder, from the author's collection*

Daffy and Dizzy before the Kansas City game with Frankie Frisch. "Dizzy is actually as shrewd as they make 'em, a born comedian, and he likes to make sly remarks, which the writers eat up eagerly," said J. L. Wilkinson, owner of the Kansas City Monarchs to a *Wichita Eagle* reporter. *Courtesy of the Missouri Valley Special Collections, Kansas City Public Library, Kansas City, Missouri*

Lee Keyser (1885–1950). As owner of the Des Moines Demons, Keyser was seeking to cash in on the Deans' success. The former soft drink vendor from St. Louis was, by 1930, one of the founding fathers of night baseball. Game four of the Dean's tour was played at night on Keyser's Holcomb Field lot in Des Moines. *From the author's collection*

Charlie Beverly (1899–1981). Lefty Beverly, a Texan, had struck out 15 of Dizzy's All-Stars in Des Moines. He had performed a similar feat at Fort Scott, Kansas; Oklahoma City, Oklahoma; and Joplin, Missouri. *Courtesy of Carroll Ray Mothell, from the author's collection*

Albert Dean (the father) and Elmer Dean (the brother). After Dizzy's Game 1 World Series win, Branch Rickey wired the pitcher congratulations, and Dizzy responded by asking Rickey to have his father on an airplane in time for the next day's game. *Courtesy of the Kansas Collection, Kenneth Spencer Research Library, University of Kansas*

(L to R) J. L. Wilkinson, Dizzy Dean, Pat Dean, Daffy Dean, and Tom Baird as the group boarded a plane for the East. When asked about their courtship Pat Dean offered, "I had a date with him Monday night. We were engaged Tuesday night. We got our wedding license Wednesday night. And we were married Thursday night. I guess when folks hear that, they'll think I'm dizzy, too." *Courtesy of the Kansas Collection, Kenneth Spencer Research Library, University of Kansas*

Paul "Daffy" Dean. A report in the *Philadelphia Evening Bulletin* stated, "Jimmy Wilson, manager of the Philadelphia Phillies, took a seat between Dizzy and Paul. 'Keep it up boys,' he encouraged. 'Grab the dough when it's hot.'" *From the author's collection*

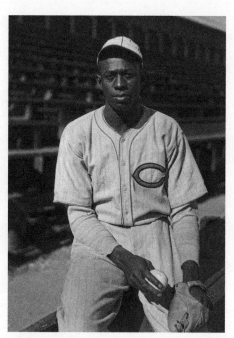

LeRoy "Satchel" Paige (1906–1982). Paige, age 27, was the ace of the Pittsburgh Craw-fords pitching staff. Dizzy said of Paige to a *Pittsburgh Press* reporter, "If you think I'm fast, you should see him." *UCLA Library Special Collections*

Mrs. Eleanor Williams. This is the face of the lady who murdered Gordon J. McNaugh-ton, one of the Deans' Chicago All-Stars. The photograph was captioned "McNaughton knew how to pick them." *From ACME Newspictures, author's collection*

CHAPTER 7

~

Milwaukee, Wisconsin

Shortchanged
Monday, October 15, 1934

Chicago to Milwaukee is a distance of 90 miles, so the Deans took the high-way. Ford Motors provided two new, spotless automobiles at no expense for transportation—one for the human cargo and another for the luggage tail-gating close behind. It looked like a chance to pick up some free advertising for the automobile company; however, upon arrival, when a Ford Motors representative desired to take photographs of the Deans in the shiny new Lincolns, Howard Purser of the *Wisconsin News* noted, "Dizzy bustled out of the car in front of the hotel and wouldn't pose."[1] Dizzy was smarter than the Ford publicity agent ever anticipated. This tour was for revenue and publicity only—not for free promotions at the brothers' expense. It was an unfortunate break for the Ford Motor Company and the start of what would become the tour's most unpredictable day of activities.

The Milwaukee stop, which was promoted by Eddie Stumpf, a local pro-moter working on a shoestring budget, was plagued by fault and blame from the onset. It suffered for a variety of factors. An early start time, inaccurate media, and competition from other local activities were soon to distract from the Deans' visit. Unlike the previous five cities where Dizzy and Daffy worked in night games, the scheduled Milwaukee event was a 3:00 p.m. start. This left little opportunity for the benefits of rest or relaxation. It most cer-tainly made Dizzy and Daffy a little jittery. Beginning at the hotel and later at the press club and during the actual contest at Brochert Field, home to the American Association Brewers, this was destined to be a stop Dizzy and Daffy wanted to put behind them—and not quickly enough. On the local sports pages they were forced to share top billing with two professional football teams. Coach Curly Lambeau's Packers had played the New York Giants at Brochert Field in 1933. Now he was back in town for a second football game.

Tickets for the Green Bay Packers versus Chicago Bears National Football League game were moving at a vigorous pace, and all indications were that they stole much of the coin that might have gone into the Deans' pockets. Almost 2,500 fans turned out on a Monday night—the very night of the Dean brothers' appearance—to watch the Packers practice under the arc lights at nearby State Fair Park, a converted racetrack.[2] The pay-per-view workout was given by Lambeau in preparation for their game at Milwaukee two days later with George Halas's Bears. The drills attracted fans more eager to line up four and five rows deep to watch football rather than baseball. The crowd, which overflowed into the grandstands, watched punting and passing for an hour and a half of big-time professional football training.

Coach Lambeau had leased State Fair Park to acquaint his Packers with night football, as his team had never played a nighttime game—they were unfamiliar with artificial lights—which accounted for their early arrival in Milwaukee. The Kansas City Monarchs had introduced Milwaukee's Borchert Field to night baseball using their portable lights on September 30, 1930. That year they came to play a team of All-Stars organized by Eddie Stumpf. That night, about 3,500 local fans were given a reason to celebrate when the Monarchs were thumped in a close-scoring 7–6 win. Borchert Field did not get permanent lights until June 1935, a year after the Deans' appearance. Milwaukee baseball was strictly a daytime venture in 1934.

Originally built in 1888, on the corners of North 7th, 8th, Chambers, and Burleigh Streets, and christened Athletic Field, it would become the home of Milwaukee professional baseball until 1952. It was built as a rectangular structure with short fences down the left- and right-field lines, and a spacious outfield. Center field was more than 380 feet from home plate.

The baseball game's early start allowed Coach Lambeau time to bring 23 members of the Packers to the park as special guests to view the baseball festivities. The football game aside, coverage of the Dean brothers' visit was uniquely different in Milwaukee, where the local media was partly to blame for the tour's lack of good fortune.

Coverage of the Deans' Milwaukee visit was among the best on the tour, and at the same time some the worst. With the exception of two words, "Charlie Beverly," the legion of upstanding Milwaukee reporters failed to mention which Monarchs pitcher had started, hurled, or completed the game. Beverly arrived with a perfect record, but we don't know the details of his Milwaukee stint. Most prominent among the Milwaukee writers, Ronald McIntyre, "Red"

Thisted, Ben Smith, Sam Levy, and Howard Purser, were critiques of Dizzy and Daffy's moral character. Moreover, none of the local newspapers printed a box score of the proceedings, which was a true illustration of these writers' lockstep adherence to race and segregation in Wisconsin.

Covering the game for the *Milwaukee Sentinel* was Amos Theodore "Red" Thisted, a tireless and dedicated writer who reportedly attended every home game played by the Milwaukee Brewers American Association team during the course of four decades.[3] You couldn't slip a white ballplayer's name past him. He knew them all, sandlot and minor leaguers included. He wasn't nearly as sharp when it came to identifying African American ballplayers. Thisted prided himself on being accurate in his writing. His coverage of the Deans was not one of his best efforts.

Born in Lindsay, Nebraska, "Red" Thisted, the son of a Lutheran pastor, was injured during World War I fighting militarism in Europe. After his return Stateside, he watched a Red Sox versus Senators game in Boston and was forever hooked. It was his first professional baseball game, and it started a love affair with the sport that lasted a lifetime. Later in life, Red hosted a radio program and surely must have talked about the Deans' whirlwind tour. On August 6, 1955, he replaced Sam Levy, who had died of a heart attack, as the official scorer for the National League Milwaukee Braves, a major-league franchise that relocated to Milwaukee from Boston in 1953.

When not talking about the Deans, Thisted summarized the game in roughly 55 words, noting,

> The Kansas City Monarchs, colored champions, rallied against Ray Wallen for four runs in the ninth, but Harry Strohm's team came right back with three to toss it into a permanent deadlock. Strohm was the leading batsman with four singles. Ralph Blatz followed Dizzy to the mound in the third and pitched until the seventh.[4]

His only praise for the Monarchs were his words "colored champions."[5] He paid much more attention to Ray L. Doan while virtually ignoring the Monarchs on the diamond. Purser, of the *News*, chose to acquaint his readers with Monarchs co-owner Tom Baird, who traveled to Milwaukee to assist the Deans.[6]

"Things went awry early that morning," said Ben Smith is his *Leader* article. "The reporters broke in on them while they were having their breakfast. That didn't set right with the Dean family." Still hoping to get a breather from the rigors of steady media interrogations and everyday baseball, orders from the Deans' hotel suite said "no interviews please." Lunch was ordered and brought to their rooms.[7] T. Y. Baird, who had been with the tour from day one, acted as the point man responsible for steering reporters away from the brothers. Tom always went by the initials T. Y. because his middle name said too much about his family's heritage. His full name was Thomas Younger Baird. Baird's mother, Japha Duncan, was the daughter of Sarah Ann "Sally" Younger Duncan, the sister of Cole Younger, the famous Missouri outlaw who rode with Jesse James.[8] Tom tried his best to keep the Younger name out of his business affairs, knowing it would be bad blood if his association with his family's outlaw heritage was ever made public. He probably understood Dizzy more than most. They had come from similar rural Arkansas backgrounds.

Tom spent his early life in Pinnacle, Arkansas, Pulaski County. Dizzy was born in Lucas, a town in Logan County. They lived little more than 100 miles apart. Tom's father, Noah, brought the family to Kansas City, Kansas, in 1902, seeking better opportunities in his plumbing occupation. They brought their Southern customs with them. Tom, who was already in his 20s, found employment as a laborer at the Procter and Gamble plant in Kansas City's Armourdale district near his home. They were forced to move again when the 1903 Kansas flood destroyed their home. Like Dizzy, Baird was accustomed to moving from place to place.

His home was located at 1213 Kansas Avenue; he later moved to 413 North 18th in Kansas City, Kansas, where his family was living at the time of the Dean tour. Tom married Francis "Frankie" Stewart and continued to play semiprofessional baseball. Tom's younger brother, Floyd, said of his older brother, "He played second base and could run. In the field he had a good arm."[9]

Tom eventually organized his own team, T.Y. Baird's Baseball Club, and leased Billion Bubble Park in Kansas City, Kansas. He made a profit on the enterprise by selling season passes. They were nicknamed the "Soapmakers" and, at other times, were sponsored by "Peet Brothers." The team featured a major-league battery in Roy "Lefty" Meeker, a pitcher who reached the majors with the Philadelphia Athletics in 1923, and catcher John Peters, who made his major-league debut in 1915, with the Detroit Tigers.[10] Baird's team played for the gate and side bets, which commanded as much as $200 a game. His team won the championship of Kansas City twice. Tom's other job kept him on the road often. He was a brakeman with the Rock Island Railroad. In his absence he hired Charlie Jenne as business manager to handle the team's affairs. Everything changed when Baird became disabled.

In 1918, Baird sustained a broken right leg while setting a brake on a Rock Island train at White City, Kansas. The fracture was above the knee, and doctors wanted to amputate. The injury was complicated by the fact that Tom had broken the same leg a few years earlier. The leg was saved, however, and after months of hobbling about on crutches, Tom was left with a horrific limp. He could walk but was unable to run, and he couldn't work at the railroad. Baird continued to manage his ball team through World War I, but he was looking for new fields to conquer. Around town he was known as a good promoter of baseball. He was well connected in Kansas City. Thanks to the efforts of researcher Tim Rives, we now know why.

Baird was active in the hooded order of the Knights of the Ku Klux Klan. According to Rives, "Kansas City's top 10 employers of Klansmen were Armour and Company, a packing house, the city government of Kansas City, Kansas, and the Chicago [based] Rock Island Railroad, where Tom was formerly employed."[11] Baird was co-owner of an African American team, but his was a melting pot not equally stirred. Tom, however, was no pure Aryan. His father was of Native American and Irish ancestry.[12] His mother was Scottish and Irish.

Baird, in room 520, flanked the Deans, in room 524. "No one can see them," was the message he relayed to the reporters. The reporters ignored Baird and kept pressing for some of those witty statements for which Dizzy had become famous. After a wait, the *News* stated, "Baird timidly telephoned next door to ascertain when they, the Deans, could see the newspapermen." There was another wait and another phone call before Dizzy "shuffled" out of his hotel room to start a conversation with the impatient writers.[13]

Dizzy was sweet-pampered into going to a meeting at the Press Club to greet a dozen or so of the newspaper writers simultaneously. "He didn't want to go," Purser advised. "It was somewhat like coaxing a baby to do a trick for a stick of candy."[14] Dizzy was about to close the door to his suite when Sheriff Joe Shinners promised to take him downtown in the squad car and deliver him back. A reluctant Dizzy grabbed his pullover sweater and was on his way, hatless and dressed without a suit coat. Along the way he told Purser, "I doan' mind goin' out there an' pitchin,' but it's all this promotin' that gets you."[15]

Dizzy's Press Club interview had barely started before it was abruptly interrupted. There was an urgent long-distance call from Sam Breadon, president of the St. Louis Cardinals. Dizzy hustled to a nearby phone booth. The conversation was centered on Paul's sore arm. Breadon requested that Paul "lay off the barnstorming," stated the *Milwaukee Journal*. Breadon's concerns were many. Another newspaper reported that he, Breadon, was more worried about Paul's arm going lame than the "nightly barnstorming."[16] "Someone apparently notified Breadon that Daffy's arm had gone dead working in exhibition games," responded Allan Sothoron, Milwaukee Brewers manager, when he learned of the Cardinals owner's call. "The younger Dean's arm is quite sore above the shoulder. When pitching arms go dead the trouble usually starts in that spot."[17] Breadon might have been equally worried about the way his two great pitchers were being roughed up by their Negro major-league opponents. Not one of the daily newspapers dared address this latter topic. Breadon's feelings about the interracial tour never appeared in print, not in Oklahoma, Wichita, Des Moines, or Chicago. Watching the events just as closely was Branch Rickey, the Cardinals general manager and team president.

Wesley Branch Rickey had been hired by the Cardinals' Sam Breadon in 1917. Rickey's introduction of the first minor-league system in sports revolutionized baseball and helped his employer to world championships in 1926, 1931, and 1934. His parents were farmers, and he tagged his new minor-league system the "farm system." Those who wanted off the farm to seek better opportunities, after signing for ridiculously low terms with the Cardinals, called the new farm system the "Chain Gang." Breadon and Rickey were the wardens who kept the inmates in line. Rickey dreamed up the farm system concept, which gathered young players and grew them like crops in a chain of minor-league franchises owned by the Cardinals.[18] According to Lloyd Johnson and Miles Wolf in The Encyclopedia of Minor League Baseball, "Rickey's approach was original because he was the first to assemble teams at different levels and push this talent through his system."[19] Rickey was once quoted as saying, "I offered mill hands, plowboys, high school kids a better way of life. They rose on sandlots to big city diamonds. They earned more in a month than they could have earned in a year."[20]

Born on December 20, 1881, in Portsmouth, Ohio, Rickey attended Ohio Wesleyan and played catcher for semiprofessional baseball teams to earn money during the summer. He was a religious lad who refused to play baseball on the Sabbath. Unique opportunities allowed for his first signing with the Cincinnati Reds in 1904, a major-league career that was short-lived because of his resistance to playing on Sundays and an overall lack of ability, but it did include a stint with the American League Browns of St. Louis. He eventually became manager of the St. Louis Cardinals before moving to the front office as general manager. Rickey was both a saint and a sinner in race relations.

Author Jimmy Breslin noted, "The only thing he [Rickey] couldn't do in St. Louis was move black fans out of the broiling one-hundred-degree sun of the bleachers and into the shaded grandstand."[21] Fast forward to 1934. In that year there was no mention of Rickey's interest in signing African American players, who were routinely beating his "farm" teams. In the late 1940s, he made mention of a former professional with the all-black Philadelphia Giants named Charles Wesley Thomas—his friend and longtime confidant. Rickey became acquainted with Thomas, an African American born in Zanesville, Ohio, when he coached at Ohio Wesleyan.

Rickey told one of baseball's most far-fetched stories in explaining how Thomas, the lone African American on the team, would influence him to sign Jackie Robinson to the Dodgers in October 1945—40 years after the fact—when he took the job as general manager and team president in 1942. By Rickey's own account, "We [Ohio Wesleyan] went to South Bend to play Notre Dame, and Thomas, a halfback on the football team and a catcher on the baseball team, could not stay at the Oliver Hotel." Rickey snuck Thomas into his room for a talk. "He was sitting on the edge of the bed pulling his fingers with great big tears running down his cheeks," recalled Rickey, "a great effort to control his emotions. He tried to pull his skin off, saying, 'If they were only white.' That was the only difference."[22]

Breslin's depiction of the story was even more outlandish. "Thomas sat in Rickey's room," he wrote, "and began crying. He rubbed one big hand over the other, saying, 'Black skin, black skin. If I only could rub it off and make it white.' Rickey said, 'Stop it. If you can't beat this, how do you expect me to?'"[23] Thomas, an outstanding player, quickly found a job among his own people with the 1905 world champion Philadelphia Giants. He appeared briefly on the roster in 1904, and returned in July 1905, to play 20 games, primarily as first baseman, between studies.[24]

Both versions of how one African American faced racial prejudice in his youth hardly ring genuine. It is impossible to accept the premise of the story, especially so when Rickey said nothing about segregation publicly for another 40 years. The message here was a simple one: African Americans could work at the Oliver Hotel, which they did as maids, porters, cooks, and waiters, but don't try to stay there or eat in their dining room or restaurants. Rickey, in his haste to tell a distorted story about Thomas, failed to mention that black labor was more valuable than its economic patronage—something he would come to appreciate many years later with the signing of Jackie Robinson and the enormous profits that followed.

When Dizzy returned to the interview, he was marking time and using as few words as possible. He half-stepped through several questions and appeared to be plotting an escape. When asked, "Did you pitch to [Greenberg's] weakness during the series?" Dizzy shook his head no, and replied, "Naw, he's a guess hitter, and I just throwed it in there."[25] Dean often called Greenberg "Mose," short for "Moses," because of his ancestry.

Roy Stockton, in a *Saturday Evening Post* article, added a further story to the Dean–Greenberg interaction. Before one of the World Series games, Dean walked by the Detroit dugout, where he paused a moment and spied

Greenberg. "Hello, 'Mose,'" said Dizzy. "What makes you so white? Boy, you're a-shakin' like a leaf. I get it; you done heard that Old Diz was goin' to pitch. Well, you're right. It'll all be over in a few minutes. Old Diz is goin' to pitch, and he's goin' to pin your ears back."[26]

When Dizzy was asked, "What are you going to do with all the money you're getting on this tour?" his reply was, "We ain't getting much dough. That's a lot of newspaper talk." Another reporter inquired, "But you're drawing thousands of people everywhere you go?" To this Dean shrugged his shoulders, licked his lips, paused, and disdainfully replied, "Yes, we don't get much though." One local writer observed that the subject of money was obviously a "painful" one to discuss, particularly in light of the national economic woes of 1934, when the average American's annual salary was $1,368 and the average net income for all Americans was little more than $3,000 per year. In the Deans' native Arkansas, the average yearly income for sharecroppers equaled $284; a teacher's annual salary averaged $489.

Another writer suggested that Dizzy was pondering what the internal revenue collectors might have to say at tax time. He was hurrying out the door when Ben Steinel waved him back to hear Press Club president John Wolf's "speech of welcome." That finished, Dizzy was back in the sheriff's car and headed for the hotel but not without making one last statement. "I tell ya, this kinda stuff almost drove Pepper Martin crazy after the first World Series he was in. He had to go off in the woods an' hide among the chipmunks to get away from the crowd. An' if this keeps up much longer I'll be shore 'nuff crazy, too." When asked, "What are you going to do in your vaudeville act, which starts next week?" Dizzy replied, "I don't know. I don't know who's writin' it for us. That won't last long. I want to get away from crowds. I like crowds in the ballparks but not on the streets."[27]

Lots of money was reportedly flowing into the Deans' personal hopper, and journalists nationwide were doing their best to keep tabs on their earnings. Paul was blown away by how easily the money was flowing. When the series ended in Detroit, someone gave Dizzy $500 just for displaying himself in a window wearing that "silly pith helmet" he picked up somewhere. Paul, puzzled by the affair, questioned his brother. "Diz, is someone kidding us about this kind of money?" he asked. "We ain't done nuthin' but win a couple ballgames."[28] One Milwaukee newspaper printed that they'd collected a "cool $5,000" for the Sunday game at Chicago's Mills Stadium.[29] An October 18 issue of the *Sporting News* estimated the brothers as having earned "something like $15,000 in five games." This same article made mention of the Deans' contract with Fanchom and Marco, theatrical producers, for a month's appearance at $5,000 a week.[30] The *Milwaukee Leader* noted,

"The bankroll of the pitching Deans has been increased by $14,000 since the World Series. They took down $5,000—more than Daffy made all season."[31] In three previous exhibition games—Oklahoma City, Wichita, and Kansas City—the Deans were rumored to have collected $9,000.[32] A column in the *Philadelphia Record* stated, "Paul gave a laugh at the estimates that run their receipts to the neighborhood of $20,000."[33] Like many of the Dean brothers' boastful rants, their financial totals were often overstated. They were, however, looking very prosperous when Dizzy and Daffy met that day's All-Stars, a team Stumpf had organized.

Long before he took the job as manager for the Rockford Peaches in the All-American Girls Professional Baseball League, Stumpf was a popular minor-league ballplayer. Born in 1894, he had been a promising young catcher in the American Association for the Milwaukee Brewers from 1916 to 1919. He was signed by the Chicago White Sox in 1919.[34] Stumpf, the baseball agent, was acting as local sponsor for Dizzy and Daffy's Milwaukee appearance. His personally assembled All-Stars were to be Dizzy and Daffy's supporting cast.

The Milwaukee version of the Deans' All-Stars was a formidable opponent. It was one of the few positive elements of the local attraction presented by Stumpf. He dropped a pretty penny to pull together a stellar All-Star combination that included future and current major leaguers playing alongside several American Association stars. A press release on October 10 said that Elmer Klumpp, who played with Syracuse in the International league, would catch Dizzy, who was slated to pitch for five innings, and Ray Thompson, who was with Louisville, would work with Daffy. Klumpp would join the Boston Red Sox the following spring.

Otto "Squeaky" Bluege, a one-time Cincinnati Reds infielder and outfielder, and John Clarence Kloza, formerly of the St. Louis Browns, were members of the local All-Stars. Kloza, nicknamed "Nap," a Polish American, had batted .326 and drove in a league-leading 148 runs for the American Association Brewers in 1934.[35] His 12-year minor-league career included two brief stints with the St. Louis Browns in 1931 and 1932. Elmer Greenwald, of the Northern League, and Fred Bedore, of the Indianapolis American Association team, formed the heart of Stumpf's All-Stars. Bedore finished the 1934 campaign with a .322 batting percentage in 150 games. Teammates Clary Hackbarth, Ray Wallen, and Ralph Blatz were signed from the Milwaukee American Association club. Hackbarth had originally signed with Milwaukee in 1930, but he only pinch-hit in the next two years. He would find his way to other minor leagues and, as late as 1940, was with

El Dorado of the Cotton States League. By far the most renowned member of the Deans' Milwaukee All-Stars was Harry Strohm.

Harry Strohm's career placed him in second place on the all-time minor-league career hit list, with 3,486. Amazingly, he spent 25 years in the minor leagues and not one day in the majors, with a record of 2,965 certified games. Born in Kansas City in 1901, Strohm broke into the minors with Topeka of the Southwest League in 1922. The following year, he hit a career-high 11 home runs for Topeka and Milwaukee, where he finished the season. In 1925, Strohm posted a career-high 214 hits for Nashville in the Southern Association, a total he would duplicate in 1927, when he collected 214 hits for Milwaukee of the American Association. He added another 202 hits in 1928, for his only back-to-back 200-hit seasons. Strohm is also rated sixth on the all-time minor-league doubles hit list, with 658; however, during his long career in the minors he only led his circuit in two offensive categories. His 53 doubles for Little Rock of the Southern Association in 1930, and 44 doubles for Lafayette of the Evangeline League in 1940, topped both leagues. Strohm became a manager, general manager, team president, and scout for minor- and major-league teams in the latter part of his baseball career.[36]

As local promoter of the Dean brothers' visit, Stumpf assembled an outstanding supporting cast of players, but his follow-through on the Deans' contract was evidently bobbled. In advertising the brothers' appearance, he wasn't attentive to the terms laid down by Mr. Doan. Stumpf made serious assumptions by suggesting the Deans would be there for the entire game in prior press releases. The announcement in the *Journal Sentinel* instructed, "Dizzy will start and after four innings will be replaced by Daffy. Dizzy will be asked to finished the game at first base."[37] Regionally, he advertised a full nine innings of the Deans on the mound.[38] Stumpf hadn't bothered to read newspaper reports that clearly showed the brothers had never pitched more than two or three innings before their Milwaukee visit. Dizzy and Daffy were not the problem—they hadn't remained in a game for all nine innings in any city—and they weren't about to pitch nine full innings at Milwaukee. It wasn't a major-league baseball problem either, as several newspapers suggested. Doan's contract was fairly straightforward.

When Doan first wired Stumpf, the offer read, "The Deans would split pitching duties." The promoter believed this to mean the Deans would pitch all nine innings. He proceeded to advertise in Milwaukee newspapers and on radio that Dizzy would pitch five innings and Paul four, and that both would be in the lineup for the full nine frames either as a pitcher or an outfielder. Regrettably, Stumpf paid little attention to Paul's well-publicized arm injury in Des Moines a few days earlier. His failure to notify the local press and the press's failure to report on Paul's inability to pitch were costly. Almost 3,500 people showed up expecting to see both Deans pitch the entire game, as had been previously advertised.

An announcement over the loudspeaker inside Borchert Field broke the news that Paul would not pitch. Those who had paid to see the star attraction were stunned. It was their first disappointment, but the fans didn't moan much at the time, and few booed the announcement—maybe they had been reading the newspapers. Paul began the game in right field and remained there for six uneventful innings. When he fielded balls hit his way, he threw them to the infielders underhanded to protect his arm. As reported, he never made it to the pitcher's mound, but Dizzy did.

Dizzy started the game and pitched to every batter in the Monarchs lineup. He allowed a run, two walks, and a single before joining Paul in the outfield. Dizzy hadn't pitched four or five innings, as advertised; he appeared in just two. The fans started to howl as if they weren't getting their money's worth. They weren't convinced that Dizzy was trying his best either—they expected him to razzle-dazzle the Monarchs as he had the Tigers in the World Series, but he hadn't. His execution was flawed. The *Leader* suggested, "They [the Deans] failed to carry out advance exploitations of what they would show against the Kansas City Monarchs, a Negro team."[39] Considerable weight was put on the words "Negro team."

Dizzy joined his brother in the outfield, where he remained for four additional innings. In the sixth frame, the crowd began to complain about the number of innings Dizzy had pitched and Daffy had played, so Charlie Beverly, Monarchs pitcher, floated up a "soft ball" to appease the crowd. He allowed Dizzy to flex his muscles as he rammed the gift pitch over the left-field wall for a home run.[40] It was the last favorable cheer of the night for Dizzy, one of the few thrills for fans, and the only mention of Beverly's name as the Monarchs pitcher. On the way to the dugout, the brothers slipped into the clubhouse and met Sheriff Shinners for what they thought would be a painless trip back to their hotel hideaway. When pinch-hitters were announced for the Deans, the crowd felt cheated. Intervals of booing and hissing could be heard throughout Borchert Field. A howl for refunds echoed from the grandstand.

Ralph Blatz relieved Dizzy on the mound and was followed to the hill by Ray Wallen. They pitched the game's final seven innings, but the fans weren't impressed. Negativity had already rocked the stands as fans scattered and overran the box office in hopes of getting their money back. They were quickly joined by others who angrily demanded a return of their cash. They paid good money to see nine innings of Dizzy and Daffy, two of baseball's biggest stars. They had gotten six at best, and only one of the Deans pitched. Outside the park there was dissatisfaction and confusion; inside the park the All-Stars and Monarchs were still putting on a splendid ballgame. Had it not been for the article that appeared in the *Wisconsin News*, one to which no writer attached their name, intimate details of the game might have been lost forever.

The game proceeded, and the *News* took note. "After that it was real baseball, no monkey business," stated the newspaper. The score stood 4–3, in favor of the Monarchs, and remained that way until the eighth inning, when umpire Harold Schiefelbein ruled Greenwald safe at first on a close play. Kansas City claimed he was out by at least a step, maybe two, and they fervently argued the call. Manager Rogan stormed out with protest on his mind, and several Monarchs followed him. He became fighting mad, and so did followers in the stands, who echoed an uneasy disposition regarding the series of events that had apparently trended toward the Dean brothers' white All-Stars, even without Dizzy in the lineup. Umpire Schiefelbein was said to have cast an "ominous glare at his ebony tormentors."[41] Rogan left the field, and play resumed. For the first time of the tour, this newspaper writer didn't change the narrative. From this point onward he called the game fairly even.

After the controversial call, the next batter, Hackbarth, tripled, and Greenwald scored. Klumpp brought him home with a drive into distant right field to give the All-Stars a 5–4 lead heading into the ninth inning. Kansas City had one last at-bat. The contest was extended when Kansas City fought back and rallied for four runs off Wallen. It was a scoring sequence that started when Giles drew a free pass, stole second base, and moved to third on a Steel Arm Davis single to right. Rogan walked to load the bases. This set the stage for Frank Duncan's triple to the outer regions of Borchert Field. Three Monarchs crossed the plate. Duncan himself came around to score when Bedore missed the relay throw to the infield. The score now stood 8–5, in Kansas City's favor.

Late-evening shadows cast a canvas over the field, and darkness flirted with the park as the All-Stars came to bat in the bottom of the inning—but no one wanted to stop the game. The All-Stars were about to stage a rally. It started with Wallen's walk. Harry Strohm singled, and Kloza doubled, scoring Wallen and Strohm. Bluege singled, scoring Kloza, which deadlocked the game at 8–8. Hackbarth fouled out to end the inning, and the game was halted due to darkness.

Dizzy and Daffy weren't there for the thrilling finish. They stepped double time in leaving the park, a cadence that left lots of questions regarding their departure. Safely in Doan's possession was a bundle of money. An article carried by the Associated Press said the brothers collected "their portion from a gate of about $3,300."[42] The local *Leader* reported the Deans as having taken a lump sum of "$1,577, or 70 percent of the receipts."[43] Levy's article said it was a "$1,700 purse."[44] Another line in the *Sentinel* reported the Deans as having escaped with "approximately $750."[45] Ronald McIntyre, in his *Sentinel's* "Between You and Me" column, advised if Paul and Dizzy had finished the game, a majority of the fans would have gone home happy, but as things worked out many were disgruntled.[46] Euphoria, a certain feeling that came from getting the money, was an emotion less satisfying than winning. The Deans hadn't tasted victory, but they were done pitching on this day. When Lynn Doyle of the *Philadelphia Evening Bulletin* heard about the hasty exit, he noted, "How the Tigers wish the Deans had been operating on that basis last week."[47]

In Dizzy and Daffy's absence, Stumpf was left holding the bag. He knew they wouldn't be returning. Their entourage was headed back to Chicago, where a plane awaited them for the trip to Philadelphia. After the game one lawyer went as far as to gather signatures on an affidavit demanding reimbursement, although nothing came of it.[48] Stumpf promised to contact Judge Kenesaw Landis, baseball commissioner, about the Dean brothers, as he had been similarly burnt by Babe Ruth and the Yankees several years prior in another exhibition game. "I think Landis should know of the Dean runout so that he can take some action against major-league barnstormers who forget the public after tickets have been bought," was Stumpf's statement. On October 25, the *Journal Sentinel* reported the results of that conversation. "Verbal agreements don't mean a thing with the judge," said Leslie O'Connor, the commissioner's male secretary. "So long as they did nothing wrong Landis won't take any action against Dizzy or Daffy."[49]

The Monarchs' portion of the tour was finished. Newt Allen recalled, "We made $1,200 a man" for the six games. Allen, the Monarchs second baseman, hadn't made big noise during the exhibition tour, but he got high praise from J. L. Wilkinson. "The greatest second basemen that ever wore a spiked shoe," said Wilkinson. "Of course, Allen is getting older now, but in his prime he never had an equal."[50] When recalling his own memories of a Negro League career that lasted from 1922 to 1946, Allen said he "cherished the good times, going state to state and seeing how the world looked at someone else's expense."[51]

The Deans had earned a large sum of money; the Monarchs had also been compensated well, but the local promoter was left holding an empty purse following game six. The next day's newspaper showed that Stumpf was impaled by his own promotion. He pocketed less than $200 after his expenses. Regrettably, some of his share probably went to refunds.

Other than the Deans, it is difficult to know who actually played in the Milwaukee game and what they achieved afield or at the plate. Who pitched the ninth inning for the Monarchs was never recorded by the local media. Evidently, none of the outstanding crew of Milwaukee writers thought it important news. Their preconceived notions of race prevailed. They wrote of just one Monarchs scoring sequence, and four runs had already tallied before this information was presented. Only five Monarchs were mentioned in the postgame wrap-ups, while nine of the local All-Stars got name recognition the morning after. Purser didn't bother with tidbits on the game; he went right after Dizzy in his "Sports Slants" column for the *News*.

Purser's *News* article discussed the Deans' appearance with several sarcastic and contemptuous statements. None of his points were positive; others were downright rancid. He titled his column, "Hillbilly Hurler Is Like a Circus Freak; They Pay to See Him." Purser went on to add, "I came away with the impression that he [Dizzy] is far behind Babe Ruth, Jack Dempsey, Bill Tilden, and Barney Ross in this respect."[52] Little patience was given to the brothers for wrestling with their overnight celebrity. Purser concluded his article by labeling Dizzy a "rawboned hillbilly who has a lot to learn about making gracious contacts with newspapermen and others who are trying to be nice to him." One of the more interesting articles about the Milwaukee stop was written by John Lardner, the oldest son of Ring Lardner, a legendary journalist in his own right. John's October 17 story was penned for NANA, Inc., and printed in the *Lincoln (Nebraska) State Journal* and other newspapers. He titled his story "Dean Boys Rusty on Barnstorming Jaunt" and subtitled it "Pitching Ability Seems to Fluctuate with Size of Gate Receipts."[53] Lardner opened his article by noting,

This is a bad time to discuss iron men in baseball, because I was going to use the Dean boys for my text and all of a sudden the Dean boys have begun to rust very fast. They pulled up at Milwaukee the other day with a complication of diseases, featuring sore arms and acute anemia of the box office.

He too announced that the brothers were to pitch "nine innings" against the Monarchs, adding, "nothing could be sweeter." Lardner continued by expressing two additional thoughts. "The crowd was shouting, 'Give us this day our money back,' and Dizzy's performance in 1934 hadn't touched any 'Iron Man' endurance records." Lardner cited the records of Joe McGinnity of the Giants, who pitched "434 innings, including a total of 44 complete games, and won three doubleheaders in a month during the 1903 season." Next, he mentioned Ed Walsh, who won both of his starts in the 1906 World Series after working almost every other day during the season and hung up an all-time mark for innings pitched with 464. Also referenced was Charles "Hoss" Radbourne, who, in 1884, with Providence, "won 60 and lost 12, of which 19 of his victories came in succession, and he pitched 22 consecutive complete games." In closing, Lardner wrote that Dizzy's "work was just as valuable to his team as Radbourne's, or McGinnity's, or even Walsh's, though he didn't match them statistically."

The tie ending in Milwaukee concluded the Monarchs' portion of the Dean tour. For all practical purposes, it wrapped up the career of Carroll Ray Mothell, one of the Monarchs' all-time greats.

Carroll Ray Mothell, nicknamed "Dink," had been an important factor in the Monarchs' success since 1924. Telling the Monarchs' story of the 1920s and 1930s without a mention of Mothell is a misapplication of this team's history. "This boy Mothell in my opinion," wrote R. H. Barber, "is just as great as [James Raleigh "Biz"] Mackey. He has also played every position on defense and played each one well. I can go back over my scrapbook and dig up some great ballplayers, but I'd rather send Mothell to bat when a run is needed that any player I know."[54] Playing eight defensive positions with all-star ability is how Mothell perfected his trade. On occasion, he hit the long ball, while compiling an impressive home run record. In a span of 10 years, from 1924 to 1934, he homered more than 125 times. He originally came to the league with Rube Foster's pennant-winning Chicago American Giants in 1920, and played an important role on Kansas City's Negro National League championship teams of 1924, 1925, and 1929, twice World Series champions.

His parents were Sammy and Scotty Mothell, who lived in Topeka, in Shawnee County. They had moved to Kansas from Tennessee. Dink was born on August 13, 1897. At age 16, he caught the attention of local manager John "Topeka Jack" Johnson of the all-black Topeka Giants. Johnson observed that Mothell, who batted from the right side, held his bat cross-handed. His manager never adjusted his hands. He simply turned his body around, put him on the other side of home plate, and made him a switch-hitter.[55] On the Topeka Giants, Mothell was joined by two brothers, Claude and Ernest.[56] Dink remained with the local Giants until the World War I draft. On August 24, 1918, he was one of 38 men given physical examinations at Board No. 1 for the draft in Topeka.

Mothell returned to baseball with J. L. Wilkinson's newly organized Kansas City Monarchs in April 1920. He came to camp as a catcher, but his stay in Kansas City ended prematurely because of a salary dispute. Wilkinson offered $120 a month; Mothell wanted pay equal to his former Santa Fe railroad job, $130 a month.[57] These demands went unmet, and Dink was forced to quit, whereupon he returned to Topeka. Foster offered the Topeka youth $125 to return, and off to Chicago he went with the more established team. He played the remainder of the 1920 season with the Giants, winners of the first Negro National League pennant. Mothell's stay in Chicago was also short-lived. Still unhappy with the pay he was getting, he stayed out of professional ball for two additional seasons.

He appeared regionally with several semiprofessional teams, mainly the Chanute Kansas Black Diamonds with his brother Ernest.[58] He also retained his relationship with Johnson's Topeka Giants before returning to the Monarchs.[59] Dink's arm troubles intensified during the 1934 season, and his batting began to suffer. After the Deans' tour, Mothell retired due to rotator cuff problems and returned home to Topeka. He never married but had a long-time girlfriend in Roma Street, who had three children he raised as his own.[60]

The Dean brothers' Milwaukee All-Stars rivalry with the Monarchs provided one more means to compare each player's talent in six total games. Unfortunately, box scores for the Wichita and Milwaukee games are missing, but there is enough detail from the four existing box scores and game notes to forcefully contend that these Negro major leaguers were being shortchanged by social and economic restrictions as they related to one's ethnicity. Where data exist, six Monarchs batted over .300. T. J. Young finished with a .471 average, going 8-for-17, with a pair of doubles and a triple. Wilber "Bullet" Rogan was also a .400 hitter, finishing 6-for-15 at bat. Frank Duncan finished with a 4-for-7 effort with a triple for a better than .500 average. Eddie Dwight went 6-for-16 for a .375 average; George Giles was a 6-for-17 and batted .353, with a pair of doubles and a triple, as well as several stolen bases. Newt Joseph also batted .300, going 3-for-10, with a couple of doubles.

Many of the Monarchs' hits and lots of the runs had come off Dizzy and Daffy, two of the best pitchers in the National League. The remainder of the hits where acquired off pitchers destined to win many more games in their minor- and major-league careers. Opportunities to achieve these records, titles, and achievements in the National League, American League, and minor leagues were denied to the players on the Monarchs roster—regardless of how well they performed against Dizzy or Daffy. Discrimination in American society, for no other reason than a thing called melanin, would continue to segregate the masses and influence U.S. sports culture for generations to come.

The *Wisconsin News* explained,

The whole barnstorming trip is based on the theory that fans off the beaten track are willing to pay just to see the Deans. And that's the way it was in Oklahoma City, Wichita, Kansas City, Des Moines, and Chicago. They pitched a couple of innings apiece and let it go at that and kicked. But they sure raised a row in Milwaukee![61]

On October 25, American League president William Harridge was quoted in an article as opposing barnstorming by major-league players except in special cases. He cited Milwaukee as an example of why it must be halted. "The unpleasantness at Milwaukee when the fans stormed the box office, demanding their money back, because the Dean brothers did not pitch as many innings as advertised," were his actual words. Underhandedly, he was blaming the Deans—Dizzy and Daffy—for the fiasco, while letting the promoter—Stumpf—take none of the blame.[62]

The *Milwaukee Journal* concluded, "When Dizzy is through exploiting his World Series fame he's going back to the hills in Arkansas and do a 'lot of sleepin' and eatin'.' He started his sleeping act at Borchert Field after pitching two innings."[63]

~

CHAPTER 8

Philadelphia, Pennsylvania

Double for Your Trouble
Tuesday, October 16, 1934

After the debacle in Milwaukee, the whirlwind tour seemed to operate without a compass. The stops had been logical up to this point of the tour. Oklahoma City to Wichita was roughly 160 miles apart, Wichita to Kansas City 190 miles, Kansas City to Des Moines about 190 miles, Des Moines to Chicago 340 miles, and Chicago to Milwaukee about 95 miles. Milwaukee to Philadelphia was a whopping 850 miles, which meant Dizzy and Daffy had to board a plane, although neither cared for air transportation. In traveling to Philadelphia, the Deans skipped over lucrative opportunities in South Bend, Fort Wayne, Toledo, Akron, Canton, Youngstown, and other cities where they might have drawn record numbers of fans in single games. The scattering of large groups of Negro citizens was responsible for Negro major-league teams having to make such long journeys between games, but the Deans could have drawn anywhere. At Philadelphia, Eddie Gottlieb, promoter of the Dean's local visit, scheduled a doubleheader—two games for the price of one, twice the work for the same money—in an effort to draw large numbers of fans. "We've been lucky on the weather," offered Dizzy. "It's nice here today."[1]

The Philadelphia festivities were scheduled in conjunction with Gottlieb, promoter and president of Philadelphia's City Baseball League. Players from the Gottlieb-run City League were to join Dizzy and Daffy at Shibe Park, home of the American League Athletics, to face Ed Bolden's Negro major league Philadelphia Stars. It would be the tour's first appearance at a major-league park, as well as the tour's only doubleheader. It is ironic that African American baseball players could not play for National and American League teams, but they could play in the same big-league parks without the slightest bit of apprehension if they paid to lease the park. Traveling and renting parks was often a segregated affair. It was not unusual to see advertisements in the North that would promote "reserved seats for colored" people.[2]

After a disastrous afternoon in Milwaukee, where they were jeered for not playing enough innings, Dizzy and Daffy could only hope for better results. To ensure there was no Milwaukee repeat, the brothers upped their participation in the outfield and increased their socializing with fans and media, showing more cooperation and lively discourse in their newspaper interviews. The tour was making history on the field, but one historical fact slipped past the legion of famous Philadelphia writers without the slightest mention. It was history—not about Dizzy or Daffy—but about an African American arbiter named Craig.

John Craig, an African American, was one of three umpires who worked both of the Philadelphia games. No one seemed to notice this important bit of history. He called the game without controversy or debate and thereby went unrecognized, as did many of the African American players on the Philadelphia Stars. These are just a few of the details missed by a reporting crew that included such well-regarded writers as Cy Peterman, Lynn Doyle, Stan Baumgartner, Paul Parris, Bill Dooly, and James Isaminger. Although he was a recipient of the J. G. Taylor Spink Award presented by the Hall of Fame in Cooperstown, New York, Isaminger deserved few nods for how he covered Dizzy, Daffy, and their African American opponents in the fall of 1934. He was fast asleep at his typewriter when discussing instruments of racial supremacy, entitlement, and negative stereotypes faced by African Americans in baseball. Notification that Dizzy had won the National League Most Valuable Player Award wasn't something Isaminger missed.

While in Philadelphia, it was announced nationwide that Dizzy had won top honors for the MVP Award. Six members of the eight-man Baseball Writers' Association of America committee gave the Cardinals pitching ace first-place votes, while two named him second. Second place belonged to Paul Waner, who finished a distant 28 points behind Dizzy. Dean's selection as MVP was based on several factors. He was the first National League pitcher since 1917 to win 30 games in a season; he led the National League in strikeouts, with 198—his third consecutive year in leading the league; and added two more wins in the World Series to lead his Cardinals to a world championship.[3] Upon receiving the news, Dizzy flippantly proclaimed, "I am the greatest pitcher in the world."[4]

Baseball's 1934 MVP and his brother Daffy arrived at the Camden airport, on the other side of the Delaware River, at 8:15 a.m. on an air sleeper from

Chicago. Dizzy complained as he stepped from the plane. "You don't get much sleep doing this jumping around the country," he murmured. "I tried to sleep on the plane last night coming here, but my ears got all stopped up, I rolled around, and I didn't get any rest."[5] He wouldn't get much rest during the day either.

At the airport he was under fire to answer some questions. According to Isaminger, Dizzy said "he was the greatest pitcher in the world and named his brother Paul as the second best."[6] Dizzy had packed their time between their arrival and the ballgame with lots of scheduled activities. On the move from the moment the airplane touched down, theirs was an itinerary that included little time for rest. Just before noon, the brothers stumbled from their hotel rooms to a waiting public and lots of stops.

Following a breakfast of ham and eggs they made a quick visit to a physician to have Paul's ailing wing evaluated. Charles J. Van Ronk, a noted specialist of the expert class, advised the obvious—rest. He suggested Paul not pitch, at least for a few days.[7] With little time for personal reflection they were off to another stop. As they headed toward Shibe Park, they visited the prestigious Franklin Institute of Science for what may have been the most uncomfortable personal appearance of the entire tour. The museum visit was a joke on the Deans—not the institute. Dizzy and Daffy were as out of place as a fish on dry land.

Their Franklin Institute visit was hosted by Dr. James Barnes, associate director of the facility. It was a fairly awkward experience for the brothers, who were dressed not as tourists, but as Cardinals baseball players, outfitted in full uniform—hat, jersey, pants, and socks—which made them the focus of everyone's attention. They were like art in the museum—a display everyone wanted to see. It was obvious, however, that Dizzy didn't care to be there. He made his feelings publicly known, and a reporter took notice. "We've only got five minutes to see this place," he told Barnes without apprehension. The visit was cut short. While receiving their celebrity certificates, recognition usually reserved for distinguished visitors of the intellectual types, Dr. Barnes made a technical comment to Dizzy about baseball. "It is very interesting that in a baseball bat there is a center of oscillation," noted the director. Dizzy looked clueless. Mystified, he fired back, "A center of what?" He stared his brother down, then whispered, "We gotta go. I think we are going to be late for the ballgame," which started at 1:30 p.m. On the way out he told reporters, "I'm going to try to duck that vaudeville tour. That would run me nuts. I'll stick to baseball. It's my game. Leave the stage to actors—that's their game."[8] With that final statement, the two men made a hasty dash for the exit, bypassed everyone, and hurried to the park without signing a single autograph.

Reporters who missed out on interviews at the hotel and museum came down to the bench to get firsthand comments while the game was being played. Dizzy and Daffy were besieged at every opportunity and could hardly focus on baseball. Dizzy's interview with Peterman of the *Evening Bulletin* was an impromptu discourse that was as candid as it was insightful. He talked about taxes, the Dean's barnstorming schedule, and their profitability while on tour. There were conflicting earnings totals appearing in many newspapers, which impelled Dizzy to ask Peterman, "Do we have to pay the government on the basis of what they're publishing in the papers? Or do we pay on what we actually take in on this tour?" Dizzy was encouraged when Peterman advised, "Just make an honest return on your rakeoff and Uncle Sam will be happy. The government hasn't started taxing according to press agents' reports. Not yet, anyhow." This "settled Dizzy's nerves," stated the article. "Well that's a load off my mind," he replied. "We're not quite millionaires, in spite of those stories."[9]

Peterman noted, "They will make, says their managing director, Ray L. Doan of Muscatine, [Iowa], about $8,000 each from barnstorming baseball, or something less than $1,000 a game." The writer took exception with Doan's totals. "The Deans should make $10,000 each at the lowest," was his response in the newspapers.[10] Even with the hefty amount they were pocketing, Paul wasn't happy. He wanted to go home.

Daffy, disillusioned because of his so-called lame limb and other undisclosed reasons, desperately wanted to end the tour long before they arrived in Philadelphia. When asked if he would pitch during the Philadelphia stop, he responded, "I wouldn't be able to pitch even if I was foolish enough to try. I wouldn't try to pitch now for $10,000."[11]

When Jimmy Wilson, manager of the Philadelphia Nationals, visited the brothers in the dugout and told Paul he was on his way to Winter Haven, Florida, the next day, Paul announced he would go with him. He was vacillating on whether to go home or finish the tour. "Dizzy put this idea out like a false alarm,"[12] the article related. Parris, writing in the *Record*, advised, "This 'getting it while the getting's good' has paled."[13] Not much was printed prior to the game regarding the Deans' opponents, the Negro League Philadelphia Stars.

By 1934, Edward Bolden was the dean of Eastern club owners. He had been in baseball longer than any of his rivals and was making a profit with his Hilldale team before the start of World War I. His practical experience in baseball was equal to Wilkinson and Baird of the Monarchs, most of the promoters in the East, and many owners of major-league teams. Bolden's Philadelphia Stars were an Eastern powerhouse fully capable of taking on the

Deans and anyone they might recruit. The Stars were heavily promoted by Gottlieb, who controlled and booked games for them at the 44th and Parkside ballpark, along with other prominent parks he controlled. His influence on the profitability of African American teams was sufficient to bury or raise a team from the dead. He had a controlling interest in the Philadelphia Stars.

Led by Webster McDonald, manager, Philadelphia had a future star in Stuart "Country" Jones, a lanky, lean, dark-complexioned right-hander who rivaled the better publicized Satchel Paige with his strikeouts. McDonald, when speaking of his young pitcher, remarked, "Jones from Baltimore, one of the sharpest little left-handers you ever saw—tall, lanky, like Satchel. I made a great pitcher out of him."[14] They also had Raleigh "Bizz" Mackey, Judson "Jud" Wilson, Rocky Ellis, Paul "Jake" Dunn, Jimmy Miles, Dewey Creacy, and Chaney White. Creacy, who once played for the Kansas City Monarchs, was nicknamed "Boot Nose" by George Giles, who had a fondness for labeling players with names other than their own.[15]

While Philadelphia's 44th and Parkside Ballpark was their home turf, on occasion they would play in the local National or American League stadiums. One such game had been played there against Ray Doan's House of David team.

When Doan brought his House of David team and 11 burros to Philadelphia's National League Park on August 11, 1934, a crowd of 5,000 fans were treated to an inning of donkey baseball and an inning of pitching by former female Olympic champion Babe Didrikson. Bolden's Philadelphia Stars ran away with that game in an 8–4 final—donkey and all. The same thing occurred in St. Louis, where the House of David played at Sportsman's Park, a game where the donkeys were witnessed from afar. In Dizzy's den, it was less about the donkeys and more about the girl tossing the baseball.

In a game won by the House of David, 11–2, on September 23, 1934, the *Alton (Illinois) Evening Telegraph* acknowledged, "The Babe's ability is no myth as she deported herself as a real baseball player slinging a mean spitball." For bizarre and twisted reasons related to racism, Babe was allowed to pitch there at a time when African American fans were restricted to the bleachers, an era when the best of the black teams, homegrown or otherwise, wouldn't spike the dirt at Sportsman's Park for another seven years. In that monumental year, on July 4, 1941, the Monarchs met the Birmingham Black Barons in the field's first Negro League contest. The playing of African American and white teams in the North was nothing unusual—but many considered St. Louis Southern territory. It was a sad commentary on St. Louis as the Monarchs and other teams from the city drew great crowds. In most states, booking agents were on the alert for such opportunities. Gottlieb, the promoter of the Stars versus House of David game at Philadelphia, was also in charge of putting together an All-Star team for the Deans. Gottlieb was always quick to promote an interracial event in Philadelphia.

Even before he became coach, manager, and owner of the original Philadelphia Warriors in the National Basketball Association, Gottlieb was knee-deep in the economics of Negro League baseball. Today, he is widely celebrated as the man who drafted Wilt Chamberlain into professional basketball and as a rules official for the NBA. Little has been written about his connection to baseball, which is where his sporting legacy began. During the 1930s, he was deeply enmeshed in the politics of segregated baseball, an era when baseball was designed for the Europeans and Jews to rule and control the Negro. "Booking agent[s] booked you to play where you couldn't book yourself," said Webster McDonald. "You had to pay him 10 percent."[16] Black teams had few parks of their own, and their movements were manipulated by a network of promoters in the major cities where they might compete for crowds that rivaled major-league teams.

Gottlieb's agency controlled the Philadelphia area, and it was he who determined where teams played and how much these teams earned in and around the city. Born in 1898, he immigrated to the United States from Kiev, Ukraine, with family, settling in New York City. Eddie's birth name was Isadore Gottlieb. He was a Jew. In a January 22, 1968, article for *Sports Illustrated*, he said plenty about his early life. Eddie's principal residence was at 107th Street at Madison Avenue, in what was later called Spanish Harlem. He "hitched rides on ice trucks over to Coogan's Bluff to see the New York Giants play." Baseball was reportedly his "first sport," before he ascended to greater heights through his long association with Philadelphia basketball.[17]

Eddie never so much as held a basketball until his mother moved the family to South Philadelphia after his father, Morris, who ran a small candy store in New York, died. He became active in South Philadelphia sports through his association with the School of Pedagogy and eventually SPHA (South Philadelphia Hebrew Association) baseball and basketball teams. SPHA was proudly stitched across the front of his team's uniforms in Hebrew letters. Gottlieb recalled the time they picked up "Rube" Chambers, an Irish junkball hurler, in an effort to win a baseball contest. Chambers "slid into second base and was dusting himself off when an Irish buddy of his—playing shortstop that day for the opposition—asked him, 'Rube, what do all those Jewish letters mean?'" "I better not tell you," Chambers said, growing more serious. His pal persisted with the questioning. "Okay," Chambers said, just before he ducked, and the fight was on.[18] Chambers was recruited for the

Deans' All-Stars based on his prior success at beating minority teams. One such game occurred in August 1932, when he defeated the New York Black Yankees while pitching for the Frankford Legion team in Philadelphia. He struck out 10 batters in that game.

As a baseball promoter, Gottlieb began by booking games for a friend, Mike Iannarella of the 2nd Ward Republican club in 1929. Later on, he began scheduling the Philadelphia Stars games at Passon Field, a park named after Harry Passon, a former associate and operator of a local sporting goods store. Passon was a childhood friend and early business associate of Eddie Gottlieb.[19] It has been written that the duo separated when Passon decided to revive the all-black Bacharach Giants but Gottlieb chose to back their rivals, the Hilldale team, headed by Edward Bolden, who later formed the Philadelphia Stars.

If a team was booked by Gottlieb, they could never forfeit or arrive late to games. By his own admission, Eddie proclaimed, "They feared me like they feared the wrath of God."[20] Gottlieb used his whiteness to move around in boardrooms, hotels, banks, and ballparks where Gus Greenlee, Cumberland Posey, and Ed Bolden never could. Webster McDonald, manager of the 1934 Philadelphia Stars, had lots to say about Gottlieb's gambling.

It was always an accepted fact that Eddie carried home much more if they won. In an interview with author John Holway, McDonald offered, "Gottlieb liked to gamble. When we're playing in Yankee Stadium or the Polo Grounds, he'd say, 'I want Slim Jones, I want both of you to pitch.'" McDonald recalled a time when they were playing the Bushwicks in Brooklyn. "Gottlieb said, 'Look, here's $250, split it up with the boys. If you win that second game, here's $500 bucks.'"[21] Men like Gottlieb "worked among blacks," wrote Rebecca Alpert in her book *Out of Left Field: Jews and Black Baseball*, "but they did not suffer the indignities of Jim Crow, nor did they refrain from their own racial prejudice and stereotypes.[22] Gottlieb found these freedoms to have great advantage. These unrestricted liberties of whiteness led to his 1972 induction into the Naismith Memorial Basketball Hall of Fame, the same year Robert L. Douglas, founder of the New York Renaissance team became the first African American enshrined in the Naismith Hall of Fame. Still, Eddie's legacy is longer lasting. The National Basketball Association Rookie of the Year Award is also named in his honor.

The Deans joined an All-Star team made up of "outstanding" players from Gottlieb's Philadelphia City League. Some, but not all, were former major leaguers. Like the other teams that backed the brothers, there were a mixture of big-league, minor-league, and one or two semiprofessional stars in the lineup.

Playing shortstop was a Polish infielder named Bill Edward Narleski. He was a World War I veteran who had broken into the majors with the last-place Boston Red Sox in 1929. Roy Tarr, the All-Stars' third baseman, had been in the minors since 1928. He had last appeared in 76 games for Buffalo of the International League in 1933, batting .269. He remained active in semiprofessional circles and, as late as 1944, was playing baseball for the Fort Monmouth Military All-Stars in New Jersey. Philadelphia-born Eddie James Silber, a future St. Louis Brown beginning in 1937, was one of the All-Stars' outfielders. Edward Benard Roetz, another Philadelphian, the Dean's second baseman, had appeared in 16 games for the St. Louis Browns in 1929. Ed was coming off a season where he had batted .353 for Johnstown of the Mid Atlantic League. Tony Parisse, who would reach the majors for 10 games in 1943–1944, was there to catch Dizzy. A lefty, Johnny Holstein, covered first base, and Yitz Crompton of the local Raphael club signed on to play center field. Crompton was a close associate of Connie Mack, owner of the American League Athletics, who eventually hired Yitz to work in their clubhouse.

Held in reserve were several pitchers who routinely appeared with the semiprofessionals. Joel Skelton, who was rumored to have gone to spring training with the Philadelphia Athletics while playing under the pseudonym Jim Duffy, was there as the Dean brothers' relief. A September 11 edition of the *Brooklyn Daily Eagle* confirmed, "Jim's [last] name is Skelton, but he would rather be called Duffy."[23] Rube Chambers, a veteran who had a "penchant for beating powerful colored teams," according to the *Inquirer*, was there to pitch in the second game. Joseph Schwartz, who pitched under the alias "Joe Schmidt" and who was reportedly on the Philadelphia Athletics roster from 1931 to 1933, pitched part of game two.

The Dean name may have drawn a number of fans, but two African American pitchers dominated the day. Webster McDonald shut out the Deans' All-Stars, 8–0, in the opener, and later, in the twilight game, Country Jones showed little pity as he captured a night-shortened seven-inning affair by a 4–3 score. It was evident from the beginning that the Dean brothers' All-Stars were no match for Edward Bolden's formidable Stars.

In the opener, neither of the Deans took the mound. Paul went out to right field and stayed there for six innings. He made a one putout. As a batter, he failed to get a hit in three trips to the plate. Dizzy joined in for a brief time in left field. At bat, Dizzy failed to get a hit in either of his two times up. In the Deans' absence from the mound, McDonald, Philadelphia's veteran submarine pitcher, became the leading man—both as pitcher and hitter.

Born in Wilmington, Delaware, on January 1, 1900, Webster McDonald, like many great African American pitchers of his generation, learned his trade while working under the baseball genius of Rube Foster, manager of the Chicago American Giants in 1926. Foster's pitchers were expected to hit as well as they pitched. Foster, who died in 1930, would have been honored to see his student's performance against the Deans' All-Stars. McDonald's deceptive underarm delivery was working to perfection.

William "Dizzy" Dismukes, formerly of the Indianapolis ABCs and other teams, taught Webster a few things about pitching in 1923. Whenever Dismukes hit town they would get together for lunch or dinner, Webster recalled. In an interview with author John Holway, McDonald advised that Dismukes was an "underhand pitcher," adding, "he's the man I learned it from."[24] Evidently he learned well. According to teammate Jake Stephens, who was also interviewed by Holway, "When he [McDonald] had one of his good days, there wasn't anybody going to lick him. When he'd throw that fastball, that thing jumped, and that curveball would come in like a whip."[25]

The accolades for McDonald's pitching were spread from East to West. In 1928, the tiny berg of Little Falls, Minnesota, reached out to him. The city fathers lured him there with a $750 a month salary and all expenses paid, making him the highest-paid ballplayer in the city's history. Time after time, they were rewarded for their cultural inclusion. When asked how he liked playing for a white team, McDonald told Holway, "I'd say, 'I'm a person, a human being, an American. I've gone to school with whites, I can command respect.'"[26] One win for which he was highly publicized occurred on August 29, 1930.

On that day, McDonald defeated an intact American Association team, the Minneapolis Millers, edging them in a 4–3 final with only an African American battery on an otherwise all-white semiprofessional squad. In that game, he allowed nine hits—one a home run by Nick Cullop—struck out nine, and walked two. The game was carried on radio station WCCO in Minnesota and witnessed by Jack Quinlan, sports editor and Halsey Hall sportswriter for the *Minneapolis Journal*. McDonald remained in Little Falls for four summers, from 1928 to 1931, recording 70 wins and nine losses, while tossing 15 shutouts.

McDonald was fairly new at managing a team in spite of getting his first shot at leading a club in 1932, while pitching for the Washington Pilots. After the sudden death of Frank Warfield, he succeeded him as manager. When that team broke up, McDonald ended up in Philadelphia. As manager of the 1934 Philadelphia Stars, he led with a Foster-like authority. He was always an expert hitter, too.

McDonald started game one as planned and showed more class than Dizzy had in the World Series. He was assiduous in working his way through the All-Stars lineup, throwing with near-pinpoint precision. On the mound, he performed the superhuman feat of holding his opponent to as few hits from the mound as he would get as a batter. The easy-throwing right-hander, who tossed them from down under, allowed three hits from the mound, then went on to collect three hits himself as a batter—a rare feat indeed, especially when you consider the forum in which it occurred. McDonald gave a first-inning single to Bill Narleski, a double to Roy Tarr in the sixth, and a single to Eddie Silber in the seventh—and that was it. He would go on to strike out four others, one of whom was Dizzy, while allowing one walk. Dizzy thought of himself as a hitter and always appreciated a pitcher who could swing the willow. "You know," said Diz, "people don't appreciate that a lot of pitchers are mighty fine hitters." Paul Parris's article in the *Philadelphia Record* told of the Cardinals pitcher's at-bat.

Dizzy, who went to left field in the fourth inning and had no hits on the day, drove McDonald's "first pitch to within a few feet of the left-field bleachers," noted Parris.[27] Cy Peterman, in his *Evening Bulletin* article, said Dean proclaimed, "[I] didn't hit that [too] good." After McDonald struck the Diz out in another at-bat, a reporter said Dizzy returned to the bench with a "sheepish grin."[28]

On the other side of the ledger, the Philadelphia Stars were pounding Jim Duffy, starting pitcher, from the mound. They knocked Jim from pillar to post. After one and two-thirds innings, during a spell where the Stars got six hits and scored six times, a new pitcher was summoned. The All-Stars' replacement, Wild Bill Durham, was a substantial improvement, as the Philadelphia Stars were limited to six additional hits in the remaining seven and one-third innings, during which single tallies were scored in the sixth and ninth frames.

Bizz Mackey's three hits, two of which were doubles, and McDonald's three hits, two of them doubles, gave the Negro major leaguers the edge they were seeking. They had run-scoring sequences in innings one, two, six, and nine. Dizzy's All-Stars never dented the scoring column. Duffy went on record as the losing pitcher in a game that took all of one hour and 58 minutes to complete. Game one was over.

Now it was Dizzy's turn at an attempted turnabout in the results. It would go down as a classic matchup—a MVP going against that year's potential best pitcher in the Negro major leagues.

Dizzy Dean opposed Stuart Jones in the nightcap. The Stars pitcher was known as "Country" Jones to those reading his hometown newspaper, the *Baltimore Afro-American*, but some newspapers nicknamed him "Slim." Tex Burnett, a peppery and energetic backstop, helped Jones hone his skills with the Baltimore Black Sox in 1932. The pitcher learned well and carried away the trophy for the best hurler in Puerto Rico during the 1933 Winter League campaign. League baseball was up in the air in Baltimore, and that allowed Jones to cast his lot with the Philadelphia Stars for the 1934 season. Those who had paid to see Dizzy were gripped by the moment. Those who came to see if Jones, the southpaw from Baltimore, could defeat the talkative Dizzy of Arkansas were waiting and wondering as they took their seats. Most remained glued to those seats until the game ended. This was the main event.

Because of the debasing loss in the opener, the All-Stars made several changes to their lineup. Paul Dean and Holstein were benched, and a new catcher, last name Sharkey, was added. Tarr, who batted leadoff in game one, was moved into the five slot, and Roetz was moved up to bat second. After much pomp and ceremony, the game began.

"All Dizzy showed during his two-inning turn were the motions that baffled the National League's strongest hitters," noted the *Philadelphia Record*.[29] Perhaps they were talking about the three men Dizzy struck out during his sojourn on the hill. This bit of rhetoric, however, failed to explain what people had seen from their pricey seats. Dizzy's pitching was no puzzle. There was much more to this story.

During Dizzy's two innings of pitching, Bolden's Stars hit safely three times. The *Philadelphia Evening Bulletin* had little compassion for the major-league MVP. "The colored sluggers were kind of sorry to see Dizzy go too," the newspaper advised. "They didn't score on him, but in those two innings they black jacked him for four hard and handsome drives."[30] Schmidt followed Dean to the mound and surrendered five hits in one-third of an inning and was quickly replaced with Rube Chambers, who allowed one hit in the remaining four and two-thirds innings. Chambers ended the day with seven strikeouts. Those 10 strikeouts—three by Dizzy—served as the highlight of this day for the All-Stars. There was reason for the hitters to celebrate, too.

Like Dizzy, Jones, although victorious, failed to live up to his enormous pregame billing. He allowed seven hits, struck out eight batters, and walked a trio of men before the contest was called at the end of seven frames due to darkness. Roetz was one of two players to collect more than one hit off Jones, who issued RBI to Rube Chambers, Price, and Ed Roetz. Durning's double was the All-Stars' only extra-base hit. Lame reporting by all of the Philadelphia dailies was prevalent. None of the newspapers listed the names of the men Jones, Diz, or Chambers struck out. To everyone's surprise, the real hitting stars weren't on Dizzy's side of the ledger. Jud Wilson, a player who would never dress out in a National or American League uniform, wouldn't be denied. He was the undisputed star of the afternoon.

Ernest Judson Wilson, born February 28, 1894, smashed baseballs all over Shibe Park. Unbeknownst to most, he was one of the most feared athletes to ever spike a baseball diamond. Some would say he was a capricious fellow, others might say he was an angry man—and his reasons for such a title were many. "He didn't hit as many home runs, but he hit so many doubles and singles," recalled Ted "Double Duty" Radcliffe.[31] As Satchel Paige would say some years later, "Nobody fooled around with Jud Wilson."[32]

As a player of superior ability, he hated to lose. It was his personal response to growing up in segregated America. He obviously deplored every minute of it. He had been on the losing side since childhood. His boyhood was tied to the city of Washington, in the District of Columbia, where his family moved in search of a better reality. They migrated from Remington, Virginia, to Washington's predominately black Foggy Bottoms neighborhood, where Wilson found it was no promised land. The area was littered with poverty. After a stint in World War I, Wilson returned Stateside, only to find that the freedoms he had so gallantly fought for abroad were denied him in his nation of birth. He was back in the racist United States, where the lack of fair play and inequality gave many a license to discriminate. It didn't matter that he was a war veteran who served his country with honors. Racial restrictions in sports limited his ability to earn a living at what he did best.

Wilson was an extraordinary baseball player. Yet, prejudice on the part of National League, American League, and minor-league owners was a forced migration that kept him out of the money in spite of his superb ability. He knew full well how segregation limited his mobility and prosperity in a sport he loved dearly.

Among Negro major-league players, Wilson is remembered as a tremendous hitting, hard-playing, and temperamental athlete. Few took the time to examine his troubling thoughts. His temperament seems to be all that contemporary writers of Negro League history care for us to know. Like many athletes of that generation, there is much more to Wilson's story. He was often misunderstood. More evident was Wilson's ability to play baseball. Jud was one of best hitters on anyone's ball field, and he surely would have written a few records in the annals of the National and American Leagues if only he had been given half a chance. Satchel Paige, a victim of Wilson's hard drives, nicknamed his friend "Boojum," and for good reason—he could hit them hard and far. He was an amazing hitter. Outfielder Ted Page was quick to tell a Wilson story. One story showed the disparity of being in the

Negro Leagues versus playing in the National or American Leagues. It took place in a rooming house in Zanesville, Ohio. "The landlady filled the tub with hot water, and the whole team, about 14 men, stood in line to use that one tubful—everyone, that is, except Wilson. 'He was first,' smiled Page, 'and I was second, because I was his roommate.'"[33]

In 1931, after joining Cumberland Posey's Homestead Grays, Wilson ripped baseballs for more than 240 hits in just 131 games—which is some kind of a fabulous record. He blemished the opposition for 50 doubles and 15 triples, although missing almost a month of play due to injuries. In May alone, he collected more than 60 hits in 25 games.[34] Wilson was equally as famous for his temper when runs meant wins. In an interview with the author, pitcher Frank Duncan Jr., son of legendary catcher Frank Duncan Sr. of the Kansas City Monarchs, recalled a story about Wilson that has never been told.

During a 1945 hitch in the U.S. Army during World War II, Duncan served in Aberdeen, Maryland, and pitched weekends for the Baltimore Elites. Frank recalled, "I was paid $52 a month in the military but was getting $200 a month playing baseball with the Elites on weekends." In a game at Baltimore versus the Grays, "Crush" Holloway was the umpire on the bases, and Phil Cockrell was the umpire behind the plate. Roy Campanella was the catcher, and Duncan was pitching. The baserunner was "Jud Wilson, who was standing on third base." Duncan recounted, "I threw a ball past Campanella, and it went back to the screen." Campanella hustled for the ball and returned it to Duncan, who was covering home plate. "Wilson slid into a cloud of dust, but I missed the tag on him by a few inches," said Duncan. Cockrell called it the best he could and waived Wilson out. A long argument followed.

"The Grays went on to lose the game." As was the custom in the Negro Leagues, the umpires always dressed in the locker room of the home team. "Cockrell was undressed and on his way to the shower when Wilson walked into our locker room and said, 'Cockrell, you cost us a ballgame today.'" The umpire gathered himself and said, "I called it the best I could." Duncan never forgot what he saw next. "Wilson grabbed Cockrell by the meat on his chest and lifted him off the ground. Blood burst from Cockrell's chest. Holloway picked up a bat and told Wilson, 'If you don't put him down I'll kill you.' Crush had those light green eyes, and he looked serious. Wilson put Cockrell down and just walked out."[35]

Against the Deans' All-Stars, there were no arguments, no umpires to grab, and no players to yell mercy, and there was a Philadelphia Stars' win. Wilson took top honors on the day by doggedly standing up to Dean and the other All-Stars pitchers. He collected four hits, one a home run; drove in six of the Stars' 12 runs; scored three runs; and stole a base. In an effort to suppress these feats, the Philadelphia newspapers left out who did what against Dizzy. We may never know if any of Jud Wilson's multiple hits, or William "Mickey" Casey's three hits, or Dewey Creacy's multiple hits could be credited to Dizzy, a winner of 30 National League games. There is, however, no guessing the final scores.

Ed Bolden's Philadelphia Stars captured both games, 8–0 and 4–3, respectively. The crowd was estimated at 8,000 to 9,000, depending on the newspaper source. One of the best articles to come out of Philadelphia was written by Parris in the *Philadelphia Record*. The worst article, without question, was penned by Isaminger.

There were stories in every Philadelphia newspaper, and several of these accounts took delight in racism and sarcasm. Stories of this nature appeared often, especially in instances where African Americans had won an important game or series over a white team. Customarily, it involved finding some Negro fans in the stands and exploiting their conversations with the worst dialect possible. This nonsense was widespread among daily newspaper reporters, whose readership not only observed the games, but also absorbed the bias and old myths of past generations. Such was the case in Philadelphia, where Lynn Doyle of the *Philadelphia Evening Bulletin* did just that. His stereotypic comments appeared in his "Close-ups on the Sports Scene" postgame column.

Doyle's article painted a picture of outright bigotry as he feverishly worked to create the "uncultured Negro" America wanted to portray:

> The grandstand was the place to sit at the Dean exhibition yesterday, downstairs with the folks, where the laughs were. The press box, a hot enough spot in the season, was a bleak and shadowy loft, fit only for things that snooze by day and fly or crawl by night. The cullah'd players were equal to their big moment, playing opposite the Deans, with 8,000 seats full and paid for. Every catch on the dusky side was made with gestures, every thrown ball was sent on its way with elaborate grace. The flavor of the cakewalk oozed for every play. A cullah'd boy and his gal arrived late. The white boys were afield. Dizzy in left, Paul in right, just serving time. "Which is they?" asked the gal. "One theah and one theah," said her man, pointing out the Deans with a sweeping sidearm delivery. He didn't know which was which, and he wasn't letting her find that out. Paul chased a single, let it pull him out of bounds, made a sleepy sore arm throw, and went back to his nap. "He ain't nuthin much," said the gal. "Why not, woman—he's the greatest pitchah they is n he's gittin a thousand bucks fo this (still thinks it's Dizzy)." "Don't c'yah," said the gal. "He ain't pitchin now, and beside he ain't fancy enough."[36]

The article was yet another case of the systemic bias African American fans and players routinely faced in the white media.

Isaminger's article was patronizing toward the Philadelphia Stars. He held his debasing compliments of the Deans in reserve, saving the worst for last. Isaminger obviously cared little for Dizzy and Daffy or their All-Stars squad. Other than the pitchers, he failed to mention any of the white All-Stars by first name, while praising the "marvelous veteran right-hander Webster McDonald" and tall youthful left-hander Slim Jones, who he advised had a "whiplash" on every pitch. His approach was a bombshell in that few saw it coming. And while it was an obvious attempt to humble the Deans in print, the comments went without debate. In the same article, he made reference to the team's cultural backgrounds. "They [the Deans] were attached to a team of Philadelphia Stars, all white players, and Eddie Bolden's Negro players, styled the Philadelphia Stars, defeated their Caucasian opponents in both games," wrote Isaminger. The things he penned about the Deans weren't at all complementary. Some were downright devilish.

Showing little compassion for the Deans, Isaminger wrote, "Dizzy and Daffy Dean did their chores at Shibe Park yesterday afternoon in a double-header, but it was nothing of which the Dean dynasty will be proud."[37] He went on to write more about Dizzy and Daffy than he had the actual game.

Parris's article in the *Record* was almost enchanting compared to the others. His story was the most detailed, and it touched on the inner workings of the game. It was he who told of Paul's three chances in the outfield and how the crowd's cheers turned to "jeers" when Dizzy stopped pitching. In his article he spoke of the Philadelphia Stars' hitting against Dizzy, and how the Cardinals pitcher "spun 'em down the alley," and how a trio of the Stars "spun 'em right back at him."[38] He told his readers how there was one Dean in "every inning of the first game." Parris seemed to have known Mackey, Bolden, and McDonald, who he gave first name or nickname recognition to in his stories. McDonald called Mackey the "best [catcher] in baseball bar none," and Parris must have known that, while writing little about what he had witnessed.[39] His article was also illustrated with pictures.

Jud Wilson was photographed stealing third base in the ninth inning of game one—a stolen base that wasn't recorded in the *Record*'s box score. As a matter of record, the *Ledger* did credit stolen bases to Paul "Jake" Stevens, Jud Wilson, and Jake Dunn, who stole two, for a total of four stolen bases in game one. Stevens added another stolen base in game two. Another photograph, this one of Stevens sliding into third base, appeared in the *Baltimore Afro-American*.

Stan Baumgartner, a former player who had taken a desk job at the *Inquirer*, focused on the Dean brothers' entertainment value:

The Deans, baseball's clever clowns, are here today to give you a little pitching—and a lot of laughs. Making people laugh in these days pays. It will pay
the Dean brothers $40,000 next season when Sam Breadon gets down to the
business of securing the Deans' autographs to a contract. Of course, Dizzy and
Daffy can pitch a little beside making the fans laugh—even Mickey Cochrane
will admit that.[40]

Baumgartner gave a quick history of the clowns' role in white professional
baseball and mentioned Nick Altrock, Al Schacht, as well as Rabbit Maran-
ville. Schacht, a Jew, was the so-called "clown prince of baseball." Baumgartner also could have mentioned John Tucker of the House of Davids, known
nationally as the "bearded Nick Altrock of baseball." Baumgartner, I'm sure,
never heard of William "Bill" Monroe, an African American, who is really
considered the greatest comedic baseball genius of all time.

Before his untimely death in 1915, Alabama-born Bill Monroe, nicknamed "Money," talked, walked, and played his way into baseball immortal-
ity. Although he was an excellent hitter, a speedy runner, and an exceptional
defensive player, his humorous frolics on the field often overshadowed his
credentials as one of baseball's greatest all-around athletes. Had the National
League or American League removed the color line, Monroe might have
been considered one of the most celebrated infielders of his generation. In
1905, the Fitchburg, Massachusetts, *Daily News* advised, "Monroe, the veteran shortstop of the [Philadelphia] Giants, has a tongue which is hung in
the middle and much ball-playing has not subdued the gayety of his spirits."
He irritated hitters by yelling, "I never miss, hit it to me, and you are out."
What's more, his zany comments were not limited to players. In the course
of a nine-inning game Money yelled benign jokes at the grandstand, offered
didactic words of encouragement to umpires, and lampooned rival managers
to the point of exasperation.[41] Monroe knew, just as Dizzy and Daffy had
quickly learned, clowns who have the right stuff always draw better than average pay no matter what line of work they undertake, and they are beloved
long after they retire.

It is safe to assume that Dizzy and Daffy never read any of these comments; they had abandoned the premises to board a 7:45 p.m. train to Atlantic City, where they received an additional $1,000 for simply showing up
and smiling broadly at an indoor softball game on the Million Dollar Pier,
and clowning around with their verbal antics one more time. Writer Lynn
Doyle advised with almost complete certainty, "One more month in these
diggings and they'll be able to endow a municipal madhouse for Holdenville,
Oklahoma."[42]

CHAPTER 9

~

Brooklyn, New York

The Other Side of Dizzy
Wednesday, October 17, 1934

Up until the time of the Dean's New York City visit, Dizzy had taken it all in fun. The pressing crowds, thousands of autographs seekers, interfering newspapermen, lost games, he laughed them all away. But something in his fun-loving spirit disappeared as they approached the New York borough of Brooklyn, where Max Rosner, manager of the Bushwicks, and legendary promoter Nathaniel "Nat" Colvin Strong were headquartered. In and around New York, there was no further mention of the Monarchs or Wilkinson or Baird—Doan had full charge of the barnstorming tour in the East. His responsibility was to count the house. Baseball fans in that region ardently awaited the brothers' arrival in spite of an ever-changing series of dates surrounding their appearance. Dizzy and Daffy's visit was to become an important day for New York baseball.

Every local newspaper was there to cover the game. The crowd that showed up, a much larger one than the day before in Philadelphia, was destined to become the largest paid admissions to see the Cardinals' pitching duo in the East. These situations, along with Dizzy's anger concerning an umpire's decisions, set the stage for what might have been the Dean brothers' worst experience in cultural awareness and race relations—ever. Dizzy and Daffy's plane had hardly touched down before Dizzy let it be known, "He and his brother would play one week of vaudeville here instead of one month."[1] In New York, the plot thickened as Dizzy reportedly earned $3,500 for an afternoon's work.[2]

Plans to lure the Deans to New York were initiated as early as September 23, when the *Brooklyn Daily Eagle* announced, "Attempt[s] to get Dizzy and

Daffy Dean as a postseason attraction at Dexter Park ha[ve] not been successful thus far. Or, if it has Nat Strong is keeping plenty mum about it. But
what an attraction the pair would be after the way they treated the Dodgers
the other day."[3] On September 24, following Satchel Paige's 1–0 win against
the Bushwicks, the same newspaper offered, "Paige will hurl against the Dean
boys on Monday, September 31, Labor Day."[4] On Wednesday, October 10,
it was announced that "Dizzy, Daffy, and Pepper Martin had consented to
appear locally for a game to be played under the arc-lights on Friday, October
12, Columbus Day."[5] Harold Parrott, in his *Daily Eagle* column, said the "brilliant trio," Dizzy, Daffy, and Pepper, was supposed to appear Friday afternoon,
Columbus Day, but the extended World Series necessitated a return to St.
Louis for the victory parade. The same article advised that both brothers
and Martin were to be paid $1,000, plus a percentage of the gate, for the ap-
pearance. These dates, as tantalizing as they were in print, were wrong. The
brothers wouldn't arrive at Brooklyn's Dexter Park until October 17.

Confirmation of the game was an occasion to mention their rivals, the
New York Black Yankees, who the *Daily Eagle* said "are the best of the colored outfits, which have some really high-grade ballplayers because of the
unwritten law which keeps them out of the big leagues."[6] That brief phrase,
as it appeared in the *Daily Eagle*, was the only such statement to touch on
the topic of why these men hadn't gotten a wink by white Organized Baseball. On October 15, an announcement in the *World-Telegram* helped make
the date official: "The Dean brothers and Pepper Martin will take to the
air in order to arrive in New York for their appearance with the Bushwicks
Wednesday night."[7] This too was misleading, as Martin, much to the public's
chagrin, had no intentions of making the trip. An issue of the *Daily Eagle*
announced that Martin was home recovering from elbow surgery.[8]

Dexter Park was dressed and well-tailored for the October 17 festivities. It
was to be another nocturnal 8:30 p.m. start played under some of the best and
brightest lights in baseball. The night before the Deans' arrival, Frankie Frisch,
the legendary Cardinals pilot, and Joe "Ducky" Medwick arrived in town
for the Crescent–Hamilton Jubilee dinner at the Pierreport Clubhouse. The
black-tie event drew celebrities from many sports, especially baseball. Steve
McKeever, president of the Brooklyn Dodgers; Dazzy Vance of the St. Louis
Cardinals; and John Heydler, president of the National League, were there to
represent the world of baseball. Frisch, a former Crescent Athletic Club product, was there with some discourse on his world champion Cardinals.

Ed Hughes's column in the *Daily Eagle* said that Frisch scored several
clean hits in the course of a "spicy address." The manager gave high praise to
Ducky Medwick and Dizzy Dean. In speaking of Medwick, Frisch acknowl-

edged, "There's a ballplayer who would have made a big hit when John Mc-Graw was at his scrappiest. I'm for him and everything he did in this series." Frankie added, "I like the way he tears into the bag when on the paths."[9] At that point everyone in the room let out a "thunderous" applause. Medwick, an able-minded player not known for his oratorical skills, stood, took a bow, and quickly sat down and "stayed down." Frisch gave equal praise when speaking of the Deans, primarily Dizzy.

When speaking of the Deans their manager declared, "They've given me many a headache and plenty of laughs, but they're a great pair of boys. That Dizzy is a wonder." He told of how Dizzy came to him with a suggestion before the World Series started and proclaimed, "You want to make this a quick series, don't you?" "Of course I do," mused a slightly puzzled Frisch. Dizzy smiled that boyish grin and uttered aloud, "Let me pitch all four of those games, hey?" Frisch said he had the "greatest faith in Dizzy's ability to beat the Tigers anytime he started." Medwick, already in town for the banquet, replaced Pepper Martin in the game against the Black Yankees. It took a bit of persuasion to get Medwick to agree to terms for the game. "Joe Medwick refused $200 a day for our games in the east," Dizzy told Cy Peterman. "Said he wouldn't play today for $500. Dumb, that guy, imagine turning down such dough for one game."[10] He was later persuaded, for one night only, putting Medwick back in the limelight at Dizzy and Daffy's request.

The brothers arrived in Brooklyn reportedly tired and weary, as the entourage set up headquarters at the Hotel Governor Clinton, opposite Pennsylvania Station. One of the first statements to reporters came from Dizzy's wife, Pat, who said that "travel by rail, auto, and sky routes is beginning to make her regret that they arranged the tour."[11] Someone hustled them out to get haircuts. While they were away, Henry McLemore of United Press International visited their room in hopes of getting an interview. "I banged on the door," he wrote, "and somebody inside yelled, 'Whatcha want?'" He proceeded to ask, "Are Dizzy and Daffy in there?" The voice behind the door responded, "You gotta appointment?" McLemore lied outright and admitted as much when he wrote, "I didn't, but I said I did," which coerced Ray L. Doan into opening the door.[12]

McLemore's article told of how the Deans, who weren't there at first, walked in after their barbershop visit. They were sporting fresh haircuts and smelling like a dozen roses, he opined. McLemore took notice of the brothers' exhaustion, saying they looked "like a couple of traveling salesmen after a three-day flier." He watched as both slumped into chairs to momentarily rest their eyelids and crooned the same old tune. "Boy, I'm a plum tired man," Dizzy muttered, eagerly. "Ain't no tireder'n me Diz," sighed Daffy. "I went to sleep three times in that barber's chair. I don't guess we ain't had a good night's sleep since Fourth [of] July, have we Diz." Dizzy fired back, "Maybe before that, but I gotta get some soon. I'm plum whupped." In yet another reference, Dizzy was quoted as saying, "When this is over, ah'm goin' down to Bradenton, Florida, and lock every durn door in mah house. They're goin' to have to shove mah fish into me through a stove pipe."[13] Doan, who was seated nearby, tried his damnedest to get McLemore to interview him, but the reporter wouldn't bite:

"I guess you musta heard of me," inquired Doan. "I'm in charge of all House of David teams east of the Mississippi. Got Babe Didrikson on one of my clubs. I'm the father of softball played on donkeys, and I thought up playing softball with the infielders and outfielders tied to goats. It's funnier'n hell." The reporter admitted, "When he told me this I had an awful time suppressing a desire to forget all about the Dean boys and interview Mr. Doan."

What Doan said next was important information. It was a rant about the Dean's fatigue and tour schedule. Doan announced,

> You pitched every day for a month before the World Series. Then you pitched four games in that, and since then you have been to Oklahoma City, Wichita, Kansas City, Des Moines, Chicago, Milwaukee, Philadelphia, and now you're here. But you won't be [for] long. Tomorrow it's Baltimore, and then Paterson, Newark, Cleveland, Columbus, and Pittsburgh. Then you got a week in vaudeville.

Dizzy interrupted Doan's verbal diarrhea by saying, "Oh lawdy, shut up! And you can tell 'em for me. I ain't gonna do no vaudeville. I jes' wants [to] get in a feather bed high as'n your head and sleep right on through to next year."[14]

The room quickly filled as other reporters poured in. Late to the party, Dan Daniel entered a room that was already full of photographers and newspapermen. In his column, "Daniel's Dope" for the *World-Telegram*, he explained how many in the room debated what to title their articles and captions. Dizzy was eating cashew nuts "out of his fist," and Daffy was "nibbling them, too." Pat Dean was chewing cashews as she complained that "she is eating too much and in danger of getting fat." Daniel observed, "Patsy dug into the box of cashews for a mite of sustenance and smiled a winsome smile." She admitted publicly, "We just can't figure this all out. The boys are mobbed wherever they go—and we got a long way to go yet." Daniel said she paused momentarily and "slew another cashew." One of the photographers yelled, "We will label it 'Dizzy, Daffy—and Nuts!'" "Label it anything you like, just so long as it keeps packing them into those ballparks," said an unyielding Dizzy, who didn't mind telling the world he was there for the money. He concluded, "Ah'm gitting to shudder every time ah see a camera."[15]

Dizzy was warming up the room with his Southern humor, and the New York writers—Daniel, Tom Reilly, James Dawson, and Parrott—clung to his every word. "I wish this was over. It was grand fun for a while," said the great Diz. After discussing the weeklong vaudeville tour, he started in on the movie contract. "We gotta go uptown to see some motion picture folks who want to put Paul and me into the flickers. Well, that's okeh with me," he sighed. "But they gotta pay—and pay plenty. We gotta cash in while this panic is on, eh Patsy?" Daffy, who was more inclined to be shy while worshiping his older brother, said, "I wish I was back home. I got a pain in my right shoulder like I had last spring, and I am afraid."[16]

Locally, the Deans, along with their Cardinals teammate, Joe Medwick, were added to a Bushwicks roster that already included a number of former major-league ballplayers. Art Smith, former Columbia University pitcher, who had a cup of coffee with the Chicago White Sox in 1932; Hank Grampp, once a member of the National League Cubs from 1927 to 1929; and catcher Charles Russell Hargreaves of the Brooklyn Nationals were Bushwicks regulars. Overton Tremper, a player once handed a $10,000 bonus for signing with the Brooklyn Nationals, and longtime Bushwicks regular William "Dutch" Woerner, also a former Dodger, were among Dizzy's All-Stars. James Calleran, a career minor leaguer with nine years of professional experience, and ex-minor leaguer William Buck Lai, who played multiple seasons with Bridgeport in the Eastern League as late as 1921, batted leadoff and played third, respectively.

William Buck Lai had come to the United States in 1912, and toured the country with one of the leading teams of Hawaii, the All-Chinese Stars. He was of Chinese ancestry, something league officials knew when he signed with the White Sox in 1915, and the Phillies in 1918. Lai was also given a personal tryout by John McGraw of the New York Giants in 1928. Buck never showed enough class to keep him in the big leagues, but he at least got a chance before being sent back to the minors—something that could not be said for any of the native-born African American players who were struggling to make ends meet in the underfinanced Negro Leagues.

Bushwicks team members weren't required to travel the entire Eastern Shore—they were called "semiprofessionals." This allowed Lai and his teammates to keep their day jobs while playing baseball. Hargreaves owned a business in Trenton, New Jersey; pitcher Rube "Lefty" Chambers was nicknamed the milkman because of his daytime employment; and Lai was a civil engineer with the Pennsylvania Railroad. Without the salaried Negro major-league teams, however, there wouldn't have been a Bushwicks legacy—but these same African American players were never compensated for their real worth. At Dexter Park, pitchers Chambers and Grampp eagerly awaited their assignments for the star-studded event, pairing them with the Deans and Medwick.

Left fielder Joseph Michael Medwick was the Deans' only Cardinals teammate to join the brothers' tour. Nicknamed "Ducky," he was a big-league star in his own right, but like the Deans, he hadn't been paid well in 1934. Reportedly, he had earned $5,000 from the Cardinals. His 1934 season had included a .319 batting average, 198 hits, and 18 home runs in 149 games. Not counting his World Series take, he earned a little more than Daffy and a lot less than Dizzy. Medwick was not an unseasoned rookie; he joined the Cardinals in 1932, as a 20-year-old with lots of promise and much vibrato. He would go on to hit 40 or more doubles in seven consecutive summers, from 1933 to 1939.[17]

Born November 24, 1911, in Carteret, New Jersey, Joe's parents were Hungarian.[18] He became a mainstay of the famous "Gashouse Gang" and remained with the Cardinals through the 1940 season. Earlier in the month, he had helped Dizzy and Daffy defeat the Tigers in his first of two World Series appearances. In the Series' deciding game, he was banished from the field for poor sportsmanship, after sliding, spikes blazing, into third base, injuring Detroit's Marvin Owen in a sixth-inning collision. Between innings, Medwick returned to the outfield, where Detroit fans indignantly showered the field with bottles, trash, and other debris.[19] The game was delayed while Commissioner Kenesaw Mountain Landis, baseball's Ebenezer Scrooge of race relations, and other league officials in attendance gathered for a powwow. After much dialogue, it was determined that Ducky should exit the game for his own safety.

Medwick hadn't played with his St. Louis teammates since that eventful Tuesday, on October 10, when the score was 9–0 against the Detroit Tigers. After a week of inactivity, he showed up wearing a Cardinals uniform and was eager to get back to one of the things he did best—playing baseball. He wouldn't have great success against his Negro major-league opponents—certainly not the kind of hitting that led to his Cooperstown induction in 1968—which was a disappointment to many who had paid good money to see his bad performance.

Gates to Dexter Park, located at Jamaica Avenue and Eldert Lane in Queens, were flung open several hours before game time to facilitate the handling of the large gathering, which was estimated to reach 20,000. Robert F. Eisen, in a letter to the author, was a youth at the time. He recalled his chance meeting with the Deans at the Dexter Park gates.

I was a teenager, and one of my friends and I waited at Jamaica Avenue (the ballpark was about 75 yards north of Jamaica Avenue) figuring that the only people coming to the ballpark in a taxi cab would be the Deans. When a cab pulled up, Dizzy Dean got out, and I asked whether I could carry his bag. My friend took Paul Dean's bag. Dizzy had his wife with him, and I thought the other lady was Paul Dean's wife. We carried the bags to the locker room passing right thru the gates of Dexter Park.[20]

It was truly a memory for a lifetime.

African American teams in and around New York had provided entertainment for generations with little national recognition. They were a force to be reckoned with long before Dexter Park reached its zenith.

Brooklyn, New York, had been a continuous haven for African American teams for almost two generations. The Royal Giants represented the borough as early as 1904. John W. Connors, an African American, was the original owner of the Giants. Two Jews, Jesse and Rod McMahon, owned the Lincoln Giants of New York. In 1911, they brought their team to Brooklyn often. That same summer, Max Rosner's Cypress Hill semiprofessionals moved into Dexter Park. In 1913, Connors sold the Royal Giants to promoter Nat Strong, who was said to have controlled and ruined many a great African American team. The next year, James J. Keenan took over ownership of the Lincoln Giants after the McMahon brothers decided their share of the gate receipts would be better in boxing. Another semiprofessional team, the Bushwicks of Brooklyn, began playing at Wallace's Grounds in Ridgewood, Long Island, as early as 1914, before moving to Dexter Park in 1918, after the Ridgewood grounds burned to the ground. Rosner purchased Dexter Park in 1921.

Each of these teams had their pick of the large numbers of immigrants who preferred a game different from those being played by the three major-league teams in New York—especially so when New York's three American and National League teams refused to install lights. Harlem's diversity was highlighted in an August 31, 1934, edition of the *Kansas City Call*. The article stated, "Contrary to the common impression that Harlem is composed principally of Negroes, there are more Jews and Italians in that section than colored persons of all nationalities." The article, which came from New York, added, "On the east side of Harlem, in uptown Little Italy, it is conservatively estimated that there are more than 150,000 Italians. [The] Spanish, Russians, French, and Polish Jews, living principally in Madison and Fifth avenues, probably outnumber the Italians."[21]

The article reported that the Negro population of Harlem was between 223,000 and 300,000, and was the largest such community in the United

States. Baseball teams were the beneficiaries of this mass population—largely Dexter Park.

Legend said that Dexter Park got its name when Dexter, a trotter of some renown, was buried in center field. Negro major-league teams, and even football and soccer teams, scheduled games at Brooklyn's Dexter Park, and the fans came out in record numbers. One of the largest crowds to visit the park showed up in 1929, when an estimated 25,000 (21,583 paid) filled Dexter Park to see the Hakoah All-Stars soccer team from Israel. Dexter Park seated 15,400. Its complex included a large parking area for teams to pull their buses along the right-field bleachers. The park's locker rooms were spacious and loaded with such modern amenities as piping-hot water for showers. The park had a lunchroom located on its grounds. There was segregation but rarely in the lunchroom, where players and fans, regardless of race, ate meals together. Visiting Negro major-league teams received the customary fee of $500. This was a major bone of contention for Negro major-league teams because they only got the guarantee, never a percentage of the gate, under Nat Strong.

Strong's booking syndicate had tied up the best-paying venues in and around New York, forcing teams in the area to accept his ridiculous fees. They were putting people in the bleachers while Strong padded his wallet at their expense. In his bid to control semiprofessional baseball in the East, Strong's double-dealing tactics ruined many Negro major-league teams. Rube Foster had made his feelings known regarding the repugnant promoter years before to the *Amsterdam News*. "I played in the East under Strong," recalled Foster. "The club received but $100 for Sunday games, yet we drew as well at that time as the present in New York. Can you imagine a colored club playing to 10,000 paid admissions and receiving only the limit of $500 and then giving 10 percent of that to Strong to play in New York?"[22] Strong controlled the bookings for Dexter Park, where big bucks were paid, putting the field on a par with the nation's best minor-league structures.

Strong and Rosner installed an impressive electric lighting system for night baseball in July 1930. Nearby Ebbets Field, home of the Brooklyn Dodgers, was not lighted for major-league play until 1938—eight years later. Yankee Stadium would not get lights until 1946. The lights at Dexter Park were said to be so bright that many called them the "Midnight Sun." Nighttime baseball games were played on Wednesday and Friday. Lights were originally placed on wooded poles in the outfield, with four additional lighting structures positioned on top of the grandstand. In the spring of 1931, the wooden poles were replaced with modern steel light towers. The light pole in right-center field was estimated to be about 440 feet from the batter's box. In straightaway center, there was a sign that read, "God Bless America." Right field was relatively short, with a wooden fence about 307 feet down the foul line. The left-field bleachers were 418 feet from home plate. Right-center was 451 feet from home plate. This was more than enough space for Dizzy to perform his wild antics in the field.

In some years, the Bushwicks were said to have averaged more than 350,000 paid admissions. The crowds in 1934 rivaled the best of these years. A doubleheader at Dexter Park against the Pittsburgh Crawfords on July 29, 1934, had drawn more than 10,000 fans, and so had a June 10 game against the Nashville Elite Giants. Rosner's Bushwicks attracted sizeable crowds in their battles against the Birmingham Black Barons and Cuban Stars. The Black Yankees, who drew a crowd of 10,000 on April 29, 1934, were as popular as any Negro major-league team at Dexter Park.

In meeting the Deans, James "Soldier Boy" Semler, a leader of the Black Yankees, chose not to fortify his club with additional talent. Adding new players to the lineup cut the pay of the men who were already there. Semler saw no need to add imported players; they were going to battle the Deans with their regular lineup, a roster strong enough to defeat American and National League teams when everyone was healthy and present—and certainly the Bushwicks—on any day of the week. Semler's team was outstanding, but he was getting little support from at least one white owner, Tom Baird of the Kansas City Monarchs, when he sought to book teams at Yankee Stadium. "They put the pressure on Yankee Stadium about two years ago to let Semler, Negro owner of the Black Yankees, promote the games there," wrote Baird.

> I am sure you know what has happened since the stadium was taken from Gottlieb and given to Semler. Semler is out of baseball, owes plenty of bills etc., but the pressure was put on the officials of the stadium and everybody lost money because Semler wasn't big enough for the job, and this may have been a big factor in the failure of the Negro National League.[23]

The Black Yankees' string of wins was worthy of national recognition, something they never received. Had they been a major- or minor-league team, a record of their consecutive wins would have been listed in history books long ago. On August 14, 1934, the Black Yankees traveled to Syracuse, New York, boasting 21 consecutive wins. They beat the Oswego Zetts, 9–0, in front of a crowd of 2,000 at local Municipal Stadium for win number 22. While they were putting together long winning streaks, they had also broken the Bushwicks' string of wins. According to the *Brooklyn Daily Eagle*, "Invariably in the past, when the Bushwicks would go out and roll up a winning streak, the traveling Black Yankees would come into Dexter Park on some Sunday afternoon and proceed to smash the winning streak."[24] Such was the case on August 26, when the Black Yankees split a doubleheader after the Bushwicks had rung up seven-straight wins. They were to meet in yet another double-header, supposedly the last game at Dexter Park for the 1934 season, on September 23, but cold weather ruined the night and the game was cancelled.

In preparation for the Deans, Manager George Scales trotted out a highly regarded aggregation of Negro major-league stars to face the big-league brothers. Bill Holland, one of his best pitchers, did not suit up for the games versus the Deans. Suited up for the Black Yankees were two players from Dizzy's birth state, Arkansas. Pitcher Connie Rector and right fielder Clyde Spearman were both from Arkadelphia, Arkansas—116 miles from Dizzy's birthplace. Spearman was considered the "best young outfielder on anybody's team," according to W. Rollo Wilson of the *Pittsburgh Courier*.[25] Rector, Holland, Roy Williams, and lefty John "Neck" Stanley were the mainstays of an impressive Black Yankees hurling crew. Stanley, a veteran southpaw who was credited with most of the team's wins, came to the Negro majors from the sandlots of Chester, Pennsylvania. There was additional talent in the outfield and infield.

Frank Blake, a Boston, Massachusetts, recruit, an excellent hitter and infielder who also pitched, was one of the Black Yankees' rising stars. They had a veteran in Walter "Rev" Cannady at second base. Rev had broken into big-time play with the 1923 Homestead Grays. Like the younger Blake, Cannady also pitched, and Rev hit for average and power. A demonstration of his durability was witnessed on July 6, 1923, in an exhibition game at Warren, Pennsylvania. On that occasion, Cannady tossed a seven-hitter, struck out a trio of batters, and hit two home runs in the Grays' 9–3 win. Billy Yancey, a two-sport professional in baseball and basketball, was their shortstop, while Manager George Scales and John Beckwith alternated at third base. Robert Clark, at catcher, alternated with Beckwith behind home plate. Spearman was joined by veterans Clint Thomas and Clarence "Fats" Jenkins in the outfield. Thomas, who was playing his final season in the Negro major leagues, was still an amazing talent. It is ironic that Clark left the team before the Deans arrived and that Tex Burnett had suffered an injury during the four-team doubleheaders in September, leaving the Black Yankees without a catcher. Jenkins and pitcher Bill Holland were also missing when the team reached Brooklyn. When Beckwith refused to go behind the plate, Thomas filled the position and Beckwith went to the outfield, replacing Jenkins, who had left to start the basketball season. At first base, the Black Yankees had a spectacular talent nicknamed "Show Boat," who wasn't caught up in the position shuffle.

Columnists in and around New York had proclaimed the arrival of David "Show Boat" Thomas in bold print. They called him the flashiest first baseman in New York. One newspaper tagged him the "cream of the Negro first basemen." These writers weren't pulling their punches in a season where the Dodgers had Sam Leslie, the Giants Bill Terry, and the Yankees Lou Gehrig—two of whom ended up in the Baseball Hall of Fame at Cooperstown, New York.

Thomas, born March 22, 1905, in Mobile, Alabama, was a master of the one-handed snatch-and-grab. He pulled in balls on the ground and plucked them out of the air with acrobatic ease. His career was distinguished long before getting to the Big Apple; it dated back to his first professional club, the Mobile Tigers, in 1923. Thomas came east in 1930, to join the Baltimore Black Sox. It is ironic that after years of little national recognition, in 1945 he finally became national news throughout the United States.

In 1945, Thomas, then a member of the New York Cubans, along with pitcher Terris McDuffie, received the first tryout for African Americans by the Brooklyn Dodgers. They wore Dodgers uniforms, and it probably took them longer to get dressed than it did to parade their talents before an insubordinate Branch Rickey, who was designing his own plan for baseball's integration. Reporters were not going to run his show. Thomas and McDuffie ran headlong into baseball's iron curtain, and the affirmative action tryout lasted all of 25 minutes. They deserved this tryout and should have gotten better results, but like other veterans of their generation and even before, they were turned away and stamped as rejects. Rickey had decided that they were not the right men to break baseball's integration barrier. He was seeking a quality that went far beyond baseball. Jackie Robinson would be his man.

Willard Brown, the fourth African American to move into the white majors, an outspoken man of immense pride, told the author, "I would have never taken the shit Jackie did," which probably explains why he was released by the last-place St. Louis Browns after a month and never returned to the National or American Leagues.[26] His sentiment was echoed by numerous others. Several of the more deserving types were members of the 1934 Black Yankees team that Dizzy and Daffy faced. John Beckwith is one fine example.

Sweet-swinging John Christopher Beckwith, born in 1900, was a premier slugger of the infield. He excelled at swinging the willow, and when hits meant runs, he would usually provide a home run. He was a shortstop during the period when men with his power and bulk weren't playing the middle infield. "Big Johnny," as he was called, was an outstanding shortstop, third baseman, and catcher. The Bambino himself, Babe Ruth, said of Beckwith, "Not only can Beckwith hit harder than any Negro ballplayer, but any man in the world."[27] Pound for pound, he was every bit the legendary Yankees' equal. One newspaper proclaimed, "Fans who have never seen Babe Ruth perform can see his double in the mighty shortstop."

At the tender age of 21, John hit the first home run to ever clear Cincinnati's Redland Stadium. That was in 1921, during a Negro major-league contest. He had been adding to that total ever since, especially in exhibitions. On July 14, 1928, Beckwith, a member of Cumberland Posey's Homestead Grays, slammed three homers in an exhibition game at Zanesville, Ohio. Other published accounts credit him with 72 home runs in 1929. In 1934, he was showing few signs of aging, as Dizzy Dean and his All-Stars would soon discover.

As the brothers stood in the vicinity of home plate before the game, they were amazed at the size of the crowd, which was estimated to be 15,000 to 16,000 rooters. "Boy, we shore pack 'em in," said Diz. "We shore do," Daffy responded. "Brooklyn's fans got sense," stated Dizzy. Their moment of reflection was rudely interrupted by the home plate umpire. "Will you boys please autograph these balls?"[28] Over the loudspeaker it was announced that "Dizzy would pitch and play right field. Paul would not pitch at all." The younger Dean was still doting on his valuable right wing, which was still aching. He was there to play three innings in the outfield during Dizzy's tenure on the mound. The announcer received a round of boos and negative statements from the stands. Had fans bothered to read the *World-Telegram* earlier that day, in which an article clearly stated, "Daffy, nursing a sore arm, will play the entire game in the outfield," the fans might have been more prepared to handle the news.[29] Unfortunately, many hadn't seen the newspaper, and it wasn't taken kindly when the statement about Paul was made.

The negative buzz continued as Art Smith, a former collegian, took the mound before Dizzy. Tom Reilly, writing in the *World-Telegram*, advised, "Nothing happened for three innings other than the strikeout of Joe Medwick. This caused much delight among the dusky opposition known as the Black Yankees."[30] Smith hurled three innings, allowing one hit, before handing a 0–0 game over to the Cardinals great. Dizzy waltzed to the mound to start the fourth inning, and all criticism appeared to be silenced, as Paul also came into the game as a right fielder. They took their positions in concert. Fans down the right-field line cheered their arrival, but those along third base, who generally heckled and taunted visiting teams and players, were plenty salty. The heckling never stopped. "You're goin'ta be dizzier 'n ever when you git done pitchin' to them eight balls," yelled a fan with more prejudices than common sense, wrote a *World-Telegram* reporter.[31] Everyone in the section knew what he was saying, as the eight ball is always black in the game of billiards.

When Dizzy whiffed fellow Arkansas native Clyde Spearman on three pitches, a supporter in the bleachers yelled, "Atta-boy, Diz, fog 'em in there." When Bill Yancy was retired for out number two, an opposition voice in the stands bellowed, "Oh-h-h-h, them bums. It's in the bag you Oklahoma Oaf. They're jus' making you look good." The first two batters were retired with ease; the third, Clint Thomas, was a bit more difficult. Dizzy had never faced him before and was unaware that Thomas feasted on fastballs. Someone yelled loudly, "Two bits he hits!" On the next pitch, the Black Yankees catcher laced a shot to right-center field, which Paul played timidly as it skipped off the wall. Tremper, in center field, retrieved the ball and propelled it back to the infield while Thomas scooted around the bases for a triple. Dizzy watched aimlessly as the baserunner circled the sacks. He was roused by another comment from an unruly and boisterous rooter. "Hey, you bum, this is Brooklyn, not Detroit," squawked the fan. "Give 'em the works, boys, he's nuttier 'n ever now."[32] Things went from bad to worse when Thomas stole home despite Dizzy's best protest. It was a dubious call followed by a harsh series of events.

In an interview with author John Holway, Thomas recalled the play.

I told Buck Lai, the third baseman, "Shit, I can steal home on him." Lai went over to the mound and told Dean. Diz said, "The hell with that son of a bitch, he couldn't beat me doin' nothing." On the next pitch Dean threw a pitchout. I didn't move. Next pitch, Dean began pumping into his windup, and I lit for home. The umpire called me safe. Dean was so mad, he knocked the next batter down, and the fans stood up and gave him hell.[33]

Thomas's theft of home became the game's first run and an embarrassing upstaging for Dizzy. A statement in the *Daily Eagle* announced, "He was infuriated when Thomas stole home on him in the fourth inning." Dizzy said, "I invited him in. I saw him coming, and then when he's on his way, I fog that ball in with plenty to spare. He is out [by] a mile, but that crooked umpire beats us. Can you imagine that! That is the first home that was ever stole on me, and one of them Black Yankees had to do it."[34] Dizzy proceeded to go to pieces after that. When Scales, next up and the last batter of the inning, stepped into the batter's box, Dizzy let go a "suspiciously wild" pitch. Parrott, writing in the *Daily Eagle*, said, "It went right by the catcher and fortunately right by the umpire, too."

Dizzy was blazing mad; he wanted to argue further about the steal of home. He said the umpire had blown the call. Bushwicks management, prepared for such debates, had hired four umpires, one at every base, to watch over the proceedings. This reduced the Cardinals' protest to a malevolent whimper. "Dizzy's Adam's apple glides with glee," Reilly explained to his readers. "Medwick's chin moves out a mile. Daffy's voice gets a high-pitched cadence. It may be Brooklyn, but it is highly reminiscent of Detroit."[35]

Dizzy was still angry as he stomped off the field between innings. He hadn't reached the dugout before an unnamed member of the Black Yankees was said to have asked for an autograph. The *Daily Eagle* cautioned its readers about what happened next. "What Dizzy said to him is unprintable, but the colored lad had to run for cover," wrote Parrott.[36] The statement lacked powerful observation and showed the inherently racist views players received on ball fields and in the media. "Dizzy has all [of] a native Oklahoman's love for the Negro," the article stated. It was loaded statement. To use "love" in such a negative context was an overreach of major-league proportions. A penchant for abuse might have summarized it better.

In Oklahoma and also Arkansas, where the Deans were born, local governments discriminated against African Americans in jobs, housing, education, income, and the criminal justice system. Advocating for one's rights in the South could get you killed. It was a harsh existence, but the North wasn't much better, illustrating the hypocrisy in Parrott's statement as he conveniently forgot about the prejudice up North and the prejudice and segregation that was occurring in New York. Robert Gregory, in his book *Diz*, interpreted what Dean supposedly said but never credited a source, which leads one to wonder if the said statements are true.

Gregory reported that Dizzy said, "This was the first time home was ever stole on me and one of them coons has to do it." Regarding the Black Yankees player who wanted Dizzy's autograph, Gregory advised that Dizzy said, "Scat, you goddamned nigger, scat."[37] Neither of these statements appeared in print that day, and neither has been attributed to any source in Gregory's work. Thus, these printed statements are not to be taken as gospel. Plenty was written in the newspapers about what Dizzy said on numerous occasions, positive and negative—but it was never racial. Dizzy's negative statements toward the umpires were well documented.

At about the same time, Dizzy started in on the umpire. "That big bum, before the game he gets a couple of autographed balls from me, like I was the only one in the world that matters, and then he pulls one like that on me," he roared. Daffy and Pat heard Dizzy's outburst. Paul, the less talkative of the brothers, tried to lower his brother's volume by asking, "If the ladies up behind the dugout could hear what was being said."[38] Cussing and fussing was a recurring event in exhibition games.

In 1932, Hack Wilson, former hone run king of the National League, had a similar outburst with a display of bitter and nasty language during a game at York, Pennsylvania. That night, September 27, 1932, Wilson was embroiled in a harsh dispute. It started when the big-leaguer came charging in from right field to argue a decision at home plate. The *York Dispatch* writer was embarrassed by what he heard spewed loudly and angrily on the field. Wilson filled the air with "deep-throated, nauseating profanity," directed at the chief umpire, and jeers from the crowd quickly followed. The writer voiced his disapproval of Wilson's actions by stating, "Judge Kenesaw Mountain Landis should have been in the stands at Eagle Park last night to hear 'one of his boys' give an exhibition of how not to raise the morals of baseball games."[39] Dizzy settled down in Brooklyn. His outburst was not heard by the spectators, but from that point onward the three Cardinals regulars questioned "every strike, ball, or decision at first," reported Reilly of the *World-Telegram.* "You'd think it was a World Series, and Medwick is so mad he fans thrice," advised Reilly. "However, they exited smiling with the fans still divided in their praises and condemnation."[40]

Dizzy's frustrations, although a bit more tempered, continued in the melodramatic fifth inning. In that frame, after Show Boat Thomas had been retired, Rev Cannady flied to right field, where Daffy bumbled the catch and dropped the ball. A *New York Times* article said that Paul was "absolutely no help" in the outer garden.[41] The official scorer gave Paul an error; Diz gave him a scolding. Upon his return to the mound, Dizzy "momentarily lost all control," a writer commented. He committed an embarrassing balk before settling down to retire Beckwith and Blake for outs two and three. Dizzy was having a lousy game, and he despised it. He wanted to win, not lose. When one of his All-Stars came to bat, he would ask the player's name and, after being told it was Bubbles, Buck, or Dutch, in a spirit of competitiveness, yell at the top of his lungs for that player to get a hit. Dizzy returned to pitch the sixth inning.

After drawing a chorus of boos for his actions two innings earlier, Diz provided more entertainment for the large crowd in the sixth after surrendering a single to pitcher Stanley. One batter later, the Cardinals ace cleverly dropped Spearman's bunt pop, then picked it up with his meat hand and served up a double play. Yancey was retired for out three to end the inning. Dizzy didn't return for the seventh frame. After three innings, a period in which he allowed two hits, a walk, a balk, three strikeouts, and a steal of home, he was done for the day. He remained in the game as a right fielder, replacing Paul. Grampp came on to pitch the seventh for the Bushwicks.

Henry Eckhard Grampp, a native New Yorker by birth, entered the game with the Black Yankees leading 1–0. Born September 28, 1903, Grampp, a right-hander, could boast of a most interesting career in the majors prior to joining the Bushwicks. He broke into professional play with Hartford of the Eastern League in 1923, and ended up on the roster of the Boston Red Sox, but was picked up by Chicago's National League Cubs following a minor-league stint in New Orleans.[42] Unfortunately for Grampp, his big-league pitching assignments were minimized to four in two years. He was on the Cubs' roster but seldom got into an actual game. During those years he became the Cubs' batting practice pitcher and pitched daily. He must have been good at it; the American League Yankees also hired him to toss batting practice for them in 1934. Fact is, he hadn't played an inning of minor-league ball since 1931, nor had he pitched in the majors since October 6, 1929. Nonetheless, to those living in and around Brooklyn he was something special. On this night, however, he was less than speculator, as all hope of Dizzy's All-Stars winning the game vanished when Grampp was treated to an early shower. Black Yankees batters raked him for five hits in two innings and were leading, 3–0, upon his exit. Additional runs were added off Chambers, who hung on until the final out. The end score favored the Black Yankees, 6–0. Dizzy, no longer in the game, settled down during the latter part of the evening and gave informative bench interviews from the dugout.

"How much are you going to ask Breadon and Rickey for next season?" asked Parrott. "That's the one question in my life I have to say I can't answer," replied Diz anxiously. He smiled smugly from ear to ear and added, "Breadon warned me not to." Dizzy went on to say, "They always treated me and Paul fair, no matter what you read in the papers. Only the other day Breadon called me up and said, 'We won't have no trouble; you pitched great ball, and we will pay you well.'"[43]

The Black Yankees finished with eight hits—one more hit than the Deans' All-Stars. They outhit their opponents in spite of Dizzy tossing three innings and Ducky taking four at-bats. Clint Thomas, age 37, was the day's real star, something you couldn't tell by reading the unrighteous commentary penned by James Dawson in the New York Times or in Reilly's World-Telegram report. Clint's banner day, which included a 2-for-4 performance at bat, a pair of runs scored, and a trio of bases stolen, received little ink. Other than the box score, Clint's name was only mentioned once in Dawson's Times wrap-up. The much-celebrated Medwick, although well-advertised and heavily promoted in the area media, was a rank failure at the plate, yet he garnered three mentions in Dawson's follow-up on the game. The World-Telegram never mentioned Thomas's name, but it did mention Medwick's name three times. Baseball writers weren't doing any favors for Thomas. He was earning every bit of recognition he could get, which wasn't much. In a professional career that ended following the Dean brothers' visit, Thomas never received the money or notoriety he was owed.

The addition of Medwick failed to supply much punch for the bewildered New Yorkers. Ducky was struck out, not once, but four consecutive times on what the *New York Times* termed "tantalizing teasers," which was Stanley's bread and butter.[44] During Medwick's entire 1934 world championship season at St. Louis, he only struck out 83 times in 149 National League contests. This was the same jumping Jerseyite who pounded out four hits, one of which was a healthy home run in the first game of the World Series, as noted by one newspaper.[45] Stanley, to his credit, handled the Hall of Fame outfielder without difficulty. He should have received national attention for his feat. Instead, few people have ever heard of the shellacking the pitcher handed the Cardinals great or the day Stanley toppled Dizzy and the Bushwicks on seven hits.

In the *Daily Eagle*'s postgame report, Stanley's performance was never mentioned, nor was his name. If not for the box score, we wouldn't even know he pitched. The *World-Telegram*'s report the day after failed to mention any of the Black Yankees by name—not Stanley, Blake, or Thomas. They used terms like "the batter," "the second batter," or "the next batter." At the Bushwicks' park there was always strife in the stands and lots of gambling. It was high stakes between the "landlords" and "tenants." Webster McDonald said in an interview with author John Holway, "The 'Landlords' sit over [on] this side, $100 bills pinned on their lapels. The 'Tenants' sit over there, with $50 bills. And they used to really give me a working out."[46]

Contrary to the journalistic rules for covering sports, more attention was paid to Country Fair Brown, who acted as a "bona fide burlesque comedian acting as 'a sideline coach'" for the Black Yankees. He got more newspaper coverage than anything that happened in the actual game.[47] And to make matters all the more insane, Reilly subtitled his *World-Telegram* article "Escaped from a Chain Gang." The coach, who was called "Country Fair Brown," was better known as "Circus Country Brown," real name, Elias Bryant. Born March 28, 1896, as a player, Bryant appeared with such illustrious New York teams as the Bacharach Giants, Brooklyn Royal Giants, Lincoln Giants, and New York Black Yankees. Four years after his appearance on the Deans' tour, Bryant died from an apparent fractured skull when he was pushed and fell, hitting his head on a curb, in an altercation on New York's Lenox Avenue. The Georgia native died on Christmas Day 1937, and was buried in Frederick Douglass Cemetery on Staten Island, where he is enshrined with a host of other well-known dignitaries. These include the likes of Sol White, legendary manager of the Philadelphia Giants; Bill "Bojangles" Robinson, co-owner of the New York Black Yankees; and Mamie Smith, a blues artist who was once married to Charles "Two Sides" Wesley, manager of the Birmingham Black Barons.

When news of the game was released to surrounding towns and cities, another tale was spun. After explaining that the "cocksure" Bushwicks were beaten by the Black Yankees, one article stated, "'Ducky Wucky' Medwick, one of the St. Louis Cardinals' World Series heroes, played left field for the Bushwicks and contributed no hits in three times at bat."[48] There was no mention of Medwick's four at-bats or the four times he struck out. Also missing was Stanley's name, the pitcher who dominated him at bat.

Missing from every article was any mention of New York's finest. Security and police officials, so prevalent in other cities, played a virtually nonexistent role in New York. Always present, however, was the mention of some player's ethnicity. This time they spoke of Dizzy's heritage. On its sports page, the Daily Eagle inserted a small headline titled "Dizzy's Two-Hyphen Descent." It stated Dizzy Dean is of "German-Irish-English descent."[49]

In hiring the Deans, Rosner and Strong got more in the way of entertainment than was originally planned. Parrott told his readers that Dizzy "chased a Negro ballplayer out of the dugout and threatened to knock an umpire down to first base."[50] Diz, still stewing after the game, prompted his wife to say to a reporter, "Diz is mad. I always know when he's mad. It's time I took him home to Bradenton to rest. We'll leave just as soon as he finishes his vaudeville act."[51]

In the dressing room after the festivities, Dizzy was a chatterbox. He said plenty. When a Daily Eagle reporter inquired about the razzing he received from Brooklyn fans, Diz was quick with a response. "I don't care," he said with a wide grin as he sat soaking wet from a shower chewing on a hotdog. "I don't care. Let 'em yell if they pay their 50 cents, that's me. I can take it," he said with cupidity.[52] The World-Telegram also twisted Dean's reply, writing, "They pay to get in, and you know I really like it when they go to work on a guy. It makes you feel like workin."[53]

Once dressed, Dizzy headed out of the locker room. He read through a special pictorial edition the Daily Eagle had printed for the occasion, then stuffed several copies into his jacket pocket and waltzed out the door. Parrott acknowledged, "He is still just a big country kid who likes to see himself in the paper."[54] It had been a productive night financially, but Diz was feeling blue. "There's one thing [that] hurts me way down to here," he admitted without interruption. "To think we autographed them baseballs for that blind umpire. That was an awful mistake."[55]

The reporters acted like bloodhounds turned loose on the Deans in their New York interviews, capitalizing on their every mistake and publicizing every controversial statement they uttered. Dizzy appeared to be taken aback and bewildered by the entire New York visit. When asked where the next stop would be, Dizzy said, "Milwaukee." Paul interrupted and said it was Baltimore. "Oh yeah," said a dazed Dizzy. "That's right Baltimore tomorrow night."[56] From that day onward, both Deans would dislike and distrust the New York sportswriters. Commenting further on his visit to New York, Dizzy said, "The fans in this heah town yell louder than anybody I ever did hear, but they know less," reported the *Daily Eagle*. "They don't know no baseball here in Brooklyn. Now you take a town like Chicago; they are smart baseball fans there."[57]

With that final insult, the brothers left Gotham to scurry off to Maryland, where the media wasn't as diabolical and proceeds from their exhibition were to help erect a memorial for a baseball idol, George Herman "Babe" Ruth.

CHAPTER 10

Baltimore, Maryland

Nasty as All Get Out
Thursday, October 18, 1934

Babe Ruth's hometown was worked in as a last-minute alternative in Doan's scheduling efforts. Local promoters struggled to assist Doan in getting together an African American team and essentially did the best they could on short notice—without success. So, instead of an African American opponent, Dizzy and Daffy were in Maryland to play an exhibition game against a team of white major- and minor-league stars bolstered by local semiprofessionals. On this night, there was no African American team to slay; the Baltimore game would be an entirely white affair that resulted in the lowest crowd turnout of the tour.

Joe Cambria, owner and operator of both the Albany club in the International League and Baltimore's Bugle Field, promoted the appearance. He allowed Don Heffner, a Baltimore native and member of the New York Yankees, to form a team to face Dizzy's All-Stars.[1] Cambria's fee was an excessive 15 percent of the Dean brothers' take, a fee he'd been extracting from African American teams for years—with lots of resistance. By starting the game at 8:15 p.m., it allowed for another full day of promotions and media interviews, which were well chronicled by Craig E. Taylor and numerous others at the *Baltimore Sun*.

Writers at the *Sun* captured the brothers in conversation as they relaxed in their lavishly decorated rooms at Baltimore's Hotel Emerson. In one article was titled "Dizzy Finds His Barnstorming Much Too Exciting for Fans," both Dizzy and Daffy expressed their desire to get to Florida and spend the winter eating "rattlesnake cutlets."[2] Daffy was dressed in a "pajama coat, a pair of dark trousers, and some brown socks." It was reported that he "wriggled his toes comfortably." When the door opened, he was said to be "lying on the bed with his legs stretched straight up into the air." Dizzy was stretched out on a davenport with his head smashed flush against a "royal gold pillow."[3] Diz took the reporters' visit as an opportunity to poke some good-natured fun at his kid brother. "When the Lord made Paul," Diz joked playfully, "he hung on a good right arm and then shut up shop for the day." As he lay relaxed on the sofa, Diz discussed his theories on barnstorming.

"This barnstorming is dangerous business," Dizzy warned. "The crowds are more nervous than we are. Three people got so excited watching us play in Philly the other night that they dropped dead." The conversation shifted to some sandwiches on the table. "Who left them sandwiches?" Diz inquired. "I did," responded Daffy. "Someone ordered 'em up for me, but I have already ate a beefsteak." Diz took the plate of sandwiches, hopped up with a sudden jolt, and headed out the door. "Dizzy, where the hell you going?" asked Ray L. Doan. "I'm going down in the lobby and peddle these to the highest bid-der," he could be heard saying as he disappeared down through the hallway corridor.[4] One of Dizzy's first promotional stops was St. Mary's.

At about midday, Dizzy visited St. Mary's. He was there by himself; Paul chose to remain at the Hotel Emerson. Evidently the younger Dean was vac-illating on resting or running while on tour; Dizzy never wavered, as he was making the most of his travels by using every minute to entertain someone. He went to Babe Ruth's alma mater and had fun with the boys during his visit. It was a fitting place to appear now that the "dizziness twins—Dizzy and Daffy Dean—had replaced Babe Ruth as one of baseball's most colorful figures."[5] Upon his arrival, Dizzy boldly told the boys, about 700 in all, "I'm proud to be with you. Until three weeks ago, Babe Ruth was the biggest figure in baseball. Now you are looking at Dizzy, the man who is walking in the Babe's shoes."[6] They had barely digested his loquacious statement when Dizzy jumped off the stage and into the orchestra pit of the school's audito-rium, where he borrowed the director's baton and proceeded to lead the band in a series of selections for more than 10 minutes.

After his band experience, Dizzy signed autographs until he got writer's cramp. These charitable activities made little impression on the *Sun's* Taylor, who wrote negatively about the visit. Instead of showing the goodwill the visit had elicited, he chose to lampoon the Cardinals pitcher. In paragraph after paragraph, he poked fun at Dean's Southern dialect, wrote disparag-ingly of his performance, and took delight when Dizzy was hit by players of little renown. This same indifference on the part of the *Sun* caused problems with Negro major-league games, thereby resulting in low profits and horrible attendance. After years of struggling to make ends meet, the Black Sox ownership group was fighting back with their own brand of boycott against the daily newspapers and Cambria's booking syndicate.

Baltimore's Negro major-league franchise had struggled mightily in 1934. After a successful opening in May, hindrance and meddling by agents of Cambria put a halt to further local games. A forced relocation to Chester, Pennsylvania, where promoter Jack Farrell, the team's new owner, lived and ran club affairs, occurred shortly thereafter. The *New York Age* acknowledged, "Joe Cambria, Baltimore Black Sox sponsor, is having league trouble on account of several of his players planning to sign with other clubs."[7]

Farrell, a former owner of the Negro League's Washington Pilots, who was also well-known in boxing circles, was the culprit, taking over Cambria's territory. In a *Baltimore Afro-American* article, he assured that his new venture was an "all-colored one." Farrell felt it better to stay out of Baltimore and out of Cambria's reach if he was going to make a go at success. He offered as his reason "interference with the management of the team by outside interests."[8]

An ailing Herbert "Rap" Dixon, released earlier in the season by Edward Bolden's Philadelphia Stars, was employed shortly thereafter to manage the revamped Black Sox. One newspaper surmised, "Rap plans to handle the reins from the dugout, having just recovered recently from a long spell of sickness which had him confined to a Philly Hospital."[9] A number of young recruits were quickly signed to shore up the roster. Tom Richardson, "Hack" Cunningham, Sonny "Sweets" Harris, "Bum" Hayes, Melvin Allen, and George Holles, along with Rap's brother, Paul Dixon, and Leon Day, joined the rejuvenated Sox. Day was 18 years old when he joined the Black Sox.

Born October 30, 1916, in Alexandria, Virginia, he would go on to an illustrious career on the mound and in the field for such teams as the Brooklyn Eagles, Newark Eagles, and Baltimore Elite Giants. Prior to joining the Black Sox, he was with the semiprofessional Silver Moons, who played out of Baltimore's Mount Winans neighborhood. Legend said he was lured into professional baseball by Rap Dixon, who offered him the pricey sum of $60 per month for services rendered. Day would have many big games thereafter. On July 31, 1942, he struck out 18 members of the Baltimore Elites, a team for which he would later play, and allowed one hit. Following his discharge from the 818th Amphibian Battalion during World War II, he returned to professional baseball and tossed a no-hitter in a big Opening Day 2–0 win over the Philadelphia Stars. Although he wouldn't play against the Deans in 1934, he was qualified for the task. Day was enshrined in the Baseball Hall of Fame in 1995—the same Hall of Fame where was Dizzy was enshrined—but 42 years later.

By leaving, the Black Sox left Baltimore without an African American league team and few major-league games. An attempt was made on July 15 to schedule a game between the Philadelphia Stars and Pittsburgh Crawfords. It was never played. Officials of the Black Sox protested and forced the cancellation of the event. When asked about the cancellation, Edward Bolden, owner of the Philadelphia Stars, called Baltimore a "poor town to support a league game or regular appearances of league teams."[10]

The crowd that gathered to see the Deans was smaller than expected. Official attendance figures were a disappointing 2,215. Since there was no African American team to draw people of color, it's safe to say that few supporters of the Baltimore Black Sox attended the event. Taylor's article alerted everyone to Dizzy's disarming response to the low turnout. Peering at the half-empty stands, Diz asked, "What are they chargin' here tonight?" Someone replied, "International League prices." Dizzy leaned back in his chair and responded, "You mean people is only payin' minor-league prices to see the greatest pitcher of all time? Well I'll be damned."[11] Cambria hadn't exercised his due diligence in promoting the Deans, and it was evident.

They say that Joseph Cambria, real name Carlo Cambria, was a super scout—"one of the most prolific scouts in major-league history"—in the opinion of Brian McKenna, a researcher for the Society of American Baseball Research. Cambria, who was born in Messina, Italy, in 1890, immigrated to America with his father after the mother's death. The family settled in Boston, where his love affair with baseball was reportedly born. He would have a distinguished career as a minor-league player, starting with Newport of the Rhode Island State League in 1909. His professional career ended in 1912, and his business career began.

One of his first business ventures was the purchase of the Bugle Coat and Apron Company in Baltimore. In 1928, he entered a team in the Baltimore Amateur League and began hiring ex-major leaguers to bolster his lineup when playing teams from the ranks of the Negro Leagues. He purchased and revamped the former Loney's Lane ballpark at Federal and Edison Highway in 1929, renaming it Bugle Field. Lights were added in 1932. He rented his park to George Rossitor's Baltimore Black Sox and other local teams when his own team wasn't active. That same year, Cambria added the Hagerstown, Maryland, Hubs of the Blue Ridge League to his growing enterprise. His goal was to find players for his team, develop them, and sell them to major-league teams.

Clark Griffith of the Washington Senators was one of Cambria's best customers. In addition to selling his players, he also scheduled games against Negro major-league teams in the region. He made a profit booking black teams, but his Hagerstown franchise was a financial failure. In 1931, his minor-league team moved twice, relocating to Parkersburg, West Virginia, and Youngstown, Ohio, finishing more than 20 games out of first place. Instead of integrating his minor-league team—something history said he could have done—the next year, 1932, he purchased the Baltimore Black Sox from Rossiter, a local saloon owner, and entered the world of African American baseball. Like many owners, he practiced the tradition of separate and unequal.

Cambria entered his Black Sox in the short-lived East–West League. Instead of paying regular salaries to African American players, he forced them to play on a percentage basis. His minor-league teams got regular pay. A good idea in a bad economy forced the East–West League to disband before season's end, and players jumped at the best opportunities available—which weren't in Baltimore. Cambria's troubles weren't over.

In 1933, he was sued by former Black Sox owners and lost ownership of the name. When Ben Taylor, a one-time leader of the Black Sox, announced plans to create a second Negro major-league team in Baltimore, Cambria was almost sunk. Before totally losing his shirt, he purchased the Albany club of the International League for the sum of $7,500. Cambria kept his secret weapon—Bugle Field. As long as he controlled the park and kept his relationship with the Baltimore Orioles for their park, no African American team could operate in Baltimore without him.

Prior to the game's 8:15 p.m. start, the celebrity brothers were feeling rejected, and it caused Dizzy to react negatively, said Taylor. "Mebbe it will rain tonight," Dizzy said. "If it rains we go back to the hotel and hev us a crap game, see?" He looked at Ray L. Doan and said, "None of that givin-back game neither," referring to rain checks. Dizzy then took this opportunity to poke fun at the Detroit Tigers and his own team, the St. Louis Cardinals. When asked about the World Series, Dizzy responded objectively, "If them American League guys are ballplayers I'm a horse." The reporter said he "whinnied slightly, either to indicate that he was or was not a horse." He then proceeded to add, "That wuz all hooey about me askin' to pitch the first and last game. I didn't ask for neither. They just had good sense and pitched me, that's all. The Tigers wuz busted after the sixth game. The last one wuz just a breeze." When speaking of the Cardinals, Dizzy cried out, "If they don't pay Paul and me what we want we just won't play, you know what I mean."[12]

Dizzy's All-Stars team consisted of players from the Cloverland Farms Dairy team. The Dairy, distinguished as the "Dairy with the Cows," formed the team, which backed the Cardinals great. As anonymous celebrities for the day, the Deans' All-Stars were there to fill seven spots on the field and not much more. They received little mention in the media. Other than Vic Keen, not one of the men on the Cloverland team was identified by first name. Keen had concluded his major-league career in 1927, with the Cardinals, but he was still an outstanding pitcher. In his column for the *Brooklyn Daily Eagle*, Tommy Holmes said that Keen was a "promising Cardinals pitcher of six or seven years ago" trying a comeback with the International League Baltimore Orioles.[13] Keen disappeared from the professional ranks shortly after he "severely" beaned Glenn Wright of the Pittsburgh Pirates.

Holmes reported that Wright's injury shook Keen's nerves. Yet, by 1934, his comeback was almost complete. On August 27 he had tossed a no-hitter for Cloverland against Glen Burnie, Maryland, winning, 3–0, in Baltimore. For the All-Stars contest, Cloverland presented a lineup that included Lunak in center field, Rosenberg at third base, Brumer in left field, Kulachi in right field, Jacobs at second base, Hess at first base, Harlege at shortstop, and Hasslut as catcher. Dizzy's club was reportedly a local sandlot team, but his opponents were major- and minor-league stars.

Dizzy's opponents were a group of professionals assembled by Heffner, a 5-foot-10, 155-pound, light-hitting second baseman of the New York Yankees. Webster McDonald, manager of the 1934 Philadelphia Stars, had lots to say about this infielder, who came from the sandlots of Baltimore to the majors, in an interview with John Holway. McDonald called Heffner a "little hot-headed guy." He continued,

> Everybody was wrong but him. He stood on top of the plate, and I pushed him back with a pitch. He'd get right back in there. He was determined to dig in and stay on top of that plate. I said, "What you gonna do about it ump?" He said, "Go ahead and push him back. Push him back." I knew that Heffner was going to get mad and want to fight, but McDonald said to himself, "I can whip five little guys like you."[14]

Just as had been in other cities, these All-Stars were not amateurs. Their roster included Henry Peter Cappola, an Albany International League hurler, and Cliff Melton, an Orioles left-hander bought by the Yankees. Jake Powell, an Albany player purchased by the Washington Senators, formed what local newspapers called a "sandlot" team—which it wasn't. Most prominent was an appearance by the iniquitous Alvin "Jake" Powell. His life is one worth further examination.

In 1933, while a member for the Middle Atlantic League Dayton, Ohio, Ducks, outfielder Jake Powell was caught trying to steal a window fan and other items from the hotel where the team had stayed by draping them in a soiled bedspread. Because the items were returned, the charges were dropped. Ducky Holmes, manager of the Ducks and a frequent witness to Powell's seedy side, believed he would have taken the mattress if he could have fit it in his suitcase. This fairly established the character of this 11-year veteran of big-league play, a player who was destined to receive national fame and a big suspension by Kenesaw Mountain Landis for his racial intolerance. Powell was no friend of the African American.

During his tenure with the New York Yankees in 1938, Powell made insensitive remarks on the radio about African Americans. On July 29, the Yankees were in Chicago to start a three-day series against the White Sox. Before the game, Powell sat down with WGN announcer Bob Elson for some dugout chatter in a segment sponsored by Old Gold cigarettes. When asked what he did in the offseason to keep in shape, Powell stated, "I'm a policeman in Dayton, Ohio, and I keep in shape by cracking niggers over the head with my nightstick." Another reference in a *Chicago Defender* article said Elson asked, "How do you keep in trim during the winter months in order to keep up your batting average?" Powell responded, "Oh, that's easy, I'm a policeman, and I beat niggers over the head with my blackjack." There may have been a debate about Powell's exact words, but everyone agreed it was a negative exchange derived from ancient racial intimidation.[15]

The live broadcast was immediately yanked off the air, but a large number of people had been listening. Within hours, the station was deluged by thousands of irate callers, leading to a half-dozen on-air apologies. Officials at WGN said the spontaneous nature of the interview allowed for some remarks to get out of control.

Three African American men representing a local organization for which no name was given attended the baseball game on July 30, demanding Powell apologize publicly or be barred from baseball for life and kept where he would not have the opportunity to exhibit his ignorance. An edition of the *Defender* added, "Powell is a dangerous man to trust with a blackjack and revolver."[16] They demanded an apology but got none. Within days, the commissioner's office was swamped with angry calls, letters, and telegrams demanding that Powell, a native of Silver Spring, Maryland, be banned from baseball for life. What they got was double talk from the office, which added its own set of inconsistent racial ethics to the discussion.

Commissioner Landis, baseball's leading disciplinarian, released statements like, "Powell was alleged to have said," and "over the air in a so-called dugout interview," and added that the remark was "carelessly and not purposely made," before handing down a 10-day suspension—the first ever in the majors for an incident related to racial intolerance.

Powell awoke the next day to a national response. In his defense, Powell said he was "thoughtless." He sheepishly claimed that "he worked in a neighborhood entirely Negro in population and that he found some of the population tough to handle, [and] as cops will, had to use his billy." To this the *Defender* suggested,

> Jake Powell, the bully of baseball, insulted a race of 15,000,000 people last Friday. If black people realize the tremendous power of their dollars, if Dayton citizens employ their ballot correctly, they can make those suffer who continue Jake Powell in baseball and on the police force.[17]

The protesters were unappeased by the suspension, and they let Powell know it at every American League park when the punishment ended. In Washington, DC, someone hurled a soda pop bottle at him during the second game of a doubleheader at Griffith Stadium, which prompted Yankees manager Joe McCarthy to say he would continue to play the disgraced outfielder even if "they throw a million pop bottles at him." Shirley Povich, writing in the *Washington Post*, responded to the bottle throwing incident on August 17, stating McCarthy: "did not distinguish himself as the possessor of any great judicial mind yesterday. He might have been wiser than to start Jake Powell in the southernmost city in the league in the first game that Powell played since being suspended for disparaging remarks about the colored race in a radio interview. In Washington, unlike other league cities, colored fans are congregated chiefly in one sector of the park. They could have been expected to work up a fury against Powell. They did, too. Powell's return to the Yankees' lineup might easily have been delayed until the Yankees were in another park."

Back in New York a petition bearing 6,000 signatures demanded Powell receive a lifetime ban as they planned for a "Beer and Cigarette Holiday" boycott. In Harlem, where Yankee's owner Colonel Jacob Ruppert sold large amounts of his beer a "holiday" against the Colonel's suds, and a change in cigarette brands would be damaging. League officials and team owners publicly decried Powell's insensitive remark, making them vulnerable to a spate of caustic commentary in the press. The *New York Post* pointed out the hypocrisy in an editorial. "[The Owners] express outward horror at Powell's hasty and uncouth comment," related the *Post*. "Then they calmly concocted their own economic boycott against this minority people." [18]

As troubling as it was, the Powell incident did shine a spotlight on the major leagues' hiring practices; however, *Kansas City Call* sportswriter Ernest Brown Jr. and others wondered how many more "Powells" were employed by Major League Baseball:

With Negro sportswriters the country over attempting to bring pressure so that Negro ballplayers will be admitted to the big leagues, this was indeed a drastic setback. If this expression by any means typifies the type of baseball players that are now present in the big leagues, it will be some time before Negroes will have the doors of Major League Baseball opened to them.[19]

Westbrook Pegler, who spoke of no wrongs in 1934, during the Dean brothers' tour, had plenty to say about Powell four years later.

Powell was only giving expression in crude, brief wordage to the unspoken but inflexible policy of the Organized Baseball industry. Moreover, his remark was thoughtless and probably untrue, whereas the men who employ him and Judge Landis have given solemn study of the problem and confirmed their decision by their conduct.[20]

Overlooked by everyone was Powell's employment. Was he really a member of Dayton's law enforcement in 1934? It was penned in a *Wisconsin State Journal* article in 1942, that Powell had "recently took a civil-service examination for appointment to the Dayton police force."[21] Policeman or not, he was known to carry a gun, a weapon he later used to kill himself.

Ten years after his rant on the radio, Powell died of an apparent suicide. The deadly series of events leading up to the suicide occurred after he was charged with passing bad checks at a hotel in Washington, DC, where he and his mistress, Josephine Amber, had stayed. After several days in the hotel, a heads-up clerk became suspicious and called the bank from which the checks were drawn, only to find Powell had no account. When the pair attempted to leave, the clerk followed Powell and his lady friend to Union Station and called for the police. Detectives took Powell and his mistress into custody on November 4, 1948. She said they were to be married the next day in Rockville, Maryland, but the wedding had been delayed after she was informed that Jake had written $300 worth of rubber checks. While in the midst of his interrogation, Powell asked to speak to his lady friend alone in a nearby room. Call it white privilege or old-fashioned celebrity treatment, he was never frisked by the local police. A gun was still in his coat. Shortly thereafter he yelled, "To hell with it—I'm going to end it all." He whipped out a .25-caliber revolver from his pocket and shot himself twice in the chest and once in the right temple.[22] It is ironic, then, that Powell would be the first hitter Dizzy faced in his Baltimore outing, a game where there was no African American opponent.

The game started with Dizzy hurling two innings. He stayed in the contest long enough to be charged with the defeat. Powell, the first batter to face Dizzy, shot a drive down the line on a three–two count. As the ball rolled to the scoreboard, Powell scampered around the bases for a triple. Fisher walked, and Heffner struck out. Rubeling followed with a fly to right, which Daffy Dean reportedly lost in the glare of the lights and dropped, allowing a runner to score. Dizzy got mad and proceeded to strike out Buscher and then forced Peters to ground out to second for the third out. Between innings the brothers discussed Paul's blunder. "Diz were you sore when I dropped that fly ball?" Daffy asked. "Naw, I expected it," Dizzy responded. "If you couldn't pitch, you wouldn't ever be a ballplayer."[23]

In the next inning, Dizzy retired the side on six pitches—something he hadn't achieved against any of his African American opponents. After that inning, the Cardinals great refused to return to the mound. Taylor's article stressed Dizzy's exhaustion. When the crowd yelled for more of the antics they had read about in the newspapers, Dizzy shrugged his shoulders and related, "I'm tard. Can't a guy get tard? I'm goin' out and sleep in left field. You know if I wuzn't a pitcher I could play anywhere on the team. Me, I'm a natural-born ballplayer."[24]

From this point onward, Dizzy and Daffy paid the fans little attention, refusing to "perform any of the customary weird antics," declared an article in the Baltimore Sun.[25] Instead, Dizzy went to the outfield for four additional innings, leaving the game in the sixth. Paul started the game in left field, shifted over to right field when his brother stopped pitching, and remained in the game until the eighth inning. As they walked onto the field between innings, both were besieged at every step by autograph hounds until halfway through the ballgame, when they called a halt to further autograph signing.

Paul, still suffering from a sore arm, did not pitch. He said his arm was "slightly sore, about as it was in training camp, but that he was concerned about it since his stay in baseball depended upon its condition and he likes to play the game." Taylor wrote, "Even there, he was a total loss, dropping a fly ball in left field and, then to show no partiality, dropping another after moving over into right field."

Taylor informed his readership that the Cardinals' two best pitchers were "far from the form that won the World Series for St. Louis." The same article noted that, Henry Cappola, who pitched for the All-Stars against the Deans, and even Vic Keen, the former Cardinals hurler, in fact, had more stuff. Keen followed Dizzy to the mound for Cloverland and allowed three hits in four innings pitched. He struck out four.

Henry Peter Cappola pitched one of the best games by a white pitcher during the entire tour and was rewarded with the win. He struck out 11 of the 15 men who faced him. Of that total, one strikeout each of Dizzy and Daffy were included. Cappola would go on to play with the Washington Senators in 1935, and for a brief period in 1936. Melton, of the International League's Baltimore Orioles, followed him to the mound and allowed two additional hits in the three innings he pitched and struck out a trio of batters.

American League president Will Harridge was obviously sharpening his own ax when discussing his disapproval for barnstorming, as could be seen in the contradictory statements he released on the Associated Press wire. "Baseball gives the player every possible protection during the regular season," he announced. "The players are provided with the best of everything, food, hotel, railroads, and playing fields."[26] His statement, however, had left out the most important element, which was financial compensation. If everything was so good in the National and American Leagues, what he announced next made little sense. "As soon as the season ends," said Harridge, "many of them immediately rush off to play exhibition games on poor fields with poor accommodations and without proper supervision." Evidently Harridge had found an ally in Daffy Dean.

Paul continued to express his displeasure with the tour. In published reports he lent his approval to the proposal made by Harridge, which called for a ban on barnstorming by major-league players. Paul said, "He has no great desire for a huge amount of money but merely wants to earn enough to buy a place in Texas and live comfortably." Dizzy disagreed, saying, "These trips gave more people a chance to see them than would otherwise be the case."[27]

Now that it was reasonably assured that the Deans were not the dominant force, as previously reported, attendance totals dropped by two-thirds. Starting with Baltimore, where the crowd consisted of only 2,215 people, a daily decrease in attendance became the norm. The newspapers blamed the low attendance on the weather. In reality, there was much more to it—like the Deans' presupposed dominance, which had rarely manifested itself. The competition didn't seem to matter—their opponents were invisible, out of sight and out of mind for national recognition.

Dave Goodman. With the Dean All-Stars in Chicago, Goodman went 1-for-2 off Chet Brewer. In a career that lasted from 1934 to 1941, Goodman appeared in more than 866 games but never reached the major leagues. *From the author's collection*

William G. Harley. In addition to booking the Deans' All-Stars at his Chicago Mills Stadium, Harley also staged boxing events. *From the author's collection*

Paul "Daffy" Dean and Jay "Dizzy" Dean. In his *Wisconsin News* article Paul Purser critiqued the Dean brothers' rapid rise to fame. "Dizzy is a good egg," he wrote, "but he's been catapulted into fame so rapidly he doesn't know what it's all about." *From the author's collection*

Chet Brewer (1907–1990) and Thomas Jefferson "T. J." Young. Brewer was the ace of a Monarchs pitching staff that included Andy Cooper, Wilber "Bullet" Rogan, and Charlie Beverly. Cooper and Rogan are in the Baseball Hall of Fame. Brewer is not. *Courtesy of Maurice "Doolittle" Young, from the author's collection*

Carroll Ray Mothell (1897–1980) and Albert Dewey Creacy (1899–1984). The final games of Mothell's 11-year big-league career were against the Dean's All-Stars. Creacy, with the Philadelphia Stars in 1934, went 3-for-6, with a trio of runs scored against the Dean brothers' All-Stars. *Courtesy of Carroll Ray Mothell, from the author's collection*

Pat and Dizzy Dean in Bradenton, Florida. "Hundreds of letters were received from all parts of the country during the World's Series [requesting] that the Deans make an exhibition tour," said Pat. *From the author's collection*

Sam Levy (1895–1955). Levy seized on the Deans' visit to write dismissively about the brothers and their barnstorming in the *Milwaukee Journal*. Levy referred to the Monarchs just once and reminded his readers that they were a "Negro team." *From the author's collection*

Thomas Younger "T. Y." Baird (1885–1962). Tom always went by the initials T. Y. in an effort to conceal his middle name, which was Younger. Cole Younger, the famous Missouri outlaw, was his great uncle. *Courtesy of the Kansas Collection, Kenneth Spencer Research Library, University of Kansas*

Eddie Stumpf (1894–1978). The popular former-minor-league-ballplayer-turned-promoter was at one time a promising young catcher in the American Association. Stumpf was the local sponsor for Dizzy and Daffy's Milwaukee appearance. *From the author's collection*

(L to R) Frank Duncan (1903–1973), Jesse "Hoss" Walker (1912–1984), and Andrew Lewis Cooper (1898–1941). Cooper hurled at least three times against the Deans' All-Stars. By the tour's fifth game, Cooper's 15.1 innings tossed exceeded Dizzy's. No one was counting how many innings Cooper pitched, and his exhaustion was never mentioned by the media. *Courtesy of Bernice Duncan, from the author's collection*

Jay "Dizzy" Dean and Paul "Daffy" Dean. At Milwaukee, people demanded refunds when the brothers left earlier than the advance advertisements stated. *From the author's collection*

Clint Thomas (1896–1990), Clarence "Fats" Jenkins (1898–1968), Clyde Spearman (1912–1955). Thomas had two hits in the Deans' game at Brooklyn, New York. Spearman came to bat five times in the two games, having one hit and scoring twice. Jenkins missed both games. *From the author's collection*

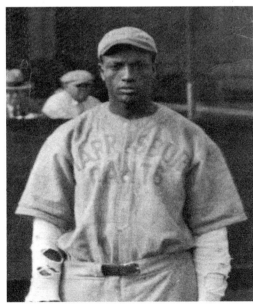

Walter "Rev." Cannady (1902–1981). In two games against the Deans' All-Stars Cannady batted .500, going 3-for-6 and scoring a run for the New York Black Yankees. *From the author's collection*

George Scales (1900–1976). Scales managed the New York Black Yankees during their two-game split with the Deans' All-Stars, in Brooklyn, New York, and Paterson, New Jersey. Scales spent more than a quarter-century in professional baseball. *Courtesy of the Tom Hardiman Collection*

Paul "Daffy" Dean. When Theron Wright, a United Press International correspondent, asked about splitting up the brothers' act, Paul shrugged and responded, "We'll go where they send us." *From the author's collection*

Kenesaw Mountain Landis (1866–1944). As a former federal judge Landis ruled against Jack Johnson in his fight against the Mann Act. That was before Landis became the first commissioner of Major League Baseball. *From the author's collection*

Ray Lambert Doan (1896–1969). Doan was in charge of the House of David teams east of the Mississippi. He was the creator of donkey baseball, where players rode donkeys. Doan also created another game played with the infielders and outfielders tied to goats. *Courtesy of the Musser Public Library, Oscar Grossheim Collection*

James Reston (1909–1995). His six-part 1934 story titled "These Incredible Deans" got a great response nationally on the Associated Press wire. He would have an outstanding 50-plus-year career at the *New York Times*, where he was twice awarded a Pulitzer Prize. *From the author's collection*

Dizzy Dean, holding twins Patricia and Virginia Lee, his godchildren. *From the author's collection*

Donald Stafford "Red" Kellett (1909–1970). Kellett, seen here in street clothes, was in Philadelphia with his mother for a ceremony honoring her son as the "Outstanding Athlete at the University of Pennsylvania for 1934." Kellett joined the Deans' All-Stars squad at Paterson, New Jersey. *From the author's collection*

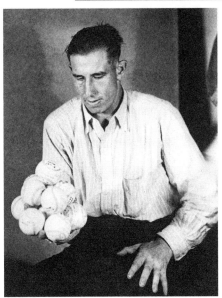

Elmer Monroe Dean (1909–1956). Everyone wanted a piece of the Dean family, which included hiring Dizzy and Daffy's older brother. Elmer was brought to St. Louis by Branch Rickey to sell peanuts on the recommendation of Fred Ankenman, president of the Houston Buffaloes. *Photograph courtesy of the Kansas Collection, Kenneth Spencer Research Library, University of Kansas*

Betty Holt (left) and Paul Dean. The caption on this photograph reads, "Two Winners." It was taken in St. Louis on October 5, 1934. From that point onward, Paul continually denied that Holt was his fiancée in numerous interviews. *From ACME Newspictures, author's collection*

Josh Gibson (1911–1947). "Gibson is perhaps the best natural hitter and the hardest slugger in Negro baseball," said an August 1932 edition of the *Pittsburgh Courier*. Gibson homered twice against the Deans' All-Stars. *Courtesy of Ted Page, from the author's collection*

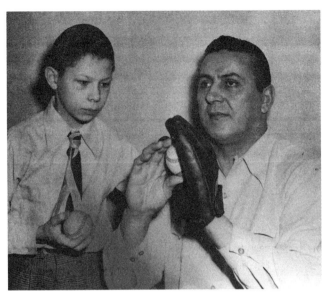

Julius "Moose" Solters (1906–1975) and son Joe. As one of Dizzy's Pittsburgh All-Stars, Solters tripled off Satchel Paige to drive in a run. In 1932, Solters led the Eastern League in RBIs when he posted 76 with Albany. *From the author's collection*

Elander Victor Harris (1905–1978). In 1931, he collected 52 hits in one stretch of 35 games. That year, Harris's multihit games accounted for 127 of his 156 total hits, leaving just 29 games in which he'd obtained one hit out of 107 games played. *Courtesy of Dorothy Harris, from the author's collection*

CHAPTER 11

Paterson, New Jersey

Night Lights and Greenbacks
Friday, October 19, 1934

The Black Yankees had whipped the Deans and their Bushwicks All-Stars in Brooklyn, and that victory prompted the *Paterson Morning Call* to write, "Taking everything in stride this season, as they have for the past three years, the Black Yankees appear to be one of the greatest Negro baseball teams of all time."[1] While they certainly weren't the greatest of "all time"—they weren't even the best of that season—no proof was provided to the affirmative. Writers at the *Evening Call* and *Paterson Morning News* thought well of the Yankees' high standing in baseball. Statements of this nature, nonetheless, allowed the newspapers to spin articles in a direction where such themes as white male chauvinism and social dominance would drive ticket sales and underline anything they wrote thereafter.

The slaughter suffered by the Deans in Brooklyn still lingered. Their currency as a social phenomenon had dimmed in the eyes of many as a result of the great defeat. The rematch, scheduled for a cold and balmy night in Paterson, New Jersey, did not help increase attendance totals. As fate would have it, the crowd shrunk to a few thousand on what promoters expected to be another record-setting evening. In Brooklyn, the *Daily Eagle* seemed to take delight in the low turnout and headlined the article "A Small Crowd of 3,500 Turned Out to See Dizzy and Daffy Perform."[2] It appeared to be another condescending attack poking fun at the Deans by the New York press. The *New York Times* made similar remarks about the crowd size.[3] The brothers' arrival in New Jersey was simultaneous with numerous national stories reverberating concerning the issue of barnstorming.

An October 19 edition of the *New York Times* and other national newspapers released comments by National League president John A. Heydler, American League president Will Harridge, and Paul Dean through the Associated Press wire. The article, an abysmal discourse in power and persuasion, served to electrify interest in the Dean brothers' barnstorming tour while leading some to fear that further All-Star tours of this nature might be banned.

Harridge was opposed to barnstorming. He said: "Major-league players owed it to their teams not to go barnstorming around the bushes." He cited the head injury suffered by Boston's Jimmie Foxx in the exhibition game at Winnipeg, Canada, and Paul Dean's sore shoulder as examples. Early reports of Foxx's injuries were full of doom and gloom. An article on the Associated Press wire from Seattle, dated October 16, said, "He was in no shape to play ball at Spokane yesterday but arrived there drowsy and wanted to sleep all the time," according to Herb Hunter, advance agent for the American League All-Star Team. "There is no chance for him to play here, and he may never don a uniform again."[4] Negative comments in the local newspapers and statements by the Deans failed to extol the benefits that barnstorming had provided for African American teams and players whose dire economic plight never entered the discussion. Even among major-league players, these extra paydays were welcomed. One could only imagine what they meant to players from the Negro major leagues.

Although he and his brother were making a small fortune by playing these barnstorming games, Daffy agreed with Harridge's negative stance against touring. "He [Daffy] doesn't like night baseball lights in his eyes or night weather on his arm," the article noted.[5] "Even Dean and Dean can't pitch as often as the fans want," Paul advised. "If there were three of us we couldn't fill all the outside engagements promoters make." They were obviously taking their cue from the St. Louis–based *Sporting News*, which warned players, "The night air is not like the day air; the man who goes to baseball after he has eaten a hearty meal is apt to have indigestion if he is nervous and excited."[6]

Heydler, of the National League, saw no reason to place a ban on barnstorming. "I can't see that it is a serious or grave matter," he said. "And unless a proposal for such a ban is forthcoming from the American League at the annual joint meeting, I am inclined to believe that our league will not touch the matter."[7] As Paul's statements were blowing up nationally, Paterson's two newspapers, the *Evening News* and *Morning Call*, were drumming up business locally. Hinchliffe Stadium was being readied as the Deans hit town. Their hotel headquarters was the posh Alexander Hamilton Hotel.

Buildup for the Dean's visit had started as early as October 15, with a photograph of Dizzy in the *Evening News*. On October 17, the *Evening News* announced, "Deans to pitch five innings here Friday."[8] The newspaper guaranteed Dizzy and Daffy would work five full innings of the regulation nine innings under the lights. For a second time, Robert Clark, Tex Barnett, Fats Jenkins, and Bill Holland were absent. This time it would cost the Black Yankees a win.

Johnny Bissett, in charge of putting the playing surface in order, worked assiduously inside and outside Hinchliffe Stadium. The stadium had no permanent lights, which prompted one local newspaper to proclaim, "The finest lighting system obtainable has been secured."[9] George Brooks, local sponsor of the game, ordered an additional 10 dozen baseballs—he wasn't going to have another night like the one in Oklahoma City, where baseballs disappeared so fast the game had to be halted after six frames.[10] An article penned by Theron Wright of United Press International captured the brothers in their talkative splendor.

When asked of their plans after the barnstorming tour and after a week in vaudeville, Daffy replied wittingly, "Two weeks in Houston, two months in Tampa, Florida, loafing in the sunshine and more loafing in the sunshine, or any place else wherever the loafing looks best, until spring training." Dizzy composed himself long enough to share, "We're sure of just one thing, we ain't gonna work no more'n we possibly can help after this trip is over. I've throwed so many baseballs the last three weeks I got myself windin' up in my sleep."

During the interview Daffy admitted his aching arm wasn't improving with these one-night stands throughout the United States. "It isn't any worse than it was last winter," he confessed, "but barnstorming doesn't help it."[11] Paul wanted nothing more than to quit the tour and leave for home, but Dizzy wouldn't let him upset the gravy train.

When asked how many games they expected to win the next year, Daffy jumped into verbal action. "We're going win all the games we can," he offered, "it may be five an' it may be 50." Daffy added, "Diz said we'd win 45 this year. We won 49 between us—30 for Diz and 19 for me. If we can do better next year, we will." When asked how tough the Tigers were in the World Series, Diz, always a sucker for media attention, laughed robustly. "They were tough for me," he joked. "But Paul—say, he just breezed through. They weren't none of 'em tough for him." Paul, sitting nearby, simply shook his head as he listened to his brother's rants. "I had good days," he said with a confident air—almost half that of the Diz. He continued, "Gehringer was the hardest one to get out, but Diz is right—none of 'em were very hard." The brothers had made similar statements in Brooklyn. "That Gehringer was the best Detroit hitter," Daffy remarked. "But then none of 'em gave me any real trouble. Hey Diz?" His older brother, seated nearby, chimed in, "No, none of 'em was real tough, like they thought they would be."[12]

The brothers kept boasting about their major-league feats; however, neither had boasted about their barnstorming achievements since Oklahoma City. They were silent for good reason, especially after they were handed a 6–0 shellacking.[13] Since Paterson had no formidable team, Nat Strong, who was getting a large piece of the Brooklyn Farmers action in New York and New Jersey, sent this team to represent the city. Unlike other cities, the promoters in Paterson offered every seat, both nonreserved and reserved, for the same price—55 cents—putting the game within financial reach of every fan. Tickets were sold on a first-come-first-served basis. The first batch of tickets disappeared like no one's business.

The October 17 headline in the *Evening News* read, "Black Yankees Priming to Batter Dean Brothers Friday." The article was subtitled "Outstanding Negro Nine Anxious to Prove Contention That Its Stars Can Hit Even the Best of Major League Hurling."[14] The statement was a familiar one that positioned African American players in a state of inferiority. The Deans had nothing to prove; society assumed they were good enough to manhandle the African American teams—it was a prevailing attitude in the era of segregated American baseball of the 1930s. The pressure was always on the Negro League team to show they could measure up to the standards of National and American League baseball. Pitting one race against the other was good newspaper copy and usually good for enhanced ticket sales.

Early on, ticket sales were brisk, but the momentum quickly slowed as the weather changed, temperatures dropped, and interest waned. George Brooks and Nat Strong had originally planned for a turn-away crowd; they were now forced to reconsider their efforts. Moving forward, every foreseeable angle would be used to promote the game. Some of the tactics were familiar; others were somewhat inimitable. Local newspapers compared the ability of the Black Yankees and their league against the Deans supposed "superiority" in the National League. They wrote that Ducky Medwick, a New Jersey boy, would be among the All-Stars. They advertised this event as the Dean brothers' only appearance in the state of New Jersey, while continually publicizing that both Deans would "take their turns" on the mound—in spite of Paul's highly publicized ailing wing.[15] They also promoted it as a home game for the Black Yankees, who visited the city often but were rarely bumped for a loss.

For the first time in their history, the Black Yankees had a "home ground," reported Rollo Wilson in a June 30, 1934, edition of the *Pittsburgh Courier*. "For the past five weeks they have been using Hinchliffe Stadium, Paterson, New Jersey, on Sundays and have played to crowds of 2,000 and more."[16] Among the teams defeated by the Black Yankees in Paterson were the Pittsburgh Crawfords, the Meadowbrooks, Grover Cleveland's House of David, the Cuban Stars, and the Brooklyn Farmers. In its October 19 installment, the *Evening News* advised, "The Black Yankees will have the same team that local baseball fans took such a fancy to in Saturday afternoon games at the Stadium."[17]

Manager George Scales had assembled a highly competitive team, and during the course of the summer this version of the Black Yankees continually improved—but they were not at full strength as they rolled into town. Missing from the lineup was catcher Robert Clark, pitcher Bill Holland, and others. Clint Thomas would remain at catcher, and John Beckwith, while not known for his speed, stayed in the outfield. Roy Williams, normally a pitcher, was also there to play right field. Scales decided to use his youngsters as pitchers in Paterson. It was a winning combination in Brooklyn, and he saw little reason for change. As skipper of the Yankees, Scales was not only a developer of young ballplayers, but also a player with many personal accolades on the field, particularly so in 1931, when he played for one of baseball's most outstanding teams, the Homestead Grays.

On July 8, 1931, Scales hit for the cycle, ripping a single, double, triple, and home run at Elizabethtown, Pennsylvania, in a Homestead Grays 15–7 win over the Klein Professionals.[18] It was just another day on the job for George Walter Scales of Talladega, Alabama. The newspapers, in their infinite wisdom, refused to discuss the African American player's college connections and other related history in drumming up interest for the big event. Subscribers to the local newspapers weren't able to read that George, at age 16, was selected by Talladega College to cover shortstop, or that shortly thereafter he began his professional career with the Montgomery, Alabama, Gray Sox. Players showered Scales with praise for his attributes as a fielder, as well as a hitter, but the *Paterson Evening News* and its rival, the *Paterson Morning Call*, only talked about the team collectively.

As one of baseball's leading second basemen, Scales could be compared with the likes of Charlie Gehringer. George had more power and more speed, and would get just as many extra-base hits. He was a brilliant leader of men schooled by some of the best coaches and managers in Negro baseball.

John F. Condon thought highly of Scales as a second baseman. Condon, a player who had witnessed the exploits of three famous Jacksons—Andrew,

Oscar, and Bob—as well as Sol White, William Selden, Clarence Williams, Charlie Grant, Bill Monroe, and others, called Scales the "peer of any of them." In building a case for Scales, Condon concluded, "It is true, Monroe, Grant, Harrison, and Clarence Williams were players par excellence in their respective positions, but Scales as a general player is to be considered favorably when the deadly parallel about stars is drawn."[19] George would have a long career as a manager in the Puerto Rican Winter League, where he led Ponce to six pennants and Caribbean Winter League titles.

When visiting Paterson, the Black Yankees used Hinchliffe Stadium as their home turf. The stadium was built to hold 10,000 when it opened July 8, 1932. Built in the shape of a large oval, it bore the last name of Paterson's mayor, John Hinchliffe, for whom it was christened. It served as a community stadium, hosting professional boxing, auto racing, midget car racing, and professional football games. The park also served as an arena for high school track events and community gatherings, for example, the homecoming of Paterson's own Lou Costello of Abbott and Costello Hollywood fame. Other Negro major-league teams played there often when the New York Black Yankees began to appear there regularly. In their game against the Deans, the Brooklyn Farmers squad, a white semiprofessional team booked by Strong, was there to back the big leaguers. Compared to Cleveland's League Park, where they were headed next, playing at the much smaller Hinchliffe Stadium was like tossing the ball around in a neighbor's backyard. The Black Yankees weren't strangers to the Brooklyn Farmers either.

During the summer of 1934, the two teams had battled on fairly even terms, with the Yankees taking five of the nine games played. When the Farmers swept a doubleheader from the Black Yankees on October 12, by 3–1 and 1–0 scores, respectively, the Brooklyn Daily Eagle proclaimed that they, not the Brooklyn Bushwicks, were the best semiprofessional team in New York. For this special game, the Farmers, augmented by several minor-league notables, some with past major-league experience, were more than ready and willing to play the Black Yanks.

Brooklyn's Farmers, now representing Paterson, had a park of their own in Brooklyn called Farmers Oval, located at Hughes and Schaelor Streets. Joe Fero was their manager. They were called Farmers, but there wasn't a plowboy or field hand among them. They were big city all the way. As was customary, the Deans' All-Stars sought players with major- and minor-league distinction to solidify their lineup. Along with promotions for the Deans, Joe Medwick, who was advertised as the game's left fielder—but never showed—was promoted heavily for his New Jersey ties. After his poor performance in Brooklyn, Joe wasn't needed, and he wasn't missed. There were others ready to take his place. Don Kellett, who had a cup of coffee with the Boston Red Sox, was one such candidate, as was Sol Mishkin, a Jew by birth. They were included with Brooklyn's regular roster of outfielder Jimmy "Lefty" Ashworth, a journeyman minor leaguer and pitcher; Dominic Torpe, who formerly played for the American Association Toledo Mudhens; Frank McGrea, a one-time Cleveland Indians catcher; and pitcher Eddie Bell. Infielder Joe Grosjean, who, in 1928, played with Greenville in the Eastern Carolina League, was there to back the Deans.

Donald Stafford Kellett's major-league career before his All-Stars appearance with the Deans wasn't eventful. In 1934, he appeared in six games as a shortstop for the Boston Red Sox. After his All-Stars appearance, he would go on to achieve many historical feats outside baseball. Kellett, nicknamed "Red," was a three-sport athlete, playing football, basketball, and baseball at the University of Pennsylvania. He would eventually become a sports broadcaster. In 1946, he became a play-by-play announcer for WFIL radio and television divisions in Philadelphia, where he announced football telecasts for the station. He also began broadcasting New York Knicks basketball games. In professional football, Kellett was named president and general manager of the National Football League Baltimore Colts and was a contender for the NFL commissioner's job in 1959. Solomon H. Mishkin was equally as famous in sports—mostly baseball.

One of the highlights of Sol Mishkin's career was his 1928 feature on a Zeenut baseball card while playing in the Pacific Coast League. He was said to be from Brooklyn, but another reference said he attended Hollywood High School and formerly attended Occidental College in the Eagle Rock area of Los Angeles. In 1932, Mishkin had led the Eastern League in runs scored, with 76.[20] He spent the 1934 season with Binghamton of the New York–Pennsylvania League, where his .338 average in 139 games ranked among the league leaders. On October 18, the *Brooklyn Daily Eagle* announced that he had been promoted to Baltimore in the International League. He would go on to spend a career in the minors, playing in the New England League, Eastern League, and International League. When his playing days were finished, he turned his skills to coaching. From 1943 to 1948 he managed New York Yankees' minor-league teams in the Ohio–Indiana Baseball League and the Canadian American League. In the 1950s, Mishkin took a job as head baseball coach at City College in New York. He was inducted into the City College Hall of Fame in 1977. Mishkin's appearance with the Deans was another career highlight.

Newspaper articles preceding the game and those that appeared afterward were loaded with rhetorical strategies. One such stated item appeared in an October 17 edition of the *Morning Call*. That article advised, "The Black Yankees, the colored players, will be out to prove that they can hit major-league pitching and hit it hard." The story stressed equality and inequality at the same time, as it suggested the African American men were working hard to prove their worth while saying nothing of the Dean brothers' preparation for the game.

When speaking of the Deans, the writer wrote with pride, stating, "They are still in top form and, loving the game as they do, are bearing down in all their exhibitions."[21] The Black Yankees had everything to prove, while the Deans played for the love of the game—is what the public was coerced into believing. Dizzy and Daffy were considered superior to the Black Yankees' best hitters and pitchers by virtue of being in the white major leagues. The newspaper made it clear that it was a test for one team and a fun and frolicking money-making opportunity for the other.

By game time, almost 2,000 fans had paid their way into the Hinchliffe Stadium to see the Black Yankees "try their best"—or merely see Dizzy and Daffy put their whammy on the Negroes. This was the total number given to the press by the *Evening News* and *Morning Call*.[22] The *New York Times*, in its report on the game, swelled the audience to 3,500.[23] Also in question was the starting pitcher for the Black Yankees. There were several to choose from, and one might have been the Dean's equal, 20 years earlier, had baseball's color line been lifted. The Yankees' choice to hurl some of the game was another Arkansas-born pitcher named Connie Rector.

Rector was among a group of outstanding ballplayers to enter Negro professional baseball from Arkadelphia, Arkansas, and for a long time he was a leading pitcher in the Negro major leagues. The aging Rector, 42 when he took the mound against the Deans, began regional play with the Arkadelphia Cuban Giants in 1910. He was no more Cuban than Caucasian. Dizzy was born in 1910, which meant Rector had been tossing a baseball for Dizzy's entire natural-born life, and he remained in baseball long enough to battle the Diz in his prime.

Like Dizzy, Rector worked his way up the ranks in Texas, but the black boy came by way of the segregated Texas Colored League—Dizzy came by way of the white minors. Rector had been a member of the Black Panthers, the baseball team in Fort Worth, not the revolutionary black nationalist and socialist organization of the 1960s, before joining the great migration of athletes leaving Texas for more prosperous fields in the North. He came North to join Edward Bolden's Hilldale club of Darby, Pennsylvania, in 1920. Before coming to the Black Yankees, he adorned the rosters of such legendary teams as the Brooklyn Royal Giants (1923–1926), New York Lincoln Giants (1928–1930), and New York Harlem Stars, forerunner of the Black Yankees.

According to folklore, Josh Gibson, the baby-faced slugger of the Pittsburgh Crawfords, was the only man to ever hit a home run out of old Yankee Stadium. Supposedly the record shot was hit off Connie Rector. It's a damn shame that newspaper accounts of the home run were never written. Rector's appearance against Dizzy also lacks documentation. We can't tell how many innings he pitched or how many hits he allowed. The box score showed that Rector issued no walks and failed to strike out any batters. It is impossible to know exactly what the legendary Arkadelphia pitcher achieved against his Hall of Fame rival. Dizzy's feats are much better chronicled.

Dizzy came to the mound in the fourth inning. Walter "Rev" Cannady, the first batter, singled. As not to have a repeat of the Brooklyn game, Dizzy whiffed John Beckwith on a trio of pitches with his famed "fog ball." He proceeded to strike out Frank Blake for the second out. Roy Williams lifted a lollipop fly to Daffy in right field, which the younger Dean caught to end the fourth inning. The Cardinals ace retuned to pitch the fifth inning. Dizzy started on a good note when he struck out Clyde Spearman, the first batter. Bill Yancey, next up, hit a humpback liner to Paul in right field, and the younger Dean corralled the ball for the second out. Unfortunately, the *Evening News* and *Morning Call* disagreed on what happened next.

The *Morning Call* advised that Dizzy "made a barehanded stop, read the signatures on the ball, and tossed to first base in plenty of time to retire Scales."[24] The *Evening News* reported, "C. [Clint] Thomas grounded to Dizzy, who caught the ball in his bare hand, played around with it a couple of seconds, and then threw to the first baseman for the putout."[25] An examination of the box score showed it was clearly Thomas, not Scales, who hit the comebacker to Dizzy and was thrown out trying to run out an infield hit. It was the final out. Both newspapers agreed that seven batters faced Dizzy, with three striking out and one hitting safely. Two men, it could clearly be seen, towered above the rest in the Black Yankees' lineup—Cannady and Thomas.

Walter "Rev" Cannady went 2-for-3, with a double and a run scored, and was perfect in the field, accepting seven chances without an error. "Show Boat" Thomas logged three singles in four at-bats while recording nine putouts and four assists, with only one error on defense. For Dizzy's All-Stars, Lefty Ashworth went 3-for-5, with a double and a perfect outing in the outfield. Three different All-Stars pitchers combined for nine strikeouts. Blake, the Black Yankees starting pitcher, and Bell, the All-Stars starter, were given the won–lost decisions.

The articles in the *Morning Call* and *Evening News* were insufficient for following much of the scoring sequences for either team. The details needed to track the game were co-opted and simply not printed. Other than the "five-run splurge" by the Deans' All-Stars in the seventh frame, few details were provided. Fortunately, much can be gleaned from two existing box scores, one printed in Brooklyn and another in Paterson from the two games.

According to these box scores, five different Black Yankees scored runs: Clyde Spearman, "Rev" Cannady, John Beckwith, Frank Blake, and Clint Thomas. Three different players, Thomas, Cannady, and John Stanley, obtained hits off Dizzy, while a total of six players obtained hits in both games—three of whom were Beckwith, as well as Thomas and Blake, obtaining two hits each. In two games against Dizzy's All-Stars, Black Yankees batters obtained 17 hits, 4 doubles, and 2 triples, compared to 19 hits, 2 doubles, and no triples for the Deans' All-Stars. For a second consecutive game, Thomas played catcher—obviously not his best position but certainly a position his durability allowed him to play on that day. He finished the game without a passed ball, and no one stole a base.

A lack of photographic images has been overlooked as a powerful tool of subliminal persuasion. As tools of prejudice, photos were certainly effective in Paterson, where images of the Deans were in abundance. The *Evening News* printed numerous photographs of Dizzy; Daffy; Pat; and Albert, Dizzy and Daffy's father. There were photographs of the family seated at a table; "pretty" Betty Holt; Dizzy as a baby; Dizzy, Daffy, and Elmer as children; Dizzy and Daffy with Albert; Pat Dean kissing Dizzy; Paul in a pitching pose; Dizzy and Daffy standing with Sportsman's Park in the foreground; and Dizzy and Daffy with Benny Borgmann, a former teammate of Paul's on the Columbus team, who lived in Paterson. These photographs ran for eight consecutive days. The New York Black Yankees, described by the *Morning Call* as one of the "greatest Negro baseball teams of all time," never had the pleasure of seeing themselves in print during the exhibitions with the Deans.[26] They weren't pictured at all—not once in the great buildup for the game or after.

The Dean brothers' appearances in Brooklyn and Paterson would be the final baseball events scheduled in Nathaniel Colvin Strong's long promoting career. The nefarious owner and promoter died at his home, 15 The Court, Rochelle Park, on the evening of January 10, 1935, from an apparent heart attack. He died after leaving his office in the Pulitzer Building on Park Row. Witnesses said he "appeared to be in great health."[27] Strong was a native of Manhattan, where he attended City College. He took an interest in baseball and, in 1913, purchased the Brooklyn Royal Giants. His association with Max Rosner's Bushwicks started prior to 1920. Additionally, Strong booked the Bay Parkways, New York Black Yankees, Brooklyn Farmers, and Cuban Stars. He was a longtime member of the New York Athletic Club and was 61 years old at the time of his passing.

Unsung at the time was Lawrence Eugene Doby, a soon-to-be student at Paterson's Eastside High School. He was born in Camden, South Carolina, but moved to Paterson in 1937, at age 14. He became a celebrated multisport athlete. After graduation he accepted an athletic scholarship to Long Island University. In 1947, he would jump from the Newark Eagles of the Negro major leagues to the American League Cleveland Indians, without spending a day in the minor leagues, and there he stayed. On March 3, 1998, at age 74, he was selected by a committee of veterans to be enshrined in the Baseball Hall of Fame.

CHAPTER 12

~

Cleveland, Ohio

World's Greatest Chunkers
Saturday, October 21, 1934

Arriving in Cleveland, Ohio, on the 8:00 a.m. train at the Pennsylvania Railroad depot on Euclid Avenue and East 55th Street, the Dean brothers' caravan exited immediately for their temporary offices at the Hotel Cleveland located near the Union Station terminal.[1] Gus Greenlee's Crawfords came storming into town from Pittsburgh, rolling the entire distance of 133 miles in a bus on four well-worn tires. It was a short jog from Pittsburgh, and upon reaching town, they washed up at the minority-owned Majestic Hotel. The Crawfords' movements before the game were obscure. Yet, Dizzy and Daffy's day of activities was well publicized.

They enjoyed the luxury of a hotel filled with splendor from bottom to top. Their rooms overlooked Cleveland's Lake Erie and other sites of this majestic American city. The Deans were living a life of luxury and leisure at a time when these same hotels barred members of the Pittsburgh Crawfords for unprincipled reasons related to race. It could have been discouraging, but men of color, travelers of highways, small towns, and large cities, had decided long before then not to be disheartened. They were, first and foremost, professional baseball players, paid athletes with talent and skills. Their ability sustained their existence.

The Deans benefited from this censorship. Yet, by virtue of their very presence on the field, they were lending their talents to expose this oppression. It was a public act of defiance that uncovered countless shortcomings in an American democracy perpetuated by racism and white privilege. This may explain why Bill Dvorak of the *Cleveland Press* and Alex Zirin and

Roelif Loveland, both of the *Cleveland Plain Dealer*, didn't treat the affair as a regulation game; they obviously weren't champions of race relations, certainly not in 1934. In the African American–owned *Cleveland Call and Post*, the Crawfords versus the Deans was front-page fodder. "Dizzy Dean to Meet Satchel Paige Sunday," rocked their page-one headline on October 20.[2] African American baseball fans had waited years for such an event after enduring more than a decade of failed Negro League franchises. Cleveland was a tough place to turn a profit.

In 1921, George J. Tate entered the Cleveland Tate Stars into the Negro National League with journeyman players and a newly built park. Tate Field, their home park, had "deficiencies," decreed Bill Finger in the *Call and Post*. "The grandstand had a roof over it but no paint. More of the seats were in the sun than should have been. The diamond was skinned, with the outfield in bad condition."[3] Their games weren't drawing well, so the 5 percent commission that Tate paid to league head Rube Foster for weekday games and the 7½ percent that was charged for holiday games soon drove the new owner out of baseball. He struggled for two seasons before going under.

The Cleveland Browns were next. They played at Hooper's Field in 1924. Because of the team's unpredictable income, the league was forced to pay for most of their transportation, supplies, and umpiring costs. The Browns went defunct after one summer. Others came and went; the 1926 Cleveland Elites, 1927 Cleveland Hornets, and 1928 Cleveland Tigers all failed. "For several years," an article stated, "the city has remained in the league as a total loss and a burden on the rest of the owners."[4] Tom Wilson, a Southerner, came north from Nashville, Tennessee, to create the Cleveland Cubs in 1931, but just like the others, he found the sledding too rough. His team took a nosedive in midsummer, but Wilson kept Paige on his payroll. During the winter of 1933–1934, Paige was the main attraction for Wilson's Elite Giants in California. "Satchel Paige mesmerized the Los Angeles populace," wrote author William McNeil, "fans and media alike, with his extraordinary pitching skills, his showmanship on the mound, and his charismatic personality off the field."[5] W. P. Young created a second version of the Cleveland Cubs in 1932, and entered the team in the failed East–West League. He lasted just a half-season before going into financial ruin. The baseball situation in Cleveland hadn't improved in 1934.

In 1934, the Red Sox became Cleveland's newest venture into professional baseball. Co-owned by Prentice Byrd, the Red Sox featured Oklahoma's Wilson Redus, former Monarchs outfielder LeRoy Taylor, and infielder Pat Patterson—both of Wiley College. They also had pitcher Bill Byrd, among others. Home games were played at the Indians' League Park at East 66th Street and Lexington Avenue in the Hough area of Cleveland. The *Call and Post* proclaimed, "Many of the abovementioned athletes can equal that displayed every day at League Park."[6] Unfortunately, there were few home games to display their talent.

In the season's Opening Day doubleheader, on May 27, the Red Sox lost to Tom Wilson's Nashville Elites 12–0 and 6–1, respectively. The Red Sox didn't play another game in Cleveland until early August. In those games, they beat the Newark Dodgers, 13–7, but lost the next contest by a 12–10 score. In mid-August, they captured a home doubleheader from the Birmingham Black Barons by 5–0 and 7–2 scores. Finally, on Labor Day, the Red Sox split a twin bill against the Homestead Grays. A complaint in the *Call and Post* said, "Just five league contests were played by the hometown entry in this so-called league. Two wins to three losses is their record."[7] The author counted eight Negro major-league games prior to the Crawfords' arrival on a cloudy Saturday, October 21. One of the top local promoters was an African American named Dave Hawkins, but he was sick with an illness and unable to participate in the scheduling of more games. His sickness did not keep him from writing letters.

The former boxing promoter for Wilson Yarbo had an equal fondness for baseball. It was Hawkins who staged the successful game in July 1933, between the Pittsburgh Crawfords and Chicago American Giants at Cleveland's League Park.[8] Hawkins had to resort to letters in the fall of 1934, as he was suffering from tuberculosis and confined to the sanitarium at Oteen, North Carolina. The happy advance agent's written language was always colorful and full of ginger. He had lots to say about racial inequality but saved his best comments for baseball and Satchel Paige.

"When white promoters kept African American fighters off the local [fight] cards," one publication noted, "Dave Hawkins, the black trainer and manager, turned racial exclusion in the ring into a civil rights issue."[9] When speaking of baseball and the Monarchs ace, Hawkins suggested, "The last time I saw long, lean, and lanky Chet Brewer, he was in Cleveland misusing and abusing the batters of the then Cleveland Stars. That day he was like a holy lady in corset, righteous and in form." When speaking of Webster McDonald, the Philadelphia Stars ace, he said, "His fastball was almost inaudible to the naked eye. I like McDonald because he will pitch to all of them; he's a great big husky guy with enough nerve to go bear hunting in the fog." Hawkins also thought highly of Willie Foster and, on his behalf, added, "Foster is the hottest thing next to a barbecued missionary. His curveball bends like a pretzel with the cramps, and he knows how to keep it away from the part of the bat that has the hits on it."[10] When speaking of the Crawfords ace, the great promoter advised,

> With all due bows to the wows named Dean, I would like to favor the good folks of Cleveland with the tip that the Pittsburgh Crawfords, the world's greatest gang of sundown baseballers, have an onion chucker who is only missing the chucking throne by a shade, pigmentarily speaking. I refer to Mistah Satchel (Black Mathewson) Paige. His manager says that Satch's Sunday speed will be too swift for ordinary horse-hide balls, so he is having some made up out of racehorse hides—race horses that have defuncted.[11]

Few could deny that this promoter had all of the color of Dizzy with some to spare. When in Cleveland, the Crawfords lodged at the segregated Hotel Majestic. Situated on the corners of East 55th Street and Central, in the Cedar-Central neighborhood, the 250-room Hotel Majestic was the place to see and be seen; however, it wasn't always a safe place to lodge. Sam Brown, traveling secretary for the Memphis Red Sox, was robbed of his billfold and $17 cash in one of the hotel's hallways. The stickup guys hadn't realized that Brown kept the team's money in his money belt, which contained $1,500 at the time of the heist.[12]

Earlier in the day there was a threat of rain. Intermittent showers and drizzle fell throughout the morning. It could have been a disastrous day, but it was not, at least not for Satchel Paige. Dizzy and Daffy took advantage of the gloomy morning by resting up for the game, which was slated to start at 2:30 p.m. The threat of bad weather and slippery conditions on the field kept the brothers inside. They relaxed at the Hotel Cleveland, using this rare opportunity to catch up on some well-deserved sleep. A reporter from the *Plain Dealer* was their only visitor. Around midday, there was a knock on the door. It was a salesman hocking liniment. Loveland, the reporter, listened and published what he heard.

"Jerome!" shouted Pat to her half-woke husband, "I think you'd better go to the door. I think this is that liniment salesman. He's been trying to see you ever since we got into town." Dizzy peaked through the cracked-open door, and indeed it was the salesman staring him in the eye. "I don't want any liniment," said Diz. "Ah, you don't know the merits of this liniment," said the persnickety salesman as he earnestly pitched his ointment. "Honest, mister," said Dizzy. "I don't want any." The salesman, determined to move his product, kept insisting he buy some. "Oh, Mr. Dean, this is a peculiarity effective liniment." Dizzy fired back, "I never use liniment." "No!" said the befuddled salesman, "No," said Dizzy, "Just hot water and alcohol."[13] The door closed, and the sales call ended. The evening start time also opened an opportunity for the bothers to meet a young fan. Dizzy and Daffy visited the young lad they had met in Detroit during the World Series at his home. The boy had been injured in a bicycle accident after returning home to Cleveland.

Both brothers visited nine-year-old Henry Zucker. The house was located at 3113 Washington Boulevard in Cleveland Heights. The boy was bedfast and wearing a cast to mend a broken leg when the brothers walked into the room. Daffy, in a playful mood, entered first. "Who am I?" asked a smiling Daffy. "You are 'Dizzy,'" the confused lad responded. "Oh," said Daffy, pointing to Dizzy, who was just walking into the room. "You mean him!" After a bit of nondescript conversation, the young boy asked Daffy if he preferred baseball over football. "I like baseball," said Daffy. "There's no money in football. All you do is get killed." They autographed a ball for their young admirer before departing for League Park. As they stepped out the door, Dizzy turned back and howled, "We'll be seeing you next year." The young boy asked, "Where?" Dizzy said, "Here! Right here in Cleveland. Cleveland is going to win the American League pennant next year, and we'll be up to play 'em for the world's championship."[14] The brothers ducked into a car and headed to the ball field, where they were to battle the Pittsburgh Crawfords.

The Pittsburgh Crawfords were owned by enterprising Gus Greenlee and managed by Oscar Charleston. They were the best Negro major-league team of the entire 1934 season. Greenlee had a policy of shuffling players as though they were a deck of cards, a process that began midway through the 1931 season with the signing of Satchel Paige. He had funds to back his new franchise, and many players took notice. In 1932, he reeled in pitchers Roy Williams and Ted Radcliffe, catcher Josh Gibson, outfielder Ambrose Reid, and Charleston from Cumberland Posey's Homestead Grays, to put his team on a high track at the start of the season. He entered his new team into the Negro Southern League when Posey blocked his entry into the Northern East–West circuit.

John L. Clark was hired as the Crawfords traveling secretary. That same year, Greenlee signed Charlie Beverly and Frank Duncan, both members of the 1934 Kansas City Monarchs. Also signed were Jake Stevens of the 1934 Philadelphia Stars; Walter "Rev" Cannady of the 1934 New York Black Yankees; and Clyde Spearman, also of the 1934 Black Yankees. These men, all former Crawfords, had battled against the Deans during their barnstorming tour as members of other teams. When these players made their exit from Greenlee's Crawfords, they were replaced with others who were just as talented. Greenlee, the baseball executive, was making his mark in sporting circles, and his legacy would not be denied.

William Augustus "Gus" Greenlee was to baseball in the eastern United States what Wilkinson and Baird had been to the West—compressed into fewer years. Gus was pushing the narrative on integration and opening doors to modern big-league stadiums—something Wilkinson and Baird avoided. He believed that black teams had to play in big-league stadiums and found some interested participants at New York's Yankee Stadium and Comiskey Park in Chicago. This ideology led to his creation of the East–West All-Star Game, which he took to Chicago, and the popular four-team doubleheaders, which he brought to New York. In addition, he built and owned his own ball diamond, Greenlee Field, in Pittsburgh, and managed a stable of professional boxers that included, most notably, John Henry Lewis, light heavyweight champion of the world. He scheduled baseball, football, and boxing at Greenlee Field, and staged the park's first night baseball game in 1932, the same year it opened. Gus was years ahead of others in his expectation for the players' and the leagues' future finances. He was the 1930s answer to the Jews and their agencies, which sought to control Negro professional sports—mainly baseball—in towns and cities throughout the nation. Greenlee's ventures made amazing profits, too. When push came to shove, he reached into his own pockets and financed events with cash from his Pittsburgh-based numbers operation. Charleston, his manager, was equally as charismatic.

Oscar Charleston was in the second season of a six-year tenure as Crawfords manager. In speaking of Charleston, the Crawfords legendary manager, Edward Bolden of the Philadelphia Stars said he "is without a technical fault and is near perfect as ballplayers ever come." Nicknamed the "Hoosier Comet," Charleston had been a professional athlete since 1915. He could be temperamental, hard-boiled, and fiery, but he was also blessed with as much talent as any left-handed hitting outfielder in baseball's long history. "Charleston was as mean as anyone who ever lived," said Ted Page of his teammate on the 1931 Homestead Grays. "He'd spike you without ever trying." Charleston's hands were massive and strong. Bill Harvey, who pitched for the Crawfords under Charleston, said Oscar "could take a ball in his hands and loosen the cover."[15] As a manager, he was a leader of men at all times. Oscar was married only once, to Jane B. Howard of Harrisburg, Pennsylvania, in 1925, but his real love appeared to be baseball, through and through down to his bones.

Charleston never played in the National or American Leagues. Yet, major-league players knew him well. In 1920 and 1921, he played in exhibition games against the St. Louis Cardinals; in 1922, he saw action in games against the Detroit Tigers; in 1923, he battled against a contingent of St. Louis Browns; and in 1926, he appeared in a contest against the Philadelphia Athletics. He had also played against Jimmie Foxx's All-Stars in 1930, and would engage Casey Stengel's All-Stars in 1932. Facing the Deans wasn't anything special—intimidation wasn't in his DNA.

Greenlee's version of the 1934 Pittsburgh Crawfords was a prolific group of ballplayers, every bit as imposing as any National or American League team. This was no ordinary roster of ballplayers. They had power in an aging Charleston and a youthful Josh Gibson; speed in James "Cool Papa" Bell and Ted Page; defense in Anthony Cooper and Judy Johnson; and a wonderful second-string receiver named Bill Perkins, who most assuredly would have been a starter on any other team. With seven great pitchers—Paige, Burt Hunter, Sam Streeter, Ernest "Spoon" Carter, Harry Kincannon, Leroy Matlock, and Wesley Barrow—they had a crop of hurlers who would have commanded big salaries in the National and American Leagues. And there were other position players, like John Henry Russell, Curtis "Popsicle" Harris, and Vic Harris, who made this Crawfords team formidable. That they were easily the most prominent team in the East was made more obvious by the way they dominated their foes. The Crawfords publicity man was Roy Sparrow. He was doing his best to put this team on par with major-league teams.

Sparrow, who was very high on Paige, called him the "black original of Dizzy Dean." "He is just as dizzy, just as modest, and probably faster," he said. The Crawfords publicity expert added, "Satchel once took Lefty Grove in his prime for seven out of seven. Hack Wilson describes Satchel as a guy that 'winds up with a baseball and pitches a pea.'" For those willing to listen longer, Sparrow warned, "Satchel can pitch a pellet all afternoon without it even being nicked."[16] What was ironic about the article, which appeared in the *Milwaukee Journal Sentinel*, was that it appeared next to an article titled "Daffy and Dizzy Here Monday." This was about as good as it got as an equalizer of race relations in a daily newspaper.

Greenlee's Crawfords were manhandling Nat Strong's best teams in and around New York—which included Max Rosner's Bushwicks, his trophy team. On June 24, the Crawfords beat the Bushwicks twice, by 9–6 and 6–4, respectively, at Dexter Park. They returned on July 30, to take another doubleheader from Rosner's team, when Paige won the 7–3 opener and Leroy Matlock applied an 8–0 whitewash in the nightcap. On September 23, they captured yet another doubleheader from the Bushwicks. In one of the games, Paige edged Rube Chambers, 1–0. The Crawfords hadn't lost a game in New York, nor had they lost in Cleveland or Columbus or a dozen other cities. They wouldn't succumb to the Rosenblums either, although second baseman

Chester Williams, shortstop Leroy Morney, pitcher Matlock, and outfielder Jimmy Crutchfield were absent.

The Deans, as pitching importations for the local Rosenblums team, were there to play the Crawfords at League Park, home of the Cleveland Indians. Tickets, which could be purchased for as low as 30 cents for general admission and $1.20 for reserved seats, were moving well. The *Plain Dealer* announced that "advance sale has been very encouraging."[17]

The Rosies were national Class-A Baseball Federation champions, a title they had won by virtue of their big victory against Birmingham, Alabama, at the national amateur championships, held in Youngstown, Ohio. They succeeded Youngtown's St. Stanislaus as national champs. They were selected to back the Deans a week earlier when Billy Evans consented to use of the Indians' baseball grounds to promoter and local businessman Max Rosenblum. Others involved in the promotion were L. R. Williams, a former publicity man of the Cleveland Red Sox; John Clark, a Negro League representative; Gus Greenlee, owner of the Pittsburgh Crawfords; and Ray L. Doan, manager of the Deans. Evans's 1934 Cleveland Indians, with a record of 85 wins and 69 losses, had finished a distant third in the American League—16 games out of first—behind the pennant-winning Detroit Tigers. They welcomed the extra income this game would produce. Cleveland's League Park was to become the Dean brothers' second stop at a major-league stadium but not the last, as Pittsburgh's Forbes Field was two games in the future. They were expecting another big crowd at the Indians' American League facility, where a capacity crowd was a meager 21,000.

A crowd, estimated to be between 10,000 and 12,000, according to various newspaper sources, assured that Dizzy and Daffy would earn their minimum guarantee. The long-awaited event pitted the much-publicized Paige, with his string of strikeouts, against Dizzy, with his great number of big-league wins. The game was well promoted; it was the match many wished to see but couldn't until now.

The Deans' visit also served as an opportunity to flip the script on race and culture. Whether it was on purpose or purely an accident, people witnessed something they hadn't expected. They watched as the Deans played the role of two jesters turned loose for a day, clowning around on the field in ways that were usually attributed to Negro teams. It was an abrupt departure from all things major league. Historically, crowds expected to see these kinds of colorful activities performed at Negro major-league games. They had to so they could draw bigger crowds. Newspapers of the time pounced on these stereotypes, taking great delight in their headlines. "Come See the Funniest Game of the Year," or "Such and Such Team to Play Clown Game," were among their favorites. At any rate, no one had expected to see such buffoonery from the Deans. These same reporters took extreme interest in the Deans' actions.

Once the game began, Dizzy looked like an understudy next to Satchel, and the writers quickly surveyed the results. They used Dizzy's comic relief as an excuse for not taking this ballgame seriously. The *Plain Dealer* tagged them as "two clowns turned loose for a day."[18] Dizzy and Daffy were also feeling the fallout from their boisterous ways. The headlines said plenty about their self-proclaimed fame and why their constant blabbing was resented by other ballplayers. Some were now speaking out publicly.

The tour arrived in Cleveland, hot on the heels of a revealing story in the *Kansas City Times*, roasting the brothers, primarily Dizzy, for their arrogance. The negative comments were spewed from the lips of Elden Auker, a rookie with an ax to grind as Detroit's losing hurler in Game 7 of the 1934 World Series. Auker had lots to say while dismissing the Deans. He told the interviewer he didn't think the Deans were such great pitchers, "despite what they did in the World Series." He added, "They're good but not nearly so good as they say they are. Babe Ruth, Walter Johnson, Lefty Grove, and the other great stars of baseball got their publicity from what they did. The Deans get most of theirs from what they say about themselves." Auker decreed he could name a "dozen American League pitchers he would rather have" and dropped the names of Detroit's Tommy Bridges and Oral Hildebrand of Cleveland as two fine examples. "I don't even think they are so fast. Why Schoolboy Rowe is two and one-half times as fast. I'm not considered fast myself, but I'm as fast as Dizzy."[19] Each of the pitchers Auker proclaimed as the equal of the Deans was in the American or National League. He wasn't arguing for Ted Trent, Slim Jones, Webster McDonald, Andy Cooper, Chet Brewer, or Charlie Beverly—he didn't know them and probably hadn't heard of them either.

When Dizzy was asked if he considered Auker a good pitcher, he said, "Sure, Elden is a fine boy and a good pitcher. You bet." The *Star* noted, "Their bombast, which has been taken by many with good-natured tolerance and by others with admiration, is resented by this former Kansas State Wildcat, principally because there is none of this type of loquaciousness in Auker."[20] Auker also might have named Paige had he been white and in the American League. Paige wasn't as chatty or prone to braggadocio as Dizzy in 1934, a year when his pitching was certainly something worth yakking about.

As great as Dizzy and Daffy had been in the National League, Paige had been equally as prolific in other baseball circles. Satchel was beating teams with such pageantry that it appeared many batters were honored to have struck out. Hitters marveled at the speed of his fastball, which seemingly exploded on batters like a combustible liquid; his control was remarkable. The public had little to compare him to, as he was unique in ability and looks. Many chose to compare him to Stepin Fetchit, a popular race actor in the movies. Both were lanky and dark, and both believed in everything in moderation. The comparisons, however, stopped there. By virtue of the publicity presented to him in the *Denver Post* Tournament, Satchel's prowess and community support had spread to the affirmative in ways Fetchit would never achieve. Similarly to the Deans, Paige, of Mobile, Alabama, was a right-handed-hitting and throwing Southern-born pitcher with little formal education. He had made his initial mark in the east with Cleveland in 1931. Two regional games against the Homestead Grays, while playing for the Cleveland Cubs and later the Pittsburgh Crawfords, stood out.

On June 20, 1931, Paige was matched in a pitchers battle against "Smokey Joe" Williams. With Paige's Cubs trailing 6–3, their game was halted by rain, with torrents in heavy display.[21] The Cubs folded shortly thereafter, and a newfound freedom allowed Paige to join any team he chose. He picked the Pittsburgh Crawfords in midseason. As a member of this team on August 1, 1931, he beat the Grays in relief of Pittsburgh's Harry Kincannon, four innings deep into a tie game at McKeesport, Pennsylvania, in a 10–7 final.[22] Paige returned to Cleveland in the fall of 1932, to defeat a team of major-league All-Stars. Facing a team that included Larry French, Hack Wilson, Tom Padden, Roy Parmelee, and others, he struck out 15 and won by a gaping 10–2 score. His reoccurring appearances in Cleveland kept his name in good standing with local fans. Paige let it be known in his own words, "Old Diz was one boy I wanted to run up against."[23]

When Paige and his Crawfords teammates arrived in Cleveland, local fans were waiting on pins and needles to see the man who replaced Rube Foster, who had died in 1930, as the most important figure among Negro major-league players. His arrival in town was not cause for celebration in the daily media. There were no feature stories, and most of all, there were no photographs announcing his presence. His arrival came unceremoniously and without celebration. Cleveland's daily newspapers had cast their lots with the Deans and their temporary teammates, the all-white Rosenblums, in hopes of a win.

A *Call and Post* article written by William Finger named other members of Max Rosenblum's team. The October 20 article noted, "Jack Bender, veteran of many black and white games, [Johnny] Mihalic, Hugger, [John] Hvisdos, Heiden, Ken Hogan, and the rest of the sandlot champs will be on hand for Max's team. These fellows in other cities would be classed as semipro, being the equal of many minor-league teams."[24] Several of the Dean brothers'

Rosenblums teammates would have significant careers in the major leagues—namely Frank Joseph Doljack, Joseph Franklin Vosmik, and Johnny Michael Mihalic. Other stories in the *Plain Dealer* said Jack Bender would make an appearance at shortstop and Earl Schamp would pitch.[25]

Nicknamed the Rosies, several were future big leaguers. Doljack, a light-hitting Slovenian outfielder, appeared in 56 games for the 1934 Detroit Tigers, batting .233. A month after his appearance with the Deans' All-Stars, he was dealt to Milwaukee's American Association Brewers. He didn't return to the majors until 1943, when he got into three games for the Cleveland Indians. Vosmik was a .341 batter for the Cleveland Indians who appeared in 104 American League games in 1934. Joe's parents were immigrants from Bohemia. Mihalic, an infielder, batted .278 in 157 games for Chattanooga in the Southern Association in a performance that landed him with Washington's American League Senators in 1935. Hogan made it out of the minor leagues but had a short-lived career in the majors.

Born October 9, 1902, in Cleveland, Kenny "Ken" Hogan was an outfielder of great ability and a speedy runner. His father's family migrated from England; his mother was the daughter of Irish immigrants.[26] As a stellar ballplayer among the semiprofessionals, he was spotted by the Cincinnati Reds. He came to the big-league club late in the 1921 campaign and got into the last game of the season. The following spring, Hogan dropped out of St. Ignatius College to join the Reds, assuming he had made the team. Much to his disappointment, he was released before the start of league play but signed to a second big-league contract by the American League Indians in late 1922. He reported to the big-league team in 1923, but his release came too quickly. After appearing in one game as a pinch-runner, his contract was optioned to the Nebraska State League, where he batted .299 in 105 games. Although Hogan played many years in the minors and numerous seasons among the semiprofessionals, he never made it back to the majors. His major-league career was all of four games in three seasons.

Other members of the Rosies were Jimmy Wasdell, Lloyd Russell, and James Schamp. Wasdell would join the Washington Senators in 1937. Russell played two games in the majors with Cleveland in 1938. At least two members of Dizzy's All-Stars had played with the Indians in 1934—pitcher Ralph Winegarner, who was in the game at Wichita, Kansas, and catcher Bob Garbark, who would join the Deans a day later in Columbus, Ohio.

It was obvious that Dizzy wanted to beat the Crawfords. He was growing weary of being on the short end of these exhibitions, night after night. During the game, a writer overheard Dizzy telling his teammates, "Hell, they only got four runs. We can beat 'em yet." Dizzy and Daffy blended in with the rest of the locals, acting as if they had known them for a lifetime. The *Cleveland Press* noted, "Diz proved himself a regular fellow, and before the game was over he was calling members of the Rosies by their first names"—names the daily newspapers never bothered to publicize before or after the game. Dizzy, however, was limited to two, maybe three innings a night. He needed his teammates to battle back.

John Hvisdos drew the starting assignment, and the All-Stars quickly fell behind in the scoring. Dizzy began the game in the outfield and remained there through the first, second, and third innings. He broke a baseball rule when he left the game to warm up in the fourth but returned in the next frame, pitching the fifth, sixth, and seventh innings. Daffy entered the game as a right fielder in the fourth and remained in the game until the seventh inning. He did not pitch. When Hvisdos turned the pitching chores over to Dizzy, the Crawfords were leading, 3–0. Dizzy entered to great applause, but his effectiveness was questionable and didn't provoke many cheers from the crowd. He allowed four hits and a run during his brief time on the mound. His myth of racial superiority was being destroyed in every at-bat. The *Plain Dealer* article related, "Dizzy didn't 'fog 'em over' very much of the time."[27] The newspapers' lousy job of covering the Crawfords as hitters illustrated how little they valued the entire team. Vic Harris was able to share at least one of his at-bats in a one-on-one interview with John Holway some years later.

Harris recalled,

> I just took picks on his [Dizzy's] first pitch. I hit a triple, and he watched me all around the bases. He called me a name, no dirty name—and said, "You'll never hit my first pitch again." Laughing, you know. It tickled him. So when I came back to bat, he threw one over the top of my head, way up—wasn't trying to hit me, just kidding.[28]

Things got interesting when the first batter to face Diz in the fifth turned out to be the light-hitting Satch, who promptly drove one of Dean's swift ones to center for a double. The next two outs were easy, but veteran Oscar Charleston drilled a single to left and Satchel crossed home plate easily.[29] Dizzy was fairly nondescript until he caught Henry Russell in a rundown between first and second base to end the sixth inning; the crowd applauded the Cardinals' effort—but rarely did they cheer Dizzy's pitching—and laughed at other events. They screamed and howled, especially when Dizzy coached first base.

While Dizzy and Daffy were putting on their comedy routine, Paige wasn't yakking or blabbing. He was keeping the Rosenblums in check by throwing smoke at the locals, while suffering another case of bad journalism. The reports in the dailies advised that Paige pitched six innings of no-hit ball and struck out 13 of the 18 men he faced.[30] Who he struck out was never printed. The articles did, however, make special mention that Dizzy, Daffy, and Frank Doljack were included in the total, which left 10 unaccounted for and without mention.[31] Newt Allen of the Monarchs wanted it to be known that, "Satchel kicked his foot way up here like Dizzy Dean, then he'd throw around that foot. Half the guys were hitting at that foot coming up."[32]

Dizzy and Daffy were reserved during the game, noted a reporter in the *Plain Dealer*. They "observed the work of Mr. Satchel Paige," as one player was retired after the other on strikeouts. "That guy must have something," said Daffy in amazement. "Yeah, he's got a hell of a fastball. Yes, sir, he's got a fastball."[33]

There was no box score to confirm anyone's participation—black or white. In Kansas City, the *Call* assured its readers, "Mister Paige didn't let the white boys see the ball he was throwing—at least while it was crossing the plate. 'Twas a wonder that the umpire saw it."[34] Finger's article, titled "Satchel Paige Dominates Game," in the *Call and Post*, provided important details that went missing in other publications. It was the *Call and Post* that advised, "The largest crowd ever to see a colored ball team in action in Cleveland witnessed Leroy stealing the show from the Deans."[35] Finger's article also announced, "Dizzy and Paul gave fans a show for their money." Additional details in the article said, "Jerome (Diz) hurled four cantos, being nicked for one run and four hits. Hvisdos, starting Rosie pitcher, gave up three runs; Schamp finished the contest." Finger also informed readers that "Tarleton Strong" finished the game for the Crawfords after Paige's exit and that the Rosenblums only run was scored on an errant throw to the plate.

In his "Passing in Review" column for the *Call and Post*, Finger spoke brashly and boldly about the Crawfords. "In our opinion Manager Charleston should have let Satchel continue," wrote Finger. "Had Paige been successful in blanking all batters who faced him, all over the country daily papers would have recorded the feat. This would prove a boon for Negro baseball."[36] The writer hadn't taken a full account of the situation; Charleston had.

As a veteran of many interracial contests, he knew how the daily press functioned, and it resulted in an ingenious tactic. In a strategy that was unexpected, Crawfords management decided to pit Satchel against the Deans for three consecutive days. Instead of pitching an entire game on one night, they limited his innings so they could continue to promote the matchup for two more games. There was also the case of Paul. Satchel hadn't faced him yet. In addition, there was also the final game of the tour—the Pittsburgh showdown in the Crawfords' hometown. Finger wrote that he had overheard a white fan remark that the Crawfords were really a big-league club. The Rosies didn't stand a chance. The white fans were convinced of the African American team's ability—but the daily newspapers, where the so-called experts loomed, remained in denial and printed little.

Dvorak acknowledged Paige in as few words as possible. "Paige is a great pitcher," he admitted. "His chief misfortune is in having been born on the wrong side of the railroad tracks in Birmingham, [Alabama]."[37] People of this generation knew exactly what the writer was saying. In most U.S. cities and towns, the African American population generally lived on the older, run-down side of the railroad tracks, where whites originally lived before moving to more affluent parts of the town on the other side of the tracks. The dividing line, the barrier called segregation, came right down the middle of most towns in the form of a railroad track. Paige's "misfortune" wasn't a misfortune at all, and it had little to do with the railroads. The reality was that Paige's exclusion from the American and National Leagues had nothing to do with where he was born. It had everything thing to do with his race. In other Cleveland dailies, much more attention was paid to Dizzy and Daffy's clowning antics.

It was evident that Dizzy had perfected a formula to amuse the crowds. He used humor to turn potential customers into loyal supporters. While visiting Cleveland, he used slapstick as a form of comic relief, effectively clowning around better than he pitched, and the fans accepted it. Here are just a few examples:

- He openly gave his brother an earful for not catching a fly ball, which dropped for a single after it smashed against the right-field wall. The ball was several feet over Daffy's head, and there was no way this catch could have been made. Dizzy used this opportunity to berate his bother for missing the ball. It was all in fun; the crowd laughed until they were holding their sides.
- Dizzy replicated Satchel Paige's windmill windup, and the crowd "loved it." An amused Roelif Loveland wrote in his *Plain Dealer* column, "[Dizzy's] arm darned near did fly off."[38]
- Dizzy was coaching first base when Daffy singled off Strong. Usurping the rules of the game, Diz called time and went after a bottle of soda for his brother. After a brief conversation, they flipped positions. Dizzy became the baserunner and his brother the first-base coach. A few pitches later, Diz was advancing on a pop fly, which was caught by Henry Russell of the Crawfords. Without delay, Dizzy dashed back to first base, but

the ball arrived first and he was doubled up. Not to be outdone, the Diz made a neat hook slide, which garnered much applause from the crowd.
• Dizzy also created an imaginary rhubarb with the umpire. The phony temper tantrum was all in fun, and each time the crowd roared with jubilation.

In effect, Dizzy and Daffy were playing fast and loose with Alexander Cartwright rules of baseball. And at the finish the Deans were rushed by hundreds of autograph hounds. They signed everything put before them—especially Dizzy. Zirin said they signed hundreds of balls and scorecards. Dvorak advised that "Dizzy Dean autographs" were "as common in town today as three-cent postage stamps." [39] When Loveland asked about all the items he had signed, Diz had plenty to say.

"Get tired [of] doing that?" he was asked.
"Yeah, drive[s] you nuts."
Yet, without whimpering or bragging or telling how good he was, he kept right at it, signing "Dizzy Dean, Dizzy Dean, Dizzy Dean."[40]

Something amazing also happened to Satchel, but it was never reported in the local dailies. Finger wrote in the minority weekly, "When Paige retired, he too was kept on the field, affixing his signature to enraptured fans' scorecards for 15 minutes."[41] Many fans had read about Satchel's exploits, but usually in a most unfavorable way. The negative imagery was often soft and subtle:

Satchel is a long, slim, lazy-looking flinger who virtually hands an invisible ball to the catcher. And he says he can work every day using only the fast one but needs a day of rest when he is up against a string of tough left-handers and has to bear down with his hook. Satchel, as you might guess, is named for his feet.[42]

Still, the autographing presented a special moment, something that hadn't happened to this extent in previous interracial contests. Paige, for one day, matched Dizzy's celebrity with his own.

Although exhaustion was a common theme among the writers, back at the hotel Dizzy continued to tell reporters he was "having a great time with this tour." It didn't keep the negative news from being reported. One report said he was 15 pounds lighter because of the heavy rubber undershirt he insisted on wearing during games to sweat off weight. It was doubtful that he had lost that much weight, and Dizzy certainly wasn't wearing the reducing shirt for free. He was being paid by the Barr Rubber Products Company. The younger Dean wasn't endorsing much of anything and wanted to go home. Reporters overheard him saying "it was senseless to waste himself in [these] exhibitions."[43] Pat Dean's quotes were made out to be equally negative.

Pat gave a revealing interview to reporters, claiming she was "maid, valet, and masseuse" for brothers who are like "two kids." Doan, who was handling the day-to-day business, demanded that the brothers and Dizzy's wife share one room to keep down expenses. Pat was obviously frustrated by the arrangements. She told Loveland of the *Plain Dealer*,

> They can't find the soap. They can't find the towels. If Dizzy goes in to bathe, he forgets to take his slippers. If he remembers his slippers he forgets his bath robe. He's always running out of shirts. His brother's just as bad. I don't know how they'd get along at all if I weren't here to tell them where things were.[44]

The Deans weren't nearly as helpless on a baseball diamond.

On the field, Dizzy and Daffy were a hit. Behind the scenes, however, it was becoming more difficult to get the brothers to comply with simple requests. Dizzy refused to take a rubdown after the game, and neither bothered to change into their street clothes at League Park.[45] At the brothers' insistence, they were driven back to the Cleveland Hotel in their soiled Cardinals baseball uniforms, where they undressed in the privacy of their rooms with no less than a $3,000 lump sum as their cut from the Cleveland visit, probably hidden away in Pat's handbag or perhaps safely tucked away in the dingy uniforms they refused to surrender. Paige got national publicity for his performance. The *Chicago Defender* headlined one of its articles "Satchel Paige Hands Beating to Dizzy Dean."[46] The *Call and Post* openly admitted that these African American Stars were being shortchanged.

> Colored diamond stars don't receive one-hundredth of the write-ups given their contemporary white brother, who is no better than the sepian. This super play-up builds in everybody's mind the superiority of the white players. Denied access to this by lack of money invested in Negro baseball comparable to that of white, our Paiges never get their due. Nor do they receive the opportunities to face complete teams where the alibi of an outfit not used to playing with each other can be resorted to when the [Afro] American clan is victorious.[47]

Little did they know, Mr. Leroy "Satchel" Paige was about to hurl on three consecutive days—in Cleveland, Columbus, and Pittsburgh.

~

CHAPTER 13

Columbus, Ohio

Plenty Daffy and Almost Dizzy
Sunday, October 22, 1934

As the tour rolled into Columbus, Ohio, for game two of the heavily touted Dizzy Dean versus Satchel Paige/Pittsburgh Crawfords matchup, the excitement continued to build. A *Columbus Dispatch* headline proclaimed, "Dizzy Dean to Be Opposed by Page."[1] They may have spelled Satchel's last name incorrectly—a journalism error that appeared to be widespread in 1934—but the spirit of the promotion was clearly evident. The *Pittsburgh Courier* said, "There should be more fireworks than one sees on the glorious Fourth."[2] Ray L. Doan raved, "I thought that Lindy [Charles A. Lindbergh] was popular when he came back after his Atlantic flight, but you have no idea the crowds that daily almost mobbed Dizzy and Paul."[3]

Ohio fans wanted to see the much-anticipated pitchers' duel that had been steadily building since Chicago, where Paige was first advertised as facing the Deans. Dizzy had battled Paige the night before in Cleveland, a war Paige easily won. As usual, there was little time for rest. And, as was always the case, exhaustion was only afflicting the Deans. The weary brothers rested and relaxed in well-publicized segregated hotels. Where the Crawfords roomed during their visit or how they felt about the announcements was no one's business. There was no mention of where they stayed in the media. The Deans gave a series of interviews at the Neil House Hotel, which appeared in local Columbus newspapers. In those articles, they announced that the Dizzy versus Satchel duel was off—but a Daffy versus Satchel duel was on.

The Capital City game at Columbus was, without question, the leading topic of the day at radio station WBNS and in local newspapers. It was a hot commodity. Yet, the night was too cool for baseball. A weeklong sampling of cold weather took top billing as fans chose not to show in great numbers. Slow ticket sales at Ben Ratner's Athletic Supply and Tyler's Community Pharmacy, absent the raving demand that had occurred in other cities, made for a disappointing turnout.[4] Not so surprisingly, Paige upstaged the younger Dean in front of those who braved the elements to see the star-studded affair.

The tour, now down to its final two days, was cause for some moderation. When the Deans checked in at the Neil House Hotel early Monday morning, they appeared tranquil and a tad chattier. Most of the tour was behind them, and they were beginning to relax in their posh surroundings when they observed something on the end table. "They saw us coming I guess when they sold us these rooms" said one of the Deans. "That radio, now. You put a quarter in it, and it plays five minutes. You can get a regular radio put in here for 50 cents. We made 'em put in the 50-cent kind."[5]

The Columbus newspapers figured people wanted to read more about Daffy than Dizzy, because of Paul's connection with the city. He had played with the Columbus Red Birds in 1933, and his supposed fiancée, Betty Holt, resided in the city. An article in the *Dispatch* included a hand-drawn insert of Miss Holt with a picture of Paul, who they called, "modest, handsome, and the most eligible member of the family."[6] It appeared in print along with Dizzy, Pat Dean, and a photograph of their father, Albert Dean. The media was seemingly making Holt a family member when she and Paul weren't even engaged. Two months later, Holt, age 19 and a student at Ohio State University, conceded the romance when Paul married another, Dorothy Sandusky, also age 19. "I wish him luck," were her final words. Of Paul's new bride it was written,

> The marriage culminated a two months' courtship, which started as Paul Dean returned from his and his brother Dizzy's conquest of the Detroit Tigers in the World Series. Dean, however, had known his bride for three years, but in her words, "He only started going with me a couple of months ago."[7]

The article never mentioned the barnstorming tour.

It is also ironic that Satchel Paige was married on October 26, to Janet Howard, in Pittsburgh. Theirs was a big celebration at Greenlee's Crawford Grill, where many received the charming couple. Paige's marriage proposal, engagement, and eventual tying of the knot, even with all of his popularity, didn't garner a fraction of the attention this one daily newspaper gave to Paul's imaginary engagement to Holt. And on the evening of his marriage, Paige signed a two-year contract with the Crawfords during the banquet to honor the newlyweds.[8] None of the Columbus newspapers made mention of Paige's marriage and signing, but they did make note of the Dean brothers' 53 wins during the season of 1934 and called them the "most impressive brother act ever."[9] On the other side of the ledger, reporters in the *Dispatch* and *Columbus Citizen* continued to slander the Deans for their unique brand of Southern dialect.

As the brothers relaxed, sprawled out on a sofa in the hotel lobby, Daffy did most of the chatting with reporters. It was a sort of homecoming for him. During the 1933 season, he compiled a 22–7 won–lost record, led the league with 222 strikeouts, and carried the Red Birds to the Junior World Series championship.[10] The year before, 1932, he led the circuit with 169 strikeouts.[11] "Ah'm plenty glad this trip is about ovah," he told a reporter from the *Citizen*, "and so is Diz. Wer're both all tiahed out. My ahm is soah, but a'hm gonna pitch two innings tonight. An's Diz will be out there too."[12] He had plenty to say about his nickname, too.

"I don't like this 'Daffy' business, because I ain't that way at all," proclaimed Paul to a writer from the *Dispatch*. "Now take 'Diz' here, that's a good name for him, and all the ballplayers call him that, but me—they just call me Paul because that's my name." Explaining further Paul said,

> Early this spring when we were down in Florida, some of these sportswriters started to call me "Harpo," but it didn't stick. Nothing'll stick 'cept just plain "Paul." I wouldn't mind being called "Dazzy" because I dazzles 'em. But I dunno. It doesn't make any difference what they call us, just so the people drop their money at the gate. Just call me for dinner and I'll be satisfied.[13]

Dizzy rarely talked during the Columbus visit, but when called upon he cut loose. "If Paul can win 30 games next year," bragged a puffed up Diz, "the Dean boys will win 60 for the Cardinals."[14] At about that time, Doan chimed in with another local event. "The Kiwanis Club wants you boys to have lunch with 'em this noon charged the promoter," he said. The response, in unison from both Deans was, "Is it free?" It was free, and the answer was a straightforward "no."[15]

On this night, their obstacle would be the Crawfords of Pittsburgh. The Deans' chance of winning in Columbus was enhanced significantly because of the All-Stars that supported them.

With the much-anticipated Dizzy versus Satchel mound duel delayed for another day, it was Daffy's turn to work against the Crawfords. The pairing brought together two of the season's most outstanding pitchers. Paul was the only pitcher in the National or American League to hurl a no-hitter in 1934, a feat he had accomplished on September 21, in a game against the

Brooklyn Dodgers. Paul's no-hitter was widely publicized. There hadn't been a no-hitter pitched in either the league since 1931. Leo Durocher, shortstop and captain of the Cardinals, told reporters after the game, "Last spring Dizzy said that he and Paul would win 45 games between them. We thought he was crazy. This is the 45th—Dizzy won his 27th, Paul won his 18th today—but even Dizzy wasn't dizzy enough to predict that the 45th would be a no-hitter."[16] Black men were achieving similar feats in their league, but these achievements were hidden in plain sight. They were gifted men with little to no publicity.

Satchel had accomplished a similar feat in his league, with practically none of the national attention. He pitched a no-hitter on July 4, 1934, against the Homestead Grays, at Greenlee Field, striking out 17 batters in the process. The *Pittsburgh Courier* wrote, "Paige was the first pitcher to hold a Grays' team hitless. Several others have held them to a few hits, but to shut the door in their faces for nine innings is something unheard-of before."[17] Paige's no-hit game was witnessed by thousands. The holiday doubleheader drew 12,000 to Greenlee Field, while a National League game at Pittsburgh's Forbes Field drew 11,000 for a Pirates–Reds Fourth of July offering. This demonstrated the drawing power of Paige, the Crawfords, and Greenlee Field. Both Paul Dean and Paige had tossed no-hit games in 1932.

Paige had tossed another no-hitter, this one against the New York Black Yankees at Pittsburgh's Greenlee Field on July 8, 1932. He struck out 11 batters in that game and chipped in with a pair of hits, one a double, in his 6–0 win against John "Neck" Stanley. It was one of those exceptional occurrences when the pitcher obtained more hits as a batter than he allowed from the mound.[18] By contrast, Paul had also pitched a no-hitter on August 30, 1932, in a night stint with the Columbus Red Birds against Kansas City's American Association Blues.[19]

News of Paige's no-hit victories had circulated among the African American communities only. Outside of these segregated communities, there was no national significance attached to his no-hitters. On the other hand, Daffy's no-hit wins were national news in newspapers throughout the United States.

Accolades or not, less than 2,000 shivering fans were interested enough to show up to watch the baseball game in weather more suited for hockey or football. Red Bird Stadium, which could hold 17,500 when full, wasn't even close to capacity on this night. The cool and extreme temperatures kept attendance totals down in spite of a hearty newspaper and radio push. In Pittsburgh, the *Courier* had tagged the series as the "dream games," in which Negro baseball's two greatest pitchers, Paige and "Country" Jones, were to oppose the big leagues' two most famous luminaries, Dizzy and Daffy Dean.[20]

The *Courier* proclaimed that record crowds were expected to turn out to see these superstars in action. In that same edition, Harry Beale, traveling secretary for the Pittsburgh Crawfords, selected a 1934 African American "Dream Team."[21] Members of the elite squad included players from the Crawfords, New York Black Yankees, Philadelphia Stars, and Monarchs. Dizzy and Daffy had faced many of them during their barnstorming tour and witnessed firsthand why Beale made these selections.

Harry Beale's selections of All-Stars featured the Crawfords Josh Gibson at catcher, Vic Harris in left field, Curtis Harris at utility, and Satchel Paige as one of the pitchers. Jud Wilson, of the Philadelphia Stars, was selected to play third base, and the Stars Country Jones was named as a pitcher. Black Yankees outfielder Clint Thomas was selected for right field; Chet Brewer, a pitcher for the Kansas City Monarchs, along with Ted Trent of the American Giants, also made the list. The remainder of Beale's team included Buck Leonard, Sammy Hughes, Willie Wells, and Turkey Stearns. Of the 13 players listed, nine would face the Deans in head-to-head competition in the fall of 1934. There were three other All-Stars team selections making the rounds, one by Tex Burnett of the Black Yankees, one by umpire Bert Gholston, and another by Cumberland Posey of the Homestead Grays, highlighting the best of 1934.

When Burnett put pencil to paper to select his All-Stars for 1934, five of the men on his list of 12 had played against the Deans. His list included Josh Gibson, Country Jones, Chet Brewer, Carroll Mothell, and Jud Wilson. Of Gholston's All-Star selections, 10 had faced the Deans. Among his pitching selections, five total, Satchel Paige, William Bell of the Crawfords, Slim Jones, Bob Evans of Newark, and Webster McDonald, three would defeat Dean All-Star teams.[22] Posey's list of 1934 African American stars had similar results.

Of the 17 players listed among Posey's elite players, 11 had been in games against Dizzy and Daffy. His list included Josh Gibson, T. J. Young, Satchel Paige, Country Jones, Ted Trent, Chet Brewer, Andy Cooper, Paul Stevens, George Scales, Jud Wilson, and Vic Harris. Five players—Gibson, Jones, Brewer, Paige, and Wilson—appeared on everyone's list as the best of 1934. Walter "Buck" Leonard was the only player to appear on everyone's list and not face the Deans in 1934. It was evident that Dizzy and Daffy were seeing the best of the best when it came to African American talent, and they had suffered dearly in the dealings.

On the field, the much-anticipated "best rookie pitcher," Paul Dean, winner of two World Series games, and Satchel Paige, the "most effective and colorful pitcher in colored ball today," as he was called by Dan Burley in the *Baltimore Afro-American*, were preparing to start for their respective teams.

The Deans' Columbus All-Stars had serious name recognition. They were selected and managed by Estel Crabtree. At least two of the All-Stars had been in the white major leagues during the 1934 season—outfielder Daniel "Danny" Taylor of the Brooklyn Dodgers and Robert "Bob" Garback, a catcher with Cleveland's American League Indians. In 120 games with the Dodgers, Taylor obtained 129 hits and batted .299. Garback had appeared in only five American League games following his call-up from the Toledo Mud Hens, where his batting average was a neat .341 in 59 American Association games. First baseman Minor Wilson Heath, known to everyone as "Mickey," had played in the National League with Cincinnati during the 1931 and 1932 seasons. He was coming off a 1934 season where he had batted .280 and led the Columbus Red Birds with 29 home runs. He helped lead the Red Birds to a Junior World Series win.[23] Henry "Nick" Cullop, another member of the championship Columbus team, also joined Dizzy's All-Stars.

Henry Nicholas Cullop's career in Minor League Baseball was more than ordinary—it was extraordinary. If there was such a thing as a hall of fame for minor leaguers, he might have been the first player inducted. Born on October 16, 1900, in the small town of Weldon Spring, Missouri, just outside of St. Louis, he ranks first on the all-time minor-league list for career RBI, with 1857, and third on the list for minor-league home runs. In his minor-league career, which spanned from 1920 to 1944, he hit 420 home runs, which included a career-high 54 in 1930, for the American Association Minneapolis Millers.[24] Bill James, writing in his *Historical Baseball Abstract*, called Cullop the "best minor-league player" of the 1930s.[25]

Cullop was both a hard-throwing pitcher and an outfielder who hit for power.[26] From 1920 to 1927, his pitching record was 49 wins and 49 losses. In 1920 alone, he won 19 games. At the same time, he was one of his league's better long-ball hitters. In the minors, Cullop had 12 seasons of 20 or more homers. In various American League trials with the Yankees, Indians, Senators, and Dodgers, he was a huge disappointment. His big-league total for home runs was only 11. In 1934, he would launch 27 round-trippers for the Columbus Red Birds.[27] The two American Association sluggers, Heath and Cullop, were joined by a pair of International League stars.

Harold "Hal" King, an infielder for the Montreal Royals, and Oliver Angelo "Ollie" Carnegie, an outfielder for the Buffalo Bisons, were both listed among the Deans' All-Stars. King, age 26, had appeared in 142 games with Montreal, where he averaged a hit per game to finish with 144. He also batted .291. Carnegie, the son of Italian parents, had been playing professionally since 1922. At age 35, he was having another superb year. He appeared in 120 games, batted .335, and homered 31 times.[28] At shortstop, they hired

Elmer Trapp, a rising International League prospect for the Albany Senators. He spent most of the 1934 summer in the Southern Association, where he had played in 109 games for Little Rock's Travelers, batting .287 in 422 official at-bats. Pitcher Bob Kline, equally as recognized in local baseball circles, was signed to pitch as the Dean brothers' relief. He was associated with various minor-league teams.

Big Robert "Bob" Kline, at 6-foot-3, was a bear of a man. His almost 250 pounds of flesh was there and ready to relieve Dizzy or Daffy if needed. Bob, born in Enterprise, Ohio, in 1909, was the son of German Irish parents.[29] In 1930, he had posted a 23–9 record for the Class-B Erie Sailors, working an amazing 305 innings. It led to his one-game appearance with the American League Boston Red Sox late in the year. He remained with the Red Sox in 1931, pitching in 28 games, while recording a 5–5 record, and was still there in 1932 and 1933, when he posted consecutive 11–13 and 7–8 records. That winter, he was dealt to the Athletics in a trade that involved Hall of Fame pitcher "Lefty" Grove. Kline's 1934 season had been a smorgasbord of sorts. He had pitched for Chattanooga in the Southern League and both the Philadelphia Athletics and Washington Senators of the American League, to finish with a combined 13–5 won–loss record before returning home to Columbus to join Dizzy's All-Stars. Dizzy and Daffy's new teammates, Taylor, Garback, Heath, and Cullop, may have been major leaguers at one time or another, but they struggled to put baseballs into play against the Crawfords Satchel Paige and Wesley Barrow.

In the first three innings, only two of the Deans' All-Stars managed to hit their way on base. Paige pitched shutout ball, allowing two hits and striking out nine All-Stars. In his write-up for the *Dispatch*, Frank M. Colley took special note of the third inning. He wrote that Paige "walked the first three men in the third and then breezed the third strike past the next three batters."[30] Colley failed to mention who the batters were, and never once did he suggest that Paige deliberately walked the bases loaded. In 1948, Ray L. Doan, in an interview with *Sporting News*, changed the narrative. It was he who started the folklore surrounding Paige by saying the pitcher loaded the bases intentionally and struck out the side. He said that Paige had "struck out Mickey Heath, Danny Taylor, and Nick Cullop in succession."[31] Nothing of the sort was printed in 1934 by the Columbus newspapers. It was evident that Paige hadn't been scored on in his first nine innings against the Deans' All-Stars—six innings in Cleveland, three innings in Columbus—while striking out 22 batters—a fact the local newspapers also missed.

Performance-wise, all of Paige's outs at Columbus resulted from strikeouts, and the list of fatalities included Heath, Cullop, Gibson, Taylor, Trapp,

Carnegie, and Daffy Dean; he struck out Heath and Cullop twice. Paige ordinarily threaded a needle with his pitches, but he wasn't as accurate as usual on this day. He walked Gibson, Taylor, and King twice. The two hits obtained off Satchel belonged to Carnegie and Garback—both were obtained in the second inning. It was, however, a fine start for Paige but not one of his best. There are lots of stories surrounding the Paige mystique, and many are yet to be told. James "Cool Papa" Bell, his teammate and roommate on the Crawfords, had seen other days when Paige's pitching wasn't at its best and the incidents that followed. Bell recalled,

> Satchel was pitching to Henry Williams of the American Giants, and he blazed a pitch inside and hit the batter. Then the next hitter, Mitchell Murray, said, "You better not hit me." Of course, Satchel did just that by putting one in Murray's ribs. Murray, hot and irritated, chased Satchel into center field. When he couldn't catch the pitcher, Murray threw the bat. It whirled through the air and hit Paige in the back of the legs. By then the police had given chase, and they broke the whole thing up.[32]

Paige's performance, regardless of results, was called a "dazzling exhibition" by Colley at the *Dispatch*.[33] In the fourth inning, the Crawfords made a pitching change, and Wesley Barrow, who pitched the remainder of the game, took the hill. Barrow, a name that is often missing when the Pittsburgh Crawfords are discussed, allowed the only All-Stars' scores, while pitching a magnificent game as Satchel's relief. He struck out Cullop twice, to give this legendary slugger four strikeouts on the afternoon and a perfect 0-for-4 day at bat.

Nicknamed "Big Train," Wesley Barrow was active in Negro professional baseball circles for more than 40 years. He is named as the manager of a dozen teams, although his appearance with the 1934 Pittsburgh Crawfords is rarely mentioned. Born in Baton Rouge, in 1902, there is a stadium named after him in his native Louisiana—a title that was well earned.[34] Barrow entered professional play in 1926, under manager William Lowe with the Chattanooga Black Lookouts of Tennessee. Two of his 1934 Crawfords teammates, Paige and infielder Anthony Cooper, were members of that team, which may account for his brief stint with Pittsburgh in 1934. Barrow's tenure in the east, however short, featured the game against the Deans' All-Stars. In 1939, he was back with the Black Pelicans in his native New Orleans, where his contributions to baseball were sewn into the fabric of the community he called home.

Barrow would go on to manage the Algiers Giants in 1940, the 1945 New Orleans Black Pelicans, and the 1946 Nashville Cubs/Black Vols. In 1950, he returned to New Orleans to manage the local Creoles team. In 1952 and 1953, he was back managing the Black Pelicans, and it also included a stint with the Mobile Alabama Shippers. Barrow's obituary says he "appeared in several Negro League all-star games and served as batterymate to Satchel Paige," but there is no mention of the Deans.[35] In 1968, local officials changed the name of New Orleans' Pontchartrain Park to Wesley Barrow Stadium. Adding to the saga, the recently named New Orleans Urban Youth Academy, a major-league training and development complex, took control of the park, which is located in the heart of the African American community, and re-named it in Barrow's honor, although he himself never played in the National or American League. Ironically, the word "urban" was soon removed from the facility. Today, it is called the New Orleans Youth Academy, and there is little mention of Barrow's name or the urban youth it was built to serve.

Paul was able to keep his promise to pitch two innings. His effectiveness was debatable. Right away, Charleston's Crawfords leaned into Daffy's best offerings. Dean, who hadn't pitched since the game in Chicago and was well rested, was no obstacle for any of the Crawfords batters. They jumped on the World Series hurler for three hits and a run after Vic Harris, the first Crawfords batter, was retired. Anthony Cooper, next up, singled. Curtis Harris followed with a double to advance the runner. An infield out allowed Cooper to score the game's first run. It was another earned run off Paul that the newspaper couldn't explain away, but the run didn't appear in the *Dispatch*'s box score, leaving one to wonder if the omission was an oversight or left out on purpose. True to his word, Daffy quit pitching after two innings. Before the game he had stated, "That story about me not wanting to pitch is all wrong. But I got a sore arm, and I ain't gonna throw. Now take tonight, if I feel a pain up here in my shoulder I ain't doin' nothin' but stop right there. I'm hoping to pitch the first inning, and Diz here will pitch the last two."[36] On this day, however, he never complained of any pain in his arm or shoulder. Pittsburgh added more runs in the third following Daffy's exit.

In the third inning, a Curtis Harris single was followed by a home run. Big-league pitcher Bob Kline made the mistake of putting a ball near Josh Gibson's wheelhouse, and two runs scored instantly. The two-run homer cleared the right-field wall of Red Bird Stadium with room to spare. Another Crawford scored in the sixth off Nick Cullop, who had taken the mound after Kline. In that inning, Bill Perkins walked, stole second base, and scored on John Henry Russell's single to give the Crawfords a 3–0 advantage. The Deans' All-Stars could do little with Paige on the mound, but they got to Paige's relief, late in the game.

Barrow allowed a run in the sixth when Ollie Carnegie slammed one of his offerings over the right-field wall for a solo home run. It was the second home run Carnegie had hit off a Crawfords pitcher. On September 23, 1932, as a member of Billy Fuchs's Minor League All-Stars, in a game played at Greenlee Field, Carnegie homered off Harry Kincannon in an 11–4 loss to the Crawfords. The Dean brothers' All-Stars tallied again in the seventh.

In that frame, King was safe on Russell's error, and Bob Gibson beat out a bounder to Judy Johnson at third. Danny Taylor followed with a single to center to load the bases, with no outs. There was a natural tension when Dizzy came to bat, but Diz went out easily, as he grounded to an infielder, who got the force on Taylor at second base. King scored on the play, and the Cardinals pitcher was credited with a RBI. Bob Gibson scored his team's third run on a dash for home when Heath grounded out. Carnegie couldn't produce in the clutch, and the scoring ended at 4–3, in the Crawfords' favor. The game was still winnable when Diz took the hill.

Dizzy came on to pitch the seventh and eighth innings. His entrance did not faze Crawfords batters, who eagerly awaited his arrival. They added their final run off the Cardinals great on eighth-inning singles by Curtis Harris, Judy Johnson, and Bill Perkins' long sacrifice fly. After a pair of innings, Dizzy retired for the night. He had struck out a batter, but the victim's name was not given. He finished his mound chores by allowing three hits. That Dizzy had played third base, pitched, and went 1-for-3 at bat, with a stolen base, and was responsible for one of his team's RBI, is all that mattered. His afternoon's work more than justified his share of the gate receipts, although Crawfords batters more than earned their day's take as well for the win.

Crawfords batters had a field day against the Deans and their aggregation of well-known All-Stars. They gathered 11 combined hits off Daffy Dean, Robert "Bob" Kline, Nick Cullop, Dizzy Dean, and finally Cullop again, before going on to win, 5–3.[37] Although every pitcher had shared in the All-Stars' loss, Cullop was named the loser. One of the Crawfords' big guns had been Curtis Harris.

Curtis Harris, nicknamed "Popsicle" and also "Moochie," was a Texan. He is vastly underrated as a hitter and speedy runner. James "Cool Papa" Bell, a speed merchant himself, recalled how Harris once hit two inside-the-park home runs in a 1932 game at Oxford, Nebraska, when both played for the Monarchs.[38] In 1932, during the time he was with the Monarchs, Harris met a young lady in Manhattan, Kansas, and shortly thereafter they married.[39]

The racial assault by baseball writers continued as the Crawfords left Columbus. Not only was Paige's name misspelled in the *Dispatch*, but also his teammates received scant first-name recognition, if any at all. Paige's proper name, Leroy, was never given; he was only listed by his nickname, Satchel. In the minds of readers, it appeared as though Paige had no first name, but the writers found it necessary to mention Dizzy as Jay H. or Jay Hanna, and Jerome Herman, and Daffy by his name, Paul, in the local newspapers while covering that city's visit. Jay was provided as Dizzy's name at least once, and Paul's first name was published three times. Even their father's name, Albert, appeared in the article, along with seven of the first and last names of their temporary Columbus teammates. Only Oscar Charleston was mentioned by first and last name in the *Dispatch*. Many of the Deans' All-Stars were provided more than creditable name recognition. The *Dispatch's* article on October 21 illustrates this point.

In the *Dispatch's* postgame wrap, an analogous observation was delivered. In that article, first names or nicknames were given for Kline, Cullop, Carnegie, King, Garback, Taylor, Crabtree, and Heath. Only initials were provided for Josh Gibson and Curtis Harris. This was done to alleviate confusion in printing the box score—not to elevate their status among local fans. The All-Stars had Robert "Bob" Gibson on their team, and the Crawfords had both Curtis and Vic Harris in their lineup. Other members of the Crawfords—Perkins, Cooper, and Russell—got last-name recognition only.

The ever-so-brief write-up in the *Columbus Citizen* mistakenly said that "Bill Bell" finished the game for the Crawfords, when it was actually Wesley Barrow. The article, which was not credited to any particular reporter, left little doubt about what the writer had witnessed. "Paul Dean started for the Dean team and allowed one run and two hits in the first two innings," penned the anonymous author.[40] "Then Bob Kline, Nick Cullop, and Dizzy Dean took turns in blazing that ball up there and ducking."[41] Frank Colley's lead line in his descriptive recap for the *Columbus Dispatch* said, "The Deans came, they saw, but didn't do much in the way of conquering, Monday night."[42]

In passing, the *Cleveland Plain Dealer* mentioned that the Deans had been the "big attraction," until a house just outside Red Bird Stadium caught fire late in the game. Having already seen the Deans, roughly 800 fans deserted the park to witness the blaze coming from the structure, essentially trading one disaster for another.[43] With the final out of the Crawfords' win, a writer advised, "The colored stars won, 5 to 3, with Satchel Paige stealing the Dean thunder before 1,650 shivering fans."[44] There were few real reasons to doubt his comment.

CHAPTER 14

Pittsburgh, Pennsylvania

Swinging and Swearing
Monday, October 23, 1934

Dizzy and Daffy arrived in Pittsburgh smiling broadly and feeling unexpectedly refreshed. Now that the whirlwind tour was down to its final game, like all athletes who love their professional occupations, they hid their exhaustion while shrouded in the comfort of the William Penn Hotel, where they gave a series of farewell interviews to celebrate the tour's ending. Looking more enthusiastic and appearing more talkative than usual, the brothers reflected on the barnstorming series, sorted through details of the tour's last game, and gave comments on their upcoming stage performance at the Roxy Theater in New York. If the brothers expected the tour's ending to be run-of-the-mill—they should have known better. The Pittsburgh ending was destined to be as climactic as the tour's Oklahoma City beginning. James Doyle of the *Pittsburgh Sun-Telegraph* wrote, "The Deans, Jay and Paul, came in like lions this year and went out the same way."[1]

Those anticipating a Dizzy versus Satchel pitching classic certainly got their wish but hardly their money's worth. Both starting pitchers left after two innings. In addition to the legendary pitchers, fans were treated to a rousing fight, a close-scoring ballgame, a come-from-behind win, and what reporters termed a "near riot." Pittsburgh's Forbes Field, with a seating capacity of 40,000, the backdrop for the Dean brothers' finale, was the tour's third visit to a major-league stadium. It would be a doozy.

Additions to the Deans' All-Stars in Pittsburgh were worth celebrating. They had an impressive lot of professional ballplayers strengthened with more add-ons from the day prior. The All-Stars' losses had been so consistent throughout the tour that rhetorical strategies were used to deceive the public once more. A writer in the *Post-Gazette* tagged the Crawfords as a "picked team of colored stars."[2] When a *New York Times* writer called Deans' Pittsburgh All-Stars a "pick-up outfit," it was evident that they were positioning themselves for a debate about the validity of the wins achieved by the Negro major leaguers. The Pittsburgh All-Stars were visibly much more than some sandlot outfit gathered together for the tour's final game. Five of the men—two of them from the major leagues—were with the All-Stars the day before at Columbus. Having played together in back-to-back contests gave them solidarity. Hal King, Ollie Carnegie, Danny Taylor, Elmer Trapp, and Bob Garback were the returnees. New to the All-Stars were John Cortazzo, Richard "Dick" Goldberg, Joseph Solters, Joe Semler, and George Susce— two were former big-leaguers and one was currently in the American League. They had the necessary manpower to deliver the win.

New shortstop John Francis Cortazzo, nicknamed "Shine," had performed for both the Johnstown Johnnies and Dayton Ducks in 1934. He could boast of playing in the majors—but only for a single day. Ironically, he batted once in his only major-league game for the White Sox in 1923, at age 19. While that one game wasn't much to celebrate, and it hardly established Cortazzo as a career major leaguer—it was certainly more opportunity than any of the Crawfords could boast. They hadn't gotten a chance at all. The only Crawford from the 1934 squad to reach the white major leagues would be Satchel Paige—and that bit of history was another 14 years in the future. Cortazzo would spend 15 years in the minors yearning to get back to the majors— which he never did. There were others signed to Deans' Pittsburgh All-Stars with equally extensive minor-league careers.

Richard "Dick" Goldberg, who split the 1934 season in the New York– Pennsylvania League and International League, was the Deans' first baseman. At Wilkes-Barre, Dick recorded a batting percentage of .323 in 89 games before being shipped to Baltimore, where he hit .282 for the remainder of the season. Goldberg spent all 11 years of his professional career in the minors. Harold "Hal" King, the Deans' second baseman, was a 1934 participant in the International League. King spent 13 years in the minors without reaching the majors. Dizzy's center fielder, Oliver A. "Ollie" Carnegie, was also from the International League. He too failed to reach the majors after spending 15 years in the minors in spite of his many impressive skills. Doyle, writing in the *Sun-Telegraph*, said of Carnegie, "[He could] outhit a flock of major-league stars."[3] Tommy Holmes, writing of Carnegie in the *Brooklyn Daily Eagle*, said of the former Pittsburgh Steel Mill worker, he "recently hit the longest home run ever seen in Buffalo. His drive hit a house 100 feet beyond a fence 400 feet from the plate."[4] After his impressive International League season of 1938—45 home runs, 136 runs batted in, and a .330 average—Carnegie would be named MVP of the circuit. Joseph Semler was hired to pitch in Dizzy and Daffy's absence.

Joseph "Joe" Semler, a pitcher for Wilkes-Barre in the New York–Pennsylvania League, with a 21–12 record in 1934, was coming off the only 20-win season of his six-year minor-league career. It is ironic that Semler had lost to the Crawfords on September 23, 1932, as a member of Billy Fuchs's Minor League All-Stars. In that game, which was played at Greenlee Field, the All-Stars lost, 11–4, as Oscar Charleston and Josh Gibson slammed home runs.

Elmer Trapp, an infielder who spent five years in the minors and retired without reaching the major leagues, was there to play third base. Four of Dizzy's All-Stars—Susce, Garback, Taylor, and Solters—spent parts of their careers in the major and minor leagues. Doyle, obviously a hometown booster for the National and American Leagues, wrote of Solters in his *Sun-Telegraph* article, calling him the "Hazelwood lad who starred for the Boston Red Sox this year."[5]

Born March 22, 1906, Julius Joseph Solters, real name Soltesz, was born to Hungarian immigrant parents. He dropped out of high school to pursue a job in the coal mines in his native Pennsylvania. He was discovered while playing for a coal-mining team and soon signed a contract with the Boston Red Sox. In 1932, Solters led the Eastern League in RBI.[6] He spent another seven years in the minors before reaching the majors. Because he weighed significantly more than 200 pounds, his teammates tagged him with the nickname "Moose."[7] In the majors he would drive in more than 100 runners for three consecutive seasons, from 1935 to 1937. He received votes for American League MVP honors in 1935, after a season of 201 hits, 11 home runs, and 112 RBI, while batting .319. It was one of his best seasons of professional play.

Solters's career was tragically cut shot on August 1, 1942, when he was struck on the temple by a thrown ball as Joe Kuhel and Luke Appling were playing catch during pregame practice. Moose had turned to look at a friend in the grandstand and never saw the ball coming. The spear landed with such a force that it knocked him unconscious, causing a serious skull fracture and damaging his vision. His eyesight never recovered, and, by 1947, the heavy-hitting outfielder who had seen action with the White Sox, Red Sox, Browns, and Indians was totally blind.

There were other big-league players among the Deans' All-Stars. Catcher George Cyril Susce, a Detroit Tiger in 1932, logged eight years of major-league play. He wasn't in the majors in 1934, the year he bounced between three minor leagues—the Texas League, American Association, and Pacific

Coast League. Susce would spend an additional nine years in the minors. His son, George Daniel Susce, pitched in the majors with the Red Sox and Tigers during the 1950s. Danny Taylor, who participated in 674 major-league games starting with Washington in 1926, finished with a big-league batting average of .297. In addition to nine years in the majors, eight in the National and one in the American, Taylor played for a dozen teams. A local favorite, Doyle, writing in the Sun-Telegraph, called Taylor "West Newton's favorite son."[8] Catcher Bob Garback, who batted .341 for Toledo in the American Association in 1934, had graduated to Cleveland's American League Indians that same season. His major-league career was all of 145 games from 1934 to 1945—a total of seven seasons, which did not include parts of nine additional seasons spent in the minors.

Dizzy was continuously interviewed prior to the game—some at the hotel and once on the radio. He was interviewed on the radio at WCAE, the Sun-Telegraph's station, during the 12:15 p.m. broadcast. There was little written about his radio interview except that it was a "humorous discourse" with announcer Louis L. Maulman heard by an army of listeners. The brothers had another impromptu interview with an unnamed Sun-Telegraph reporter inside their swanky rooms at the William Penn Hotel after breakfast. The reporter tried his best to show readers "how out of place" and "unnatural" the brothers were in their posh surroundings. Awakened from their naps, the reporter gloated, "Dizzy shouted as he yawned," before saying, "It's a great relief to get this thing over with. We have too much at stake for me and Paul to be fiddling around the country playing night games and taking chances. We've had a good time, but just as soon as we put in a week of vaudeville in New York we're gonna make ourselves scarce."[9]

The writer took lots of liberties in describing Paul. The interviewer told readers that Daffy "landed on the carpeted floor with his substantial bare feet, wearing what would pass for a country night gown." He added, "The boys have not let the city take the country out of them." During the interview, Paul proceeded to explain that his arm was not injured and that it was in "perfect condition," despite reports flashed throughout the county to the contrary. "I did get a few little pains from pitching night baseball," he offered without being asked, "but listen—I know that our living depends on our arms, and neither of us is going to take any long chances. I'm fine again, and I want to stay that way."

Dizzy excitedly interrupted his younger brother to say, "We've had a good time, though."[10] When asked about their Cardinals salaries and league rival, the Pittsburgh Pirates, it started a dozen comments. The brothers had plenty to say. Volney Walsh of the Pittsburgh Press took special interest in their comments.

Asked about their salary negations with the Cardinals for the upcoming season, Dizzy explained, "We ain't worrying about that. We won't have no trouble, but right now we ain't thinking about it."[11] The *Sporting News* learned from private sources close to the Deans that Dizzy was "determined to Buck Messrs. Breadon, and Rickey for $25,000 in 1935, and that Paul will insist on not less than $15,000."[12] Diz was also watching how Detroit took care of Mickey Cochrane.

Cochrane practically conceded Game 1 of the World Series to the Cardinals when he pitched veteran Alvin Crowder against Dizzy Dean instead of using his own ace, "Schoolboy" Rowe. For leading his team to the pennant and the World Series, the Tigers management presented him with a $10,000 bonus.

When speaking about the Pirates, Daffy called them the "best club in the league, except for pitching." He added, "I don't understand how those pitchers fold up every summer when it gets hot." Dizzy supported his brother's comments with a few of his own. "Yeah, it's a swell club," he added. "Nice people in Pittsburgh, but that ballclub is tough." During the brothers' conversation with Walsh they made note of the cars that were given to them. Turns out that Henry Ford had given each of the Deans new automobiles. Dizzy boasted that he had "three autos."[13]

As publicized, the final barnstorming event matched two of baseball's best pitchers against one another. Dizzy toed the mound for the All-Stars, and Satchel took the hill for the Crawfords. Both pitchers were closing fabulous seasons during which they had won many important games, and both had appeared in their respective league's All-Star Games, although neither was selected to start.

In the American League versus National League All-Star Game at New York's Polo Grounds, Carl Hubbell of the Giants received the starting nod and made baseball history by striking out Babe Ruth, Lou Gehrig, Jimmie Fox, Al Simmons, and Joe Cronin in succession. Dizzy didn't warm up until the fifth inning, entering in the sixth frame and leaving with a combined effort of five hits (two had been lost in the sun) and four strikeouts (Foxx, Averill, Harder, and Gehrig) in three innings of pitching. Paige hadn't started in his league's All-Star Game either. In the East–West Classic, played at Chicago's Comiskey Park, Stuart "Country" Jones was given the starting assignment. Paige entered the game in the sixth inning, striking out five and walking none before leaving with the win.

Dizzy and Satchel may have been big stars in 1934; however, Edward F. Balinger, in his sports column for the *Post-Gazette*, gave Vic Harris more print for rousing an umpire than Dizzy or Satchel combined. More concerned with things not related to baseball, Balinger failed to list Dizzy's Pittsburgh totals, and little was said about Paige's achievements on this day. As a result, for the first time in his career, Harris became nationally recognized—an overnight sensation after 11 years of unrecognized accomplishments.

Elander Victor Harris, or "Vic," as he was known in baseball circles, was an outfielder who threw from the right but batted on the left. He was a graduate of Pittsburgh's racially and ethnically diverse Schenley High School, located in the North Oakland neighborhood near the Hill District. He appeared on the roster of his first professional team, the Cleveland Tate Stars, in 1923. The next season, he joined Rube Foster's Chicago American Giants. As a student of the legendary Foster, Vic turned from athlete to strategist as his baseball philosophy was elevated to an entirely new level after just one season in Chicago. In 1925, Harris returned to Pittsburgh to join Cumberland Posey's Homestead Grays, for whom he would play the rest of career, except the 1934 season when he jumped to the rival Crawfords.

Harris, who was born in Pensacola, Florida, on June 10, 1905, and died in Mission Hills, California, on February 23, 1978, was an amazing hitter and manager with Hall of Fame credentials. In 1931, he collected 52 hits in one stretch of 35 games. That year, Harris's multihit games accounted for 127 of his 156 total hits, leaving just 29 games where he'd obtained one hit out of 107 games played.[14] Later, as manager of the Homestead Grays, he led them to nine league championships in 10 seasons. Prior to the Dean brothers' tour he was known only by those who followed Negro major-league players. Among them he was a great player and a big star. His star status, like that of many others on the team, was dwarfed next to that of his 1934 teammate, Leroy "Satchel" Paige, who was supposedly too inferior for the major leagues.

Paige started the Pittsburgh exhibition for the Crawfords. Although he wasn't as sharp as the day before, he outpitched Dizzy and Daffy for a third consecutive day. Satchel was shooting them over and striking out batters in grand fashion. His strikeout feats are worth repeating—13 in six innings at Cleveland, 9 in three innings at Columbus, and 3 in two innings at Pittsburgh. By comparison, Dizzy hadn't struck out any batters in three innings at Cleveland and only two in five combined innings at Columbus and Pittsburgh. Daffy's strikeout totals weren't any better. He had only recorded two.

Unfortunately, the weather was mostly frigid before the game. Cool October winds blew across the diamond, lessening the class of entertainment. Attendance totals suffered as a less-than-capacity crowd passed through the turnstiles. Edward Balinger, writing in the *Pittsburgh Post-Gazette*, reported a crowd of 2,500 gathered to see the Deans.[15] These fans were described by the *Pittsburgh Press* as mostly "Negroes" and "half frozen."[16] Those in attendance were treated to an exciting event that lasted all of an hour and 42 minutes. The umpires were making controversial decisions from the first pitch in a match that provided all the thrills of an important baseball game with lots of offense. All totaled, 12 batters struck out and four walked. Five doubles were hit, as well as two triples and a home run. One batter was hit with a pitch, one batter sacrificed, and a pitcher balked.

The Deans' All-Stars played with bats and gloves, then smiled smugly as the questionable calls appeared to be in their favor. In the early innings, Crawfords players "complained about these decisions," advised the *Sun-Telegraph*.[17] They were not happy with umpire in chief Jimmy Ahearn. In the fifth inning, a questionable call caused a ruckus between the normally mild-mannered Vic Harris and Ahearn, who was working behind the plate. Players from the All-Stars hurried to Ahearn's defense carrying heavy artillery. The game had been an interesting one up until this point.

Paige was ragged at the start, and as a result, the Crawfords quickly fell behind. In the first inning, a Paige pitch struck Cortazzo in the ribs after one out had been recorded on King's fly-out to Vic Harris in center. Paige proceeded to strike out Taylor. Solters, next up, tripled to drive Cortazzo home for the game's first score. Doyle, writing in the *Sun-Telegraph*, observed, "He [Solters] has the kick of a mule at the plate. He raised one of Satchel Paige's swifters against the right-field fence."[18] Satchel got out of the inning before another run scored but continued to struggle in the second.

The first man up in the second inning, Goldberg singled. Trapp walked, and Susce fanned. Dizzy got hold of a Paige pitch for a double to push Goldberg home for another run. Paige exited the game after two innings, having allowed two hits and a pair of runs. The *Post-Gazette* inappropriately labeled Taylor, Susce, and Solters Paige's strikeout victims when it was actually Taylor, Susce, and Semler. Solters had hit safely in his only at-bat against Paige. After two innings, Satchel was done. Dizzy's All-Stars were leading, 2–0. He was relieved by Harry Kincannon, who yielded to Burt Hunter, the final Crawfords pitcher. Kincannon and Hunter would combine for five more strikeouts.

They gave Dizzy the ball, and he pitched a pair of innings to open the game. Statistics are crucial for any game, but these important details were absent from every newspaper's accounts—all three daily publications. The *Press*, the *Sun-Telegraph*, and the *Post-Gazette* deserved a failing grade for their journalistic coverage of this contest.

Vic Harris, Dizzy's only strikeout victim, was the leadoff batter—and even that call was questionable. Vic, who went down looking, left feeling cheated and sat alone on the bench. He said little as he lamented the call. How and to whom Dizzy pitched after the first batter was not recorded. It was a tragic miscarriage of statistics. Since Dizzy did not walk a batter, we can reasonably assume by the printed box score that he faced Anthony Cooper and Oscar Charleston for outs two and three in the opening frame. In the second, he would have faced Josh Gibson and William "Judy" Johnson, two future Hall of Fame batters, in succession, and Curtis Harris. Dizzy faced a total of three future African American Hall of Fame inductees in the two innings he pitched before turning the mound chores over to Semler with the score 2–0 in the All-Stars' favor. Semler took the mound to start the third. Outfielder Danny Taylor moved to the bench, and Dizzy went to left field. Both Deans were in the game at this point. Paul stayed in right field and never approached the mound. Semler completed the game and received credit for his team's loss as the Crawfords picked at him constantly.

In the All-Stars' portion of the fourth, King singled through the middle of the infield and advanced to second on Cortazzo's sacrifice. Semler rolled out to the right side of the diamond, allowing King to reach third. Solters followed with a double to left center, which scored King. The Deans' All-Stars were leading, 3–1. Likewise, the Crawfords had scored in the top-half of the frame.

Pittsburgh got on the board in the fourth when Josh Gibson singled to left, then went out on Judy Johnson's fielder's choice at second for putout number one. Johnson remained on first but stole second base and made such a hullabaloo with his great lead off the bag that Semler balked, allowing Johnson to amble on to third base. Curtis "Popsicle" Harris followed with a single to center, which scored Johnson. The Crawfords won the contest with a scoring burst in the eighth inning.

Stringing together four straight hits was the deciding factor, and it occurred after two were out. Charleston doubled to right and trotted home when Josh Gibson launched a massive home run over the left-field wall to tie the game at 3–3. Carroll Ray Mothell of the Monarchs aptly described the elation Gibson might have felt, saying, "That was a thrill to hit a home run in a big-league park."[19] Chet Brewer recalled, "Josh had two stances. One in which he [Gibson] was in a slight crouch. The other he would stand with straight back. The latter was his long-distance hitting stance. If you threw anything up high you could kiss it goodbye." [20] Judy Johnson followed with a triple to right, and Popsicle Harris drove him home with a single to extreme left for another Crawfords run and the win. In between the Crawfords' scoring in the fourth and eighth innings, there was a scuffle between Vic Harris and umpire James Ahearn that included ballplayers and fans.

The *Post-Gazette* and other local newspapers showed how Dizzy instigated the mess. Having already pitched his two innings, Dizzy went to left field. In the bottom of the fifth, Vic Harris rapped a soft bounder in front of the plate and was ruled safe when the All-Stars catcher, George Susce, "threw rather wild to first base," reported Balinger in the *Post-Gazette*. "The ball got away from the [first baseman], and Harris dashed to second." Dizzy took issue with the call. Taking it a step further, he came running in from left field and called personal attention to the batter, telling the arbiter that Harris ran "inside the base line" and thus interfered with the catcher's throw.[21] Another newspaper report quoted Dizzy as saying Harris had not "touched first base."[22] How Dizzy got a better angle from left field than Ahearn, the umpire behind the plate, or Steve Cox, who was umpiring bases on the infield, was anyone's guess. What happened next was a classic case of jingoism that has come down through history like one of Paige's fastballs. The result was like gas and a lighted match. Harris had every right to complain.

It came as a great surprise when Ahearn sided with the celebrity pitcher and waved a confused and puzzled Vic Harris out to end the inning. Dizzy had waged a similar revolt in New York, but the umpire there refused to reverse the call. Things were different in Pittsburgh, where the highly touted Dizzy, crying and complaining like a baby, got his way. Within moments of the reversal, Harris, a right-hander, attacked the umpire with both mitts— a hard right and a corking good left. Both benches cleared, benchwarmers and all, as the combatants on the ball diamond turned from competitive to hostile. Balinger noted, "Within a few seconds the rumpus was in full sway with fists flying, players gripping their bats in menacing fashion, and everything [was] in turmoil." Harris reportedly marched in from second base and headed directly to home plate, allegedly "picking up a mask" en route. He "smacked the umpire on his dome with it."[23] "Out of the Deans' dugout rushed players charging and swinging," wrote Charles J. Doyle in the *Sun-Telegraph*.[24] "Harris and catcher [Josh] Gibson were their principal targets. Then the Negroes grabbed bats to protect themselves."[25] Many aggressive blows were thrown. Fortunately, most missed their marks. Some of the spectators liked the ruckus better than the ballgame and couldn't resist joining in the action.

African American spectators, far from the action in their segregated seating along the left-field line, leaped over railings to get into the midst of the melee. They were met by white fans who were charging the field from the nearby box seats. Ahearn grabbed a bat for protection as he was jostled about by Harris before cooler heads from both teams got between the men and prevented what could have been a serious brawl.

Police officers huddled up inside Forbes Field and at the gates were on the field almost immediately, but there were too many people mixed up in the commotion. The *Pittsburgh Courier* advised, "The fight became too much for the field police to handle, and a hurried call was put in to the Oakland police station for reserves."[26] Within minutes, a squad had rushed over from a nearby police station armed with guns, blackjacks, and billy clubs. Thank goodness they arrived too late. Peace already had been restored. The *Sun-Telegraph* informed its readers that the Deans kept their heads.[27] Dizzy, who provoked the mess, "sought to break up the fight."[28] The *Courier* added, "Star pitchers from both sides, Paige and [Dizzy] Dean, entered the fracas unarmed in an effort to quiet the ruffled players and get the game underway. Many of the more levelheaded [people] in the stands made an effort to do likewise."[29] Balinger wrote in his *Post-Gazette* article that the affair "was said to be the renewal of an old feud between Harris and Ahearn that started some 10 years ago when they clashed during a ballgame at Jeannette [Pennsylvania]."[30] The *Courier* said, "Vic and the same ump had an argument which later resulted in a tie-up that caused no little comment."[31] Both newspapers believed much of the animosity was the result of their previous fight. These statements were publicized versions of the same event that appeared in the daily newspapers. Another less-publicized version, with Vic's own comments, appeared much later in the African American–owned *Courier*.

Vic did not deny hitting Ahearn; he said he "simply defended himself." Commenting further he added, "Players of both teams poured from the dugouts with bats and other weapons onto the field and engaged in a free-for-all, hitting in all directions. The fans took up the fracas, and many [in] the boxes armed with pop bottles and chairs made a mad dash to the field, leaping over the railing and engaged in the fight."[32]

Harris was escorted off the field and replaced by James "Cool Papa" Bell in center field. After peace had been restored, the contest continued. Ahearn reluctantly returned to his place behind the plate. Steve Cox, his assistant, who also had been in the thick of the turmoil, went back to the bases. It was not until after the end of the ballgame that Ahearn claimed injury. He complained of pain in his head and back, and a physician reported that the chief ump was suffering from a wrenching of the body and bruises on his head. Ahearn informed the media of his plans to file a lawsuit the next day charging Harris with assault and battery.[33]

The *Pittsburgh Press* offered a unique approach to its coverage, and the theme of their intent went national. "Yesterday's exhibition game was dizzier than Dizzy," wrote the *Press*. "A team of colored all-stars won, 4 to 3, but not until after there had been a near riot which threatened to extend among the

1,500 customers, most of whom were Negro rooters."[34] It was an old refrain—where the *Press* called out African American rooters for something negative as to project the message of violence onto an entire race of people. Using unruly crowd behavior at unsegregated baseball games as a method to justify segregation was an old strategy—it was always effective.

There are additional reasons to examine coverage of the game as it went on the wire to newspapers throughout the country. The power of the press took over when the Associated Press sent stories across the wire to their members, associates who seemly cared little about how these articles could, and would, impact others. These pieces were virtually the same in every newspaper; however, newspaper editors could take liberties and personalize the release as they saw fit. The basic AP reports read, "Dizzy and Daffy, backed by a 'local pick-up outfit,' were involved in a free-for-all fight involving the Pittsburgh Crawfords, fortified by several other clubs in the Colored National League."[35] It was a loaded missive with lots of subliminal messages.

By saying "several other clubs," the entire Negro National League was stigmatized, when actually there were no additional players from other teams on the field. The statement about Dizzy's supporting cast was also biased. This team was much more than a loosely knitted group of semiprofessional "pick-ups." The polarization continued, as each article gave Vic Harris full-name recognition and was robustly distributed nationally—same story, different headlines throughout the nation.

Kansas City Times—"Players Use Fists; Dean's Exhibition Game Marred by a Free-for-All"[36]

Monroe (Louisiana) News-Star—"Fight Enlivens Deans Game at Pittsburgh Park"[37]

Butte (Montana) Standard—"Riot Marks Game of Deans and Pittsburgh Negro Club"[38]

New York Times—"Police Stop Fight at Deans' Contest"[39]

Sheboygan (Wisconsin) Press—"Dizzy Almost Starts Riot as Trip Ends"[40]

Hartford Courant—"Free-for-All Fight as Dean Boys Lose"[41]

Chicago Tribune—"Fight Features Final Game of Touring Deans"[42]

Logansport (Indiana) Press—"Free-for-All Fight Marks End of Deans' Barnstorming"[43]

For added insult, only three photographs of African American players were printed in daily newspapers during the Dean brothers' entire barnstorming tour—two were from the fight in Pittsburgh—which appeared in an edition of the *Sun-Telegraph*. The images sparked more negativity toward the

Crawfords, who were rarely seen in print. The caption that accompanied the photograph read, "Note the swinging arms of the player on the ground at the right."[44] The captions also named George Susce as was one of the main figures in the scrap. These writers were influencing American culture through their literature right down to the captions.

What became of Ahearn's charges against Harris was anyone's guess. There were few follow-ups in any of the Pittsburgh dailies documenting this story. In late February, long after the Deans' tour had ended, and with periodic delays at the courthouse, a rescheduled date for the case was published. This caused Cumberland Posey, a longtime associate of both Ahearn and Harris, to comment in his *Courier* article dated February 23, 1935.

In the case of "Jimmy Ahearn vs. Vic Harris," said Posey, "as in most cases of this kind, it never looks well for the defendant when appearing before a jury, especially in an assault and battery case." Posey recalled how he repeatedly warned Grays players not to assault umpires, especially those who were members of the local Umpires' Association. "The Association keeps a certain amount of money on hand to prosecute any person, or persons, who assault any member of their Association," stated Posey.

> In addition to this, one of their associates, a former official in the Basketball Officials Association, which is very closely allied with the Pittsburgh Umpires' Association, is a justice of peace, located in Dormont. This justice of peace is Marty Weitzel, and Marty can be depended upon to see that the plaintiffs in these cases are well satisfied or he holds the case for court.[45]

Moreover, Posey took issue with the highly advertised report claiming Harris and Ahearn were angry with one another for past deeds. Posey recalled an important series between the Homestead Grays and the Altoona Penn Centrals in 1931, where a winner-take-all game was scheduled. Vic Harris made the suggestion that Ahearn umpire the game. "Had there been any bad feeling whatsoever between players and Ahearn over an incident which occurred in 1925, at Jeannette, it is an assured fact that Ahearn would not have been permitted to work a game of this kind," wrote Posey. "Whatever was done at Forbes Field," informed Posey, "was done on the spur of a moment in the heat of anger by both parties."[46]

Some years later, Harris told author John Holway, "The Umpires' Association was going to appear against me. Art Rooney, the owner of the Pittsburgh Steelers, and a friend to Pittsburgh African American athletes, calmed everyone."[47] Rooney wanted to know why no one informed him of the situation. Quite honestly, I can't see how he missed it.

CHAPTER 15

~

Amazing Outcomes

The legendary tour had finally ended; however, the legacy of Dizzy and Daffy Dean's direct interaction with African American ballplayers and teams was just beginning. In a period of almost two weeks, from October 10, 1934, to October 23, 1934, Dizzy and Daffy accomplished a feat that no other white American baseball players had ever achieved. During a span of 14 games, they ducked and bobbed in and out of hotels, restaurants, and dugouts in a dozen different cities while barnstorming against representatives from the African American baseball universe on consecutive days. It was a feat like no other and one they could surely boast about as being completely unique.

They had faced men on diamonds outside the boundaries of the "lilly" white National League, American League, and minor leagues, and witnessed firsthand how African American men were placed in disadvantaged, segregated, and undervalued situations, and simultaneously deemed too inferior for the major leagues' talent pools. The powers that be in baseball had barred and padlocked them out, not only from big-league play, but also big-league pay, potential endorsements, and the equitable national notoriety from which many white players benefited. Daily news sources—national and local—which also included the emerging media of radio and magazines, had taken a non-supportive stance on the issues of racism in sports. Other than a few minority weeklies, their allies were few. During the Dean brothers' tour, reporters were abnormally distant and actually aided the curse of segregation in baseball.

In 1934, the best of the Negro major-league stars were still playing their game in near isolation. Their success against Dizzy and Daffy, and their All-

Stars, had not alleviated their dilemma. Breaking down the ideology of bias and the practice of institutional segregation would take a marathon effort. Dizzy and Daffy might have helped the situation had they spoken out more, which they rarely did. Almost anything the brothers said was national news. When it came to the plight of their opponents in baseball, they were tight-lipped and muffled for most of the tour. Dizzy, the most talkative member of the Dean family, was mum on the topic except for a few rare exceptions. After the 1934 season, Dizzy became one of Paige's biggest boosters, and he talked about him in uncharacteristic fashion. "The best pitcher he ever saw was Satchel Paige," was his published remark after seeing Paige in 1934. He added to that bold statement by saying, "If he and Satch were on the same team they would win 60 games, clinch the pennant by the Fourth of July, and go fishing until the World Series starts."[1]

One of Dizzy's most famous conversations about race and baseball wasn't quoted until 1938. "A bunch of the fellows gets in a barber session the other day, and they start to argue about who's the best pitcher they ever see, and some says Lefty Grove and Lefty Gomez and Walter Johnson and old Pete Alexander and Dazzy Vance," he said. "I know who's the best pitcher I ever see, and it's old Satchel Paige, the big lanky colored boy. Say, old Diz is pretty fast back in 1933 and 1934, and you know my fastball looks like a change of pace alongside that little pistol bullet old Satchel shoots up to the plate."[2]

As the brothers traveled from city to city, reporters never inquired as to why these African American men were barred from National and American League play. Reporters were committed to America's other national pastime—racism. They worked in unity and never printed one word against segregation or the promoters that had exploited these men in every region of the nation. As a result, some of the most egregious coverage in history was printed in newspapers throughout the United States during the fall of 1934. Clearly prevalent are the articles, written by reporters who would not discuss what they had witnessed in honest, open dialog. Their state of mind was illogical. They had seen the large crowds and witnessed firsthand the abilities of the African American players but said nothing in defense of these outstanding athletes. This illusion of racial superiority, ever-present in their minds, set the stage for one of the most dispiriting legacies of economic inequality in U.S. sports history, in spite of the tour's many achievements.

The Dean's jaunt against the unrecognized stars of Negro baseball after the 1934 World Series drew in excess of 107,150 fans in spite of often-unfavorable late October weather. The amount Dizzy, Daffy, and their promoters earned was big news to the media, who, on a daily basis, attempted to summarize the totals. Ray L. Doan went public with the following announcement: "I thought that Lindy [Charles Lindberg] was popular when he came back after his Atlantic flight, but you have no idea the crowds that daily almost mobbed Dizzy and Paul." One sports organ let it be known that on the "basis of an $8,500 income from the club, Dizzy has so far realized in round numbers $24,000 for the year."[3]

What the African American players earned was never revealed in print, although the brothers' take was publicized often. After the game in Chicago, the *Tipton (Indiana) Daily Tribune* reported that the bankroll of the Deans had increased by something like $14,000 since the end of the World Series. The article stated they had taken in $5,000—more than Daffy made all season—for pitching two innings each for the Mills semipros Sunday against the barnstorming Kansas City Monarchs. An article in the *Pittsburgh Sun-Telegraph* on October 24 stated, "The Deans estimate that their barnstorming trip, which ended here yesterday, netted them between $10,000 and $12,000" each. Following each game, Doan took half of the Deans' share and, out of that total, paid their expenses. Dizzy and Paul got the remainder, which usually meant about "25 percent of the gross receipts. After all expenses had been settled, Doan shelled out another $3,358 to the Deans, a total separate from the amount they had already received." "Diz and Paul," Mrs. Dean predicted, "will be $35,000 richer at the conclusion of their vaudeville tour."[4]

Having collected all of the baseball coin they could before the winter, Dizzy and Daffy left the outdoors for the indoors, going directly to New York for a one-week engagement at the Roxy Theater—where Negroes weren't welcome as paid customers, except probably in the area called the peanut gallery, far away from the stage. There, the brothers earned an additional $1,625 each for their weeklong vaudeville engagement. During their New York visit, they also appeared in a baseball short with Shemp Howard of Three Stooges fame, for which they were further compensated.

An additional $2,250 to $2,750 was paid to the brothers for an appearance in an Artagraph Pictures Company movie short. The movie was directed by Lloyd French and featured actors Roscoe Ates, Shemp Howard, and Dick Cramer. It was the first attempt to tell part of Dizzy and Daffy's real story in movie form, although many liberties were taken. The Deans played themselves. Howard appeared as "Lefty" Howard, using his physical comedy, prate talk, and slapstick stunts throughout. The poorly written script included a stuttering umpire and Howard as a half-blind veteran pitcher. In one scene, actors wore Brooklyn Farmers uniforms, on loan for the segment, filmed at Erasmus Field in Brooklyn. Final scenes showed the Cardinals winning the World Series and included actual film footage from the fall classic. One of the best lines in the movie came when an almost-blind Howard went to bat and stood on home plate instead of in the batter's box. The umpire stopped the game and said, "Put your feet where they belong." Howard responded, "If I did you wouldn't sit down for a week."[5]

The tour had ended, but the debate concerning Dizzy and Daffy's earnings was just getting started. There were few public arguments regarding their effectiveness on the field. Arguments about what agents were to be paid continued into early 1935. This agent was taking the brothers for as much as he could, as Dizzy was required to pay a small commission on his barnstorming receipts to a St. Louisan, according to an agreement that expired in 1935.[6] These so-called small commissions turned into a major squabble that ended up in court. Bill DeWitt, a former peanut and soda vendor, and later a long-time administrative secretary to Branch Rickey of the Cardinals, claimed unpaid commissions from Dizzy and Daffy's earnings.

In a 1941 team-issued history of William Orville DeWitt, who was then serving as vice president for the St. Louis Browns, his biography said he had started in baseball by hustling soda at old Sportsman's Park. The year was 1916. In late 1934 and early 1935, he was hustling the Deans—especially Dizzy. Dizzy's take from the legendary season was presented in a court case, showing he may have earned more money than anyone knew when DeWitt filed a lawsuit claiming unpaid commissions. An article in the *Sporting News* tried to guess the Deans' take for the fall of 1934, and so had others. It was estimated that the amount of the brothers' individual earnings included $5,389 each from the World Series, $2,750 each from the movie they filmed, $5,716 each from the barnstorming tour, and $1,625 each for a week of appearing at the Roxy Theater in New York.[7] We need not estimate some of Dizzy's earnings, as they are public record.

Thanks to DeWitt, who served as Dizzy's agent at Rickey's covetous insistence, we have some of the totals almost down to the penny. As the pitcher's so-called agent, DeWitt was to be paid a 10 percent commission on some items and a one-third commission on others. He sued for his agent's commission in a St. Louis court. If not for Commissioner Kenesaw Mountain Landis, whose investigations into DeWitt's backdoor activities with the Deans' outside income brought many things to light, Dizzy and Daffy would have suffered greatly. Commissioner Landis reportedly reduced some of DeWitt's larger cuts.

DeWitt presented evidence that Dizzy cleared at least $7,000 from the barnstorming tour—a figure significantly less than the total Pat Dean made public. The extent of Dizzy's profitability from May 1933 to November 1934 illustrates the extent to which Negro major-league players were economically pickpocketed in the era of segregation. There was much more money in baseball than they knew, especially when it came to endorsements—deals they would rarely get. Dizzy's earnings were astronomical for the time, and the endorsement deals were many. He earned more than most fans could imagine, almost tripling his annual baseball salary from the Cardinals.[8] Listed among his annual income were the following items for 1934 and early 1935:

General Foods advertisement, $500.00
Christy Walsh News syndicate, for a World Series column, $728.34
General Mills, Grape Nuts cereal funny paper cartoon, $300.00
M. Hohner Incorporated, harmonica endorsement, $250.00
Caradine Hat Company, use of name, $500.00
Nunn-Bush Shoe Company, radio commercial, $100.00
Western Table and Slate Company, use of name on writing tablet, $500.00
A. Cohen and Sons, $233.29
Barr Rubber Products Company, rubber reducing suit, $187.60
Young & Rubicam, Inc., integrated marketing (1934), $15,000.00
Young & Rubicam, Inc., integrated marketing (1935), $15,000.00
J. C. Ayling kite factory, $67.00
Rice-Stix Dry Goods Company, shirts and baseball cards, $2,089.52
Marx & Hass Clothing Company, men's wear, $538.60
M. D. Dreyfach, $885.60
W. C. Schneir, $19.36
Hall Brothers, for a line of Greeting Cards, Kansas City, $ 6.57
Nok-Out Baseball Company, $250.00
Beech-Nut Tobacco Company, $250.00
Dick Slack, Slack Furniture, Tom Daily, KWK radio (1934), $1,450.00
Dick Slack, Slack Furniture, Tom Daily KWK radio (1935), $5,000.00
Kate Smith, radio broadcast, $600.00
Al Jolson, radio broadcast, $450.00
J. G. T. Spink, Sporting News Publishing Company, $100.00
A. G. Spalding & Brothers, $4,260.71

In addition to the endorsement money there were also other valuable considerations to examine. The tour had served as a wake-up call for generations to come. In 1947, while employed as general manager of the St. Louis Browns, this same William DeWitt would sign Hank Thompson and Willard Brown from the Kansas City Monarchs, making them the third and fourth African Americans taken into the National and American Leagues behind

Jackie Robinson and Larry Doby. When they failed to bring in an abundance of cash-paying customers, DeWitt dropped them from the roster of the last-place team as if they were scorching pieces of black charcoal.

The Deans' 1934 tour proved that there was a serious disparity in the economics of baseball; an inequality in player recognition; a lack of creditability in the media; and discrimination and unfairness in living and traveling conditions that worked against the profitability and advancement of African American players, teams, and owners. There was little difference in the ability of those playing in the minor leagues, major leagues, or Negro professional leagues; however, the earnings gap, lack of endorsement opportunities, and poor media coverage was significant. It was destined to remain that way for many years, although Dizzy and Daffy reaffirmed that men of all ethnicities could play baseball together—which was ancient history for most.

Furthermore, the Deans' barnstorming tour demonstrated that men in the Negro major leagues were equal to the best in the National and American Leagues. These were proud African American men, the sons and grandsons of former slaves toiling in a game called baseball. The pattern in American society was to persuade the public to view them as inferior human beings, unqualified for the task of big-league play and unworthy of recognition for major-league stardom—and it worked and continues to do so. Some of the most renowned and celebrated writers in the United States pushed this ideology through their reckless neglect and prejudiced reporting. They elected to ignore what they had seen on the field, choosing instead to continue their lampooning of the Deans for their loquacious and amusing comments while ignoring the plight of African American players almost in unison. If they had been asked, Dizzy and Daffy most certainly could have named an All-African American team based purely on what they had witnessed.

Dizzy and Daffy had witnessed not only the Crawfords Satchel Paige strike out 13 in six innings at Cleveland, which was well publicized, but also other things equally spectacular but rarely discussed. In Brooklyn, Dizzy had seen Clint Thomas steal home. And he watched helplessly as "Neck" Stanley whiffed "Ducky" Medwick four consecutive times. In Philadelphia, they had seen submarine pitching artist Webster McDonald get more hits as a batter than he allowed in nine innings as a pitcher. The Deans had also seen Josh Gibson homer, not just once but twice, in Pittsburgh and Columbus, and in Oklahoma City they saw every batter in the mighty Monarchs lineup get hits off both Deans in a game that only lasted six innings. And don't forget about Charlie Beverly, who struck out 15 All-Stars in Des Moines.

By embarking on the tour, Dizzy and Daffy had made their own kind of history, history that was achieved in a most monumental way, both on the field and off. They fostered hope that the National and American Leagues might someday unlock their gates and let African American players into the fold. It would take 12 more years before "Uncle Branch" Rickey, as he was often called by his team, the man who had originally signed Dizzy and Daffy, and was obviously watching the results, to sign Jackie Robinson, an African American, to the Brooklyn Dodgers. In the meantime, there was lots of money to be made by the brothers and other men in the National and American Leagues, not necessarily for men outside these leagues who were African American. In 1935, both Deans signed large contracts. It wasn't the money they were hoping for; it was a compromise figure.

In 1935, Dizzy and Daffy cashed in on their success. The Cardinals upped Dizzy's salary to $17,500, plus a $1,000 bonus—double what he had been paid the year before. Daffy also saw a healthy increase, which was said to be $8,500, plus a $500 bonus—double his Cardinals pay rate of 1934. How do we know this? We know because Dizzy and the media told us so.

In keeping with the antics of mainstream media and their customary biased reporting, we have no idea what the stars of the Negro major leagues were earning in any year—not Paige, not Beverly, not Gibson, and certainly not Clint Thomas. These men had all played well against Dizzy and Daffy, but their performances, once the legendary barnstorming tour ended, were seldom newsworthy. What they achieved from that day onward was inadequately reported. Perhaps now we finally know how and why such a thing could happen.

~

Notes

Preface

1. James P. Dawson, "15,000 See Deans Play Exhibition," *New York Times*, 18 October 1934.

Introduction

1. David Craft, "Meet George Giles: The Negro Leagues' Other First Baseman," *Sports Collectors Digest*, 21 June 1991, 113.

2. Al Monroe, "Speaking of Sports," *Chicago Defender*, 6 October 1934, 16.

Chapter 1

1. Mark Ribowsky, *A Complete History of the Negro Leagues, 1884 to 1955* (New York: Carol, 1995), 189.

2. "Daniel's Dope," *New York World-Telegram*, 18 October 1934, 36.

3. Ira Berkow, *Hank Greenberg: The Story of My Life* (New York: Times Books, 1989), 31.

4. "Serious Paul Dean to Learn Brother 'Dizzy's' Technique," *Wichita Eagle*, 12 October 1934, 8.

5. "Dean Boys Big Stars in American Comedy," *Brooklyn Daily Eagle*, 16 October 1934, 21.

6. "Dizzy Dean's Rise Began Four Years Ago," Associated Press, *Philadelphia Evening Bulletin*, 16 October 1934, n.p.

7. "Oh-Oh We'se A-commin to Springfield," *Illinois State Journal*, 15 March 1928.

8. "Dean Boys Once Called Horrors of the Town," *Brooklyn Daily Eagle*, 19 October 1934, 19.

9. Bill James, *The Bill James Historical Baseball Abstract* (New York: Villard, 1986), 149.

10. Vince Staten, *Ol' Diz: A Biography of Dizzy Dean* (New York: HarperCollins, 1992), 19.

11. Bill James, *The Bill James Historical Baseball Abtract*, 146.

12. "Dizzy Rivaling Ruth as Money Maker This Season," *Brooklyn Daily Eagle*, 3 October 1934, 18.

13. Herbert Simons, "Did Dean Do It? Will Don Do It 30 Wins," *Baseball Digest*, May 1963, 6.

14. Edward J. Neil, "Missus Dizzy Tells about Fiery Diz and Quiet Daffy," *Raleigh (NC) News Observer*, 19 October 1934.

15. Herbert Simons, "Did Dean Do It? Will Don Do It?" *Baseball Digest*, May 1963.

16. Bill Finger, "Passing in Review," *Cleveland Call and Post*, 2 June 1934, 6.

17. George Giles, personal interview, 1984.

18. John Snow, "Antique Dealer's Hobby Keeps Him on the Road," *Springfield News Leader*, 3 May 1936, B4.

19. Ernest Mehl, "Sporting Comment," *Kansas City Star*, 29 January 1956, 32.

20. Mehl, "Sporting Comment," 32.

21. Al Monroe, "Panic Is Seen within the Ranks of Organized Baseball," *Abbott's Monthly*, August 1932, 48.

22. Paul Mickelson, "Dizzy and Daffy to Keep Right On Pitching in Exhibition Tour," *Biloxi Daily Herald*, 10 October 1934, 3.

23. "Famous Den Brothers May Come to Muscatine," *Muscatine (IA) Journal and News Tribune*, 10 October 1934, 8.

24. Bill Finger, "Passing in Review," 6.

Chapter 2

1. Meredith Williams, "Dizzy and Nutsie Dean Are Both Proved Sane as 15,000 Fans Go Delirious in City Ball Park," *Oklahoma News*, 11 October 1934, 1.

2. "Dizzy and Paul Dean to Rush Here by Plane," *Oklahoma News*, 9 October 1934, 8.

3. "Dizzy Sent Wire Collect," *Brooklyn Daily Eagle*, 4 October 1934, M1.

4. "Tulsa Date for Deans Canceled," *Tulsa Daily World*, 9 October 1934, 10.

5. "Dizzy and Paul Show City Fans How They Tamed Tigers in Game with Monarchs at Texas League Park Tonight," *Daily Oklahoman*, 10 October 1934, 13.

6. Karl Wingler, "These Were the Firsts," *Baseball Digest*, May 1963.

7. "Monarchs Again Win from Colts in Game at R.I. Park, 10 to 3," *Kansas City Kansan*, 8 October 1934.

8. Bill Finger, "Passing in Review," *Cleveland Call and Post*, 5 May 1934, 6.

9. "Monarchs vs. Colts Clash Here Today," *Kansas City Kansan*, 7 October 1934, 9A.

10. Bus Ham, "A Column of Sports," *Daily Oklahoman*, 10 October 1934, L3.

11. "Baseball Runs Out as Deans Capture Town," *Vidette-Messenger*, 13 October 1934, 6.

12. "Great Men of Baseball Get Eye of Public," *Daily Oklahoman*, 11 October 1934, 16.

13. "Great Men of Baseball Get Eye of Public," 16.

14. "Great Men of Baseball Get Eye of Public," 16.

15. "Great Men of Baseball Get Eye of Public," 16.

16. Meredith Williams, "Dizzy and Nutsie Dean Are Both Proved Sane, As 15,000 Fans Go Delirious in City Ball Park" *Oklahoma News*, 11 October 1934, 1.

17. "Great Men of Baseball Get Eye of Public," 16.

18. "Dizzy Finds His Barnstorming Much Too Exciting for Fans," *Baltimore Sun*, 19 October 1934, 26.

19. Ham, "A Column of Sports," 13.

20. "Great Men of Baseball Get Eye of Public," 16.

21. "Dizzy and Nutsie Dean Are Both Proved Sane as 15,000 Fans Go Delirious in City Ball Park," 1.

22. Ham, "15,000 Storm Park to See Dizzy and Daffy," 17.

23. "Deans Go to Wichita after Entertaining 15,000 Here," *Oklahoma News*, 11 October 1934, n.p.

24. Ham, "15,000 Storm Park to See Dizzy and Daffy," 17.

25. "Baseball in Oklahoma," *Cleveland Call and Post*, 20 October 1934, 4.

26. "Negro Hurler Fans 14 Men, Blanks Stars," *Daily Oklahoman*, 12 October 1933, 12.

27. Bill Finger, "Passing in Review," *Cleveland Call and Post*, 29 September 1934, 6.

28. Chet Brewer, personal interview, 6 July 1987.

29. George Giles, personal interview, 1984.

30. Brewer, personal interview.

31. "Dizzy and Paul Dean to Rush Here by Plane," 8.

32. "The Famous Dizzy Dean Will Be with the League," *Negro Star*, 28 September 1934, 5.

33. "Paul Dean to Start, Dizzy to Follow in Game Here Tonight," *Oklahoma News*, 10 October 1934.

34. Lloyd Johnson and Miles Wolf, *The Encyclopedia of Minor League Baseball* (Durham, NC: Baseball America, 1993), 182.

35. Chris Rainey, "Uke Clanton," *Society for American Baseball Research*, https://sabr.org/bioproj/person/e895b6e6 (accessed November 18, 2017).

36. "Deans' Ticket Sale Delayed," *Oklahoma City Times*, 8 October 1934, 14.

37. "Pepper Martin Faces Knife," *Brooklyn Daily Eagle*, 13 December 1934, 1.

38. *Kansas City Star*, 5 August 1926, n.p.

39. Williams, "Dizzy and Nutsie Dean Are Both Proved Sane as 15,000 Fans Go Delirious in City Ball Park," 1.

40. Williams, "Dizzy and Nutsie Dean Are Both Proved Sane, As 15,000 Fans Go Delirious in City Ball Park," 1.

41. "Dizzy and Nutsie Dean Are Both Proved Sane as 15,000 Fans Go Delirious in City Ball Park," 1.

42. Ham, "15,000 Storm Park to See Dizzy and Daffy," 7.

43. Johnson and Wolf, *The Encyclopedia of Minor League Baseball*.

44. "Dean Crowd of 11,976 Barely Fails to Top Record," *Oklahoma City Times*, 11 October 1934, 16.

45. Ham, "15,000 Storm Park to See Dizzy and Daffy," 17.

46. John Holway, *Voices from the Great Black Baseball Leagues* (New York: Dodd, Mead, 1975), 101.

47. "Deans on Mound against Monarchs Tonight," *Kansas City Call*, 12 October 1934, unknown.

48. "Deans Refuse to Be Separated," *Wichita Eagle*, 11 October 1934, n.p.

49. Frances Corry, "Jerome Not So Dizzy, Says Loyal Wife of Great Pitcher," *Oklahoma News*, 11 October 1934, 11.

50. Ham, "15,000 Storm Park to See Dizzy and Daffy," 17.

51. Ham, "15,000 Storm Park to See Dizzy and Daffy," 17; "Dean Crowd of 11,976 Barely Fails to Top Record," *Oklahoma City Times*, 11 October 1934, 16.

52. Ham, "15,000 Storm Park to See Dizzy and Daffy," 17.

53. Meredith Williams, "Dizzy and Daffy Sane Ones There, Says Williams," *Oklahoma News*, 11 October 1934, 11.

54. "Dizzy and Daffy Are Backed by 7,000 Infielders," *Wichita Beacon*, 11 October 1934, n.p.

55. Bill Finger, "Baseball in Oklahoma," *Cleveland Call and Post*, 20 October 1934, 4.

56. Jake Cornwell, personal interview, 1 July 2018.

Chapter 3

1. "Game Certain," *Wichita Beacon*, 10 October 1934.

2. "Famous Deans Will Pitch against Monarchs at New Field," *Wichita Eagle*, 11 October 1934, 8.

3. Bernie Williams, "K.C. Monarchs Play an All-Star League Cast in Wichita," *Negro Star*, 28 September 1934, 5.

4. "Monarchs Play Major Leaguers, Oct 10," *Negro Star*, 5 October 1934, 5.

5. "Two Deans Will Face Monarchs," *Wichita Eagle*, 5 October 1934.

6. "Deans May Take Plane to Wichita," *Wichita Eagle*, 8 October 1934.

7. "10,000 Will Jam Lawrence Stadium to Greet Dean Brothers, Heroes of World Series," *Wichita Beacon*, 11 October 1934, 15.

8. "Huge Crowd Sure to Be Out When Deans Play Here," *Wichita Eagle*, 10 October 1934, 8.

9. "Night Baseball to Get Trial in Wichita Tonight," *Wichita Beacon*, 2 June 1930, 12.

10. "Major Leaguers Beat Monarchs," *Wichita Eagle*, 13 October 1933, 20.

11. "All-Stars Defeat Monarchs 8 to 3," *Negro Star*, 19 October 1934, 5.

12. "Stars Scores," *St. Louis Argus*, 10 October 1930.

13. George Giles, personal interview, 1986.

14. "Monarchs Claim They Beat Dizzy," *Wichita Eagle*, 10 October 1934, 8.

15. "Dizzy Dean to 8,000," *Kansas City Times*, 3 October 1933.

16. "Monarchs Down an All-Star Selection," *Concordia Blade-Empire*, 4 October 1933, 4.

17. "'T' Baby Young Says Dizzy Dean Is a Hard Nut to Crack," *Negro Star*, 12 October 1934, 4.

18. "Deans Refuse to Be Separated," *Wichita Eagle*, 11 October 1934, n.p.

19. Frank Duncan Jr., personal interview, 15 November 1986.

20. Giles, personal interview.

21. Denise R. Harvey, "A Baseball Memoir: George Giles: A Young Man's Dream, a Nation's Shame," *Manhattan Mercury*, 27 May 1984, D1.

22. David Craft, "Meet George Giles: The Negro Leagues' Other First Baseman," *Sports Collectors Digest*, 21 June 1991, 112.

23. Craft, "Meet George Giles," 112.

24. Giles, personal interview.

25. Giles, personal interview.

26. "Living Legend," *Kansas State Collegian*, 25 January 1991, 12.

27. "House of David Certain of Win over Monarchs," *Wichita Beacon*, 26 August 1934.

28. "Monarchs Win before Huge Crowd," *Wichita Beacon*, 27 August 1934, n.p.

29. "Riot Marks Victory of Cards; Deans Start on Tour of West," *Wichita Eagle*, 10 October 1934.

30. "Base Ball News," *Negro Star*, 19 October 1934, 5.

31. "Monarchs Win before Huge Crowd," *Wichita Beacon*, 27 August 1934, n.p.

32. "Dean Boys Entertain Vast Crowd by Baseball Feats," *Wichita Eagle*, 12 October 1934, 8.

33. "Base Ball News," *Negro Star*, 19 October 1934, 5.

34. "Base Ball News," 5.

35. "Dean Boys Entertain Vast Crowd by Baseball Feats," 8.

36. "Base Ball News," 5.

37. John Holway, *Blackball Tales: Rollicking, All New, True Adventures of the Negro Leagues by the Men Who Lived and Loved Them* (Springfield, VA: Scorpio Books, 2008), 58.

38. "Deans Make Hit with Fans Here," *Wichita Eagle*, 12 October 1934, 16.

39. "Huge Crowd Sees Famous Deans in Exhibition Appearance," *Wichita Beacon*, 12 October 1934, 15.

40. "Deans Make Hit with Fans Here," 16.

41. "Base Ball News," 5.

42. "Dockum Drug Store Sit-in," *Kansas Historical Society*, https://www.kshs.org/kansapedia/dockum-drug-store-sit-in/17048 (accessed November 18, 2017).

43. "Dockum Drug Store Sit-in."

44. Debs Myers, "Sitting In in the Sports Game," *Wichita Eagle*, 12 October 1934, 16.

45. "Dizzy Likely to Start," *Kansas City Star*, 12 October 1934, 22.

Chapter 4

1. "Deans on Mound against Monarchs Tonight," *Kansas City Call*, 12 October 1934, 1.

2. "Dean Brothers to Attend Dinner Here," *Kansas City Journal-Post*, 11 October 1934, 16.

3. Georgia Dwight, personal interviews, 1982–2003.

4. "The Deans Here Tonight," *Kansas City Times*, 12 October 1934, 12.

5. "Deans May Draw Huge Crowd Here," *Kansas City Kansan*, 11 October 1934, 6.

6. George Giles, personal interview, 1986.

7. "Dean Brothers Here to Pitch against Monarchs," *Kansas City Journal-Post*, 12 October 1934, 18.

8. "Dizzy Ready for Work," *Kansas City Star*, 2 October 1933, 8.

9. "Deans Here Friday," *Kansas City Journal-Post*, 7 October 1934.

10. "Dizzy Dean Boys to Pitch Here Tonight," *Kansas City Kansan*, 12 October 1934, 12.

11. Sec Taylor, "Monarchs Batter Demons, 14 to 3," *Des Moines Register*, 8 August 1933.

12. "Monarchs, Davids play 10 Frames to 8–8 Deadlock," *La Crosse Tribune*, 21 September 1934.

13. "N.Y. Giants Just Hit Slump, Explains Bowman," *Kansas City Journal-Post*, 7 October 1934, 13A.

14. Frank Weitekamp, "Just Below the Majors," *Brooklyn Daily Eagle*, 9 September 1934, 11.

15. "Rogan's Hit to Right Breaks Up a Ball Game That Almost Gives the Fans Heart Disease," *Kansas City Call Southwest Edition*, 6 October 1933.

16. "Monarchs Win in Ninth," *Kansas City Times*, 16 October 1933, 10.

17. "Steel Arm Davis Is Killed," *Chicago Defender*, 3 December 1941, 23.

18. "Trading of Davis Hit by Ball Fans," *Chicago Defender*, 24 March 1934, A4.

19. "11 to 0 Count on Famous Men from Big Teams," *Jamestown Sun*, 8 October 1934, 6.

20. "Paul Dean Is Silent," *Kansas City Times*, 13 October, 1934, 14.

21. "By Paul Dean," *Wichita Beacon*, 11 October 1934, n.p.

22. "By Paul Dean," 15.

23. "Paul Dean Is Silent," *Kansas City Times*, 13 October 1934, 14.

24. James B. Reston, "Those Incredible Deans," *Milwaukee Journal*, 22 October 1934, 32.

25. "Frisch Here Friday," *Kansas City Journal-Post*, 10 October 1934.

26. "Dizzy Keeps Up His Fun," *Kansas City Times*, 13 October 1934, 2.

27. Andy Anderson, "He's Not So Dizzy," *Kansas City Kansan*, 16 October 1934, 6.

28. "Party for Baseball Stars," *Kansas City Times*, 13 October 1934, 2.

29. "Party for Baseball Stars," 2.

30. "The Dean Boys Attend Frank Frisch's Party," *Kansas City Times*, 13 October 1934, 8.

31. "Dizzy Keeps Up His Fun," 2.

32. "Both Deans Will Hurl," *Kansas City Star*, 11 October 1934, 14.

33. "Dizzy Keeps Up His Fun," 1.

34. Fay Young, "Deans on Mound against Monarchs Tonight," *Kansas City Call*, 12 October 1934, 1.

35. "Dizzy Keeps Up His Fun," 1.

36. "Dean Brothers Pitch Two Innings Each before 15,000 Fans in K.C., MO," *Kansas City Kansan*, 13 October 1934, 5.

37. "Monarchs Beat Deans," *Kansas City Times*, 13 October 1934, 14.

38. L. Herbert Henegan, "Monarchs Win from the Dean Brothers 7–0," *Kansas City Call*, 19 October 1934, 1.

39. Chet Brewer, personal interview, 6 July 1987.

40. Brewer, personal interview.

41. "Monarchs Beat Deans," *Kansas City Times*, 13 October 1934, 14.

42. Elden Auker, with Tom Keegan, *Sleeper Cars and Flannel Uniforms: A Lifetime of Memories from Striking Out the Babe to Teeing It Up with the President* (Chicago: Triumph, 2001), 94.

43. Andy Cooper, "Hot Stove League," *Negro Star*, 30 November 1934, 5.

44. "Monarchs Beat Deans," 14.

45. Jack Etkin, "Memories of Early Days with Monarchs Still Fresh for Two Survivors," *Kansas City Star*, 23 July 1985, 3C.

46. Timothy M. Gay, *Satch, Dizzy, and Rapid Robert* (New York: Simon and Schuster, 2010), 84.

47. "Talk to 'The Great,'" *Kansas City Star*, 13 October 1934, 2.

48. "Sez Ches," *Pittsburgh Courier*, 20 October 1934, A4.

Chapter 5

1. "Police for Deans Here," *Des Moines Tribune*, 12 October 1934, 11A.

2. "Dean Obliges Kansas City Nut Vendor," *Des Moines Tribune*, 13 October 1934, 6.

3. "Dean All-Stars Beaten 9–0 by Monarchs Team," *Des Moines Register*, 14 October 1934, 1.

4. James Reston, "These Incredible Deans," *Paterson Evening News*, 16 October 1934, 21.

5. Lee Lowenfish, *Branch Rickey: Baseball's Ferocious Gentleman* (Lincoln: University of Nebraska Press, 2009), 211.

6. Edward J. Neil, "Goofy and Dizzy Dean Will Share $30,000 for Exhibitions; Deans Take Rest after Vaudeville Act," *Baton Rouge State Times Advocate*, 18 October 1934, 20.

7. C. C. Johnson Spink, *Daguerreotypes of Great Stars of Baseball*. St. Louis, MO: Sporting News, 1981.

8. "Famous Dean Family Team Pays Visit to Wichita," *Wichita Eagle*, 12 October 1934, 8.

9. "Famous Dean Family Team Pays Visit to Wichita," 8.

10. "Famous Dean Family Team Pays Visit to Wichita," 8.

11. "Daffy's Hat Pays Loser on Tigers," *Washington Evening Star*, 19 October 1934, C-6.

12. "Police for Deans Here," *Des Moines Tribune*, 12 October 1934.

13. "Local Semipro Stars to Play with Dean Boys," *Des Moines Tribune*, 11 October 1934, 4A.

14. "Dean Brothers on Air Today," *Des Moines Tribune*, 13 October 1934.

15. "Cowles Media Company History," http://www.fundinguniverse.com/company-histories/cowles-media-company-history/ (accessed November 18, 2017).

16. "Dizzy Learns," *Des Moines Register*, 14 October 1934, 3.

17. Vince Staten, *Ol' Diz: A Biography of Dizzy Dean* (New York: HarperCollins, 1992).

18. Karl Wingler, "These Were the Firsts," *Baseball Digest*, May 1963.

19. Pete Lightner, "Just in Sports," *Wichita Eagle*, 11 October 1934, 8.

20. "K.C. Monarchs Bow to the Inevitable," *Oxford (NE) Standard*, 5 October 1933, 1.

21. "K.C. Monarchs Bow to the Inevitable," 1.

22. "Baseball Jockeys," *Baton Rouge Advocate*, 16 September 1952, 10.

23. George Kirksey, "'How Am I Doing, Edna?' Cardinals Query Rowe," *Miami Herald*, 11 October 1934, 14.

24. Rollo S. Vest, "'Schoolboy' Rowe Denies Rumors," *Detroit Tribune-Independent*, 13 October 1934, 2.

25. "Schoolboy Rowe Denies He Slurred Colored," *Baltimore Afro-American*, 27 October 1934, n.p.

26. "Local Semipro Stars to Play with Dean Boys," *Des Moines Tribune*, 11 October 1934, 4A.

27. "In Exhibition Contest Here Tonight," *Des Moines Tribune*, 13 October 1934, 6.

28. "Dean Brothers on Air Today."

29. Doyl Taylor, "Holdenville Horrors Here Tonight," *Des Moines Register*, 13 October 1934, 5.

30. Taylor, "Holdenville Horrors Here Tonight," 5.

31. Troy Black, personal interviews, 1985.

32. Phil S. Dixon, Dixon's Negro League Greats, Card #4.

33. Georgia Dwight, personal interviews, 1982–2003.

34. "St. John Defeated by All-Stars, 6–3," *Kansas City Times*, 21 October 1929, n.p.

35. Black, personal interviews.

36. Marriage certificate in Phil Dixon's records, Jackson County, Missouri, #86219.

37. Phil Dixon and Patrick J. Hannigan, *The Negro Baseball Leagues: A Photographic History* (Mattituck, NY: Amereon House, 1992), 105.

38. John Holway, *Blackball Tales: Rollicking, All New, True Adventures of the Negro Leagues by the Men Who Lived and Loved Them* (Springfield, VA: Scorpio Books, 2008), 70.

39. "Dean All-Stars Beaten 9–0 by Monarchs Team," 1.

40. "'Old Diz' Names Paige Greatest Pitcher," *Chicago Metropolitan Post*, 24 September 1938, 15.

41. Holway, *Blackball Tales*, 77.

42. "Ohio Girl Denies She's Engaged to Paul (Daffy) Dean," *Des Moines Register*, 14 October 1934, 3.

Chapter 6

1. "Deans Sign to Play Here," *Kansas City Times*, 9 October 1934, n.p.

2. "Monarchs Seek Page to Oppose Dean Brothers," *Chicago Tribune*, 13 October 1934, 22.

3. "Seek 'Satchel' Page to Face Dean Boys," *Chicago Herald and Examiner*, 13 October 1934, 20.

4. John Holway, *Voices from the Great Black Baseball Leagues* (New York: Dodd, Mead, 1975), 143.

5. C. C. Johnson Spink, *Daguerreotypes of Great Stars of Baseball* (St. Louis, MO: Sporting News, 1981), 218.

6. Pat Gannon, "Is He Bragging?" *Milwaukee Journal Sentinel,* 14 October 1934, 21.

7. Satchel Paige, *Maybe I'll Pitch Forever* (Lincoln: University of Nebraska Press, 1993), 96.

8. Bill Finger, "Passing in Review," *Cleveland Call and Post,* 25 August 1934, 6.

9. "Deans Pitch for Mills Today in Exhibition Game," *Chicago Tribune,* 14 October 1934, A4.

10. "Dean on Slab for Semipros," *Chicago Herald and Examiner,* 14 October 1934, 21.

11. "Deans Pitch for Mills Today in Exhibition Game."

12. "Deans on Slab for Semipros," *Chicago Herald and Examiner,* 14 October 1934.

13. "Paul and Dizzy Dean Pitchers against Monarchs at Mills," *Chicago Defender,* 13 October 1934, 17.

14. Bill Nowlin, "Gordon McNaughton," *Society for American Baseball Research,* https://sabr.org/bioproj/person/044f718c (accessed October 15, 2017).

15. "Jilted Platinum Blonde Slays Athlete," *Omaha World Herald,* 7 August 1942, 1.

16. Chet Brewer, personal interview, 6 July 1987.

17. Brewer, personal interview.

18. Phil Ellenbecker, "Brewer: Cooperstown-bound?" *Leavenworth (KS) Times,* 30 August 1987, 8A.

19. Chet Brewer, personal interview, date not recorded.

20. "Dean and Dean Get $5,000 Pitching for Mills Team," *Chicago Tribune,* 15 October 1934, 19.

21. "Deans Capture Semipro Game," *Chicago Tribune,* 15 October 1934, n.p.

22. "Deans Play to 20,000," *Kansas City Star,* 15 October 1934, n.p.

23. "Monarchs Bow to the Deans in Chicago," *Kansas City Call,* 19 October 1934, n.p.

24. Lynn Doyle, "Close-Ups on the Sport Screen," *Philadelphia Evening Bulletin,* 17 October 1934, n.p.

25. "Injury May Keep Foxx Out of Game for Good," *New York World-Telegram,* 16 October 1934, 27.

26. "By Harry Grayson," *Stamford (CT) Daily Advocate,* 17 October 1934, 4.

27. Albert W. Keane, "Calling 'Em Right," *Hartford Courant,* 17 October 1934, 15.

28. Jacob Pomrenke, "John Sullivan," *Society for American Baseball Research,* https://sabr.org/bioproj/person/22fde3cf (accessed September 3, 2017).

29. "20,000 Watch Deans Capture Semipro Game," *Chicago Herald and Examiner,* 15 October 1934.

30. "20,000 Watch Deans Capture Semipro Game," n.p.

31. Julius J. Adams, "Twenty Thousand Fans See Deans Beat Monarchs," *Chicago Defender,* 20 October 1934, n.p.

32. "Dean and Dean Get $5,000 Pitching for Mills Team," 19.

 Notes ⌒ 227

Chapter 7

1. Howard Purser, "Sports Slants," *Wisconsin News*, 16 October 1934, 16.

2. "Packers Arrive; Workout for Bears Game Here," *Milwaukee Journal Sentinel*, 16 October 1934, 18.

3. Bob Buege, "Red Thisted," *Society for American Baseball Research*, https://sabr.org/node/30734 (accessed June 18, 2017).

4. Red Thisted, "Crowd Riots after Dean Exhibition Here," *Milwaukee Sentinel*, 16 October 1934, 13.

5. Thisted, "Crowd Riots after Dean Exhibition Here," 13.

6. Purser, "Sports Slants," 16.

7. Ben Smith, "Sports Editor," *Milwaukee Leader*, 16 October 1934, 7.

8. Floyd Baird, personal interview, 11 June 1986.

9. Baird, personal interview.

10. "Leading K.C.K. Team Two Decades Ago," *Kansas City Kansan*, 22 May 1940, n.p.

11. Timothy Rives, "The Second Ku Klux Klan in Kansas City: Rise and Fall of a White Nationalist Movement," *PendergastKC.org*, http://pendergastkc.org/article/second-ku-klux-klan-kansas-city-rise-and-fall-white-nationalist-movement (accessed June 18, 2017).

12. Baird, personal interview.

13. Purser, "Sports Slants," n.p.

14. Purser, "Sports Slants," 16.

15. Purser, "Sports Slants," n.p.

16. Purser, "Sports Slants," n.p.

17. "Police Called to Quiet Crowd as Deans 'Run Out,'" *Milwaukee Journal Sentinel*, 16 October 1934, 18.

18. Jimmy Breslin, *Branch Rickey* (New York: Viking, 2011), 47.

19. Lloyd Johnson and Miles Wolf, *The Encyclopedia of Minor League Baseball* (Durham, NC: Baseball America, 1993), 151.

20. Bill James, *The Bill James Historical Baseball Abstract* (New York: Villard, 1986), 149.

21. Breslin, *Branch Rickey*, 6.

22. Lee Lowenfish, *Branch Rickey: Baseball's Ferocious Gentleman* (Lincoln: University of Nebraska Press, 2009), 22.

23. Breslin, *Branch Rickey*, 28.

24. Phil Dixon, *Phil Dixon's American Baseball Chronicles: Great Teams: The 1905 Philadelphia Giants*, Vol. 2 (Booksurge: 2010), 265–66.

25. Dixon, *Phil Dixon's American Baseball Chronicles*, 265.

26. Ira Berkow, *Hank Greenberg: The Story of My Life* (New York: Times Books, 1989), 69.

27. "Diz Not Talking Anymore; Boss Breadon Puts on Gag," *Milwaukee Journal Sentinel*, 16 October 1934, 18.

28. "Diz Not Talking Anymore," 18.

29. "Deans Get $14,000 Since Card Series; Pitch Here Today," *Milwaukee Journal*, 15 October 1934, 4.

30. "Deans Still Dazzle 'Em," *Sporting News*, 18 October 1934, 1.

31. "Deans in City Post Series Take $14,000," *Milwaukee Leader*, 15 October 1934, n.p.

32. "Dean Brothers Collect Cash on New Tour," *Ogden (UT) Standard-Examiner*, 15 October 1934.

33. "Dooly," *Philadelphia Record*, 17 October 1934, 16D.

34. "Eddie Stumpf Is Signed by Chicago," *Montgomery (AL) Advertiser*, 20 January 1919.

35. Lloyd Johnson, *The Minor League Register* (Durham, NC: Baseball America, 1994).

36. Johnson, *The Minor League Register*.

37. "Dizzy, Daffy Dean to Pitch Exhibition Game Here Monday," *Milwaukee Journal Sentinel*, 14 October 1934, 21.

38. "Famous Brothers to Pitch Entire Game at Milwaukee Monday," 11 October 1934.

39. Ben Smith, "Dizzy Hurls Two Innings," *Milwaukee Leader*, 16 October 1934, n.p.

40. "Fans Boo the Deans," *Kansas City Times*, 16 October 1934, 11.

41. "Deans Skip Early; Police Called to Quiet Angry Fans Demanding Money Back!" *Wisconsin News*, 16 October, 1934, n.p.

42. "Deans Are Jeered by Fans in West," *New York Times*, 16 October 1934, 33.

43. Smith, "Dizzy Hurls Two Innings," n.p.

44. Sam Levy, "Police Called to Quiet Crowd as Deans 'Run Out,'" *Milwaukee Journal*, 16 October 1934, n.p.

45. Thisted, "Crowd Riots after Dean Exhibition Here," n.p.

46. Ronald McIntyre, "Between You and Me," *Milwaukee Sentinel*, 16 October 1934, n.p.

47. Lynn Doyle, "Close-ups on the Sports Screen," *Philadelphia Evening Bulletin*, 17 October 1934, n.p.

48. Smith, "Dizzy Hurls Two Innings."

49. "Landis Clears the Dean Boys," *Milwaukee Journal Sentinel*, 25 October 1934, 27.

50. John Holway, *Voices from the Great Black Baseball Leagues* (New York: Dodd, Mead, 1975), 101.

51. Newton Allen, personal interview, 11 August 1985.

52. Purser, "Sports Slants," n.p.

53. John Lardner, "Dean Boys Rusty on Barnstorming Jaunt," *Lincoln (NE) State Journal*, 17 October 1934, 9.

54. R. H. Barber, "R. H. Barber Writes in the *Philadelphia Tribune*," *Kansas City American*, 21 February 1929, 5.

55. John Holway, *Blackball Tales: Rollicking, All New, True Adventures of the Negro Leagues by the Men Who Lived and Loved Them* (Springfield, VA: Scorpio Books, 2008).

56. Carroll Ray Mothell, personal interview, 1980.

57. Holway, *Blackball Tales*.

58. "Flashy Ball Artist," *Iola (KS) Daily Register*, 28 May 1921.

59. "Topeka Giants 12; Overbrook 3," *Topeka State Journal*, 25 July 1921.

60. Celois Street, personal interview, 1980s.

61. "Deans Skip Early," n.p.

62. "Harridge Opposes Barnstorming," *Sporting News*, 25 October 1934, 8.

63. "Diz Not Talking Anymore," n.p.

Chapter 8

1. "Touring Racket Has Dean Down," *Philadelphia Evening Bulletin*, 16 October 1934, n.p.

2. "The Champions are Here!!!" *Hagerstown (MD) Daily Mail*, 16 July 1934, 8.

3. "Dizzy Dean Is Honored Again," *Charleston (SC) Evening Post*, 17 October 1934.

4. "Dizzy Dean Chosen as 'Most Valuable in National League,'" *Philadelphia Record*, 17 October 1934, 16D.

5. "Touring Racket Has Dean Down," *Philadelphia Evening Bulletin*, 16 October 1934, n.p.

6. James Isaminger, "Dizzy-Daffy Stars Lose Double Bill," *Philadelphia Inquirer*, 17 October 1934, 17.

7. Paul Parris, "Deans Fail to Bring Luck to All-Stars," *Philadelphia Record*, 17 October 1934.

8. "Professor Has Too Much on Ball for Deans," *Chicago Daily Tribune*, 17 October 1934, 21.

9. Cy Peterman, "Viewing the Sports Parade," *Philadelphia Evening Bulletin*, 17 October 1934, n.p.

10. Peterman, "Viewing the Sports Parade," n.p.

11. Bill Dooly, "The Deans Discover All Isn't Gold That Glitters," *Sporting News*, 25 October 1934, 7.

12. Peterman, "Viewing the Sports Parade," n.p.

13. Parris, "Deans Fail to Bring Luck to All-Stars," 16D.

14. John Holway, *Voices from the Great Black Baseball Leagues* (New York: Dodd, Mead, 1975), 83.

15. George Giles, personal interview, 1985.

16. Holway, *Voices from the Great Black Baseball Leagues*, 82.

17. "Eddie is the Mogul," *Sports Illustrated*, 22 January 1968, 42.

18. "Eddie Is the Mogul," 44.

19. Rebecca T. Alpert, *Out of Left Field: Jews and Black Baseball* (New York: Oxford University Press, 2011).

20. "Eddie is the Mogul," 42.

21. Holway, *Voices from the Great Black Baseball Leagues*, 84–85.

22. Alpert, *Out of Left Field*, 11.

23. "Just Below the Majors," *Brooklyn Daily Eagle*, 11 September 1934, 19.

24. Holway, *Voices from the Great Black Baseball Leagues*, 71.

25. Holway, *Voices from the Great Black Baseball Leagues*, 75.

26. Holway, *Voices from the Great Black Baseball Leagues*, 80.

27. Parris, "Deans Fail to Bring Luck to All-Stars," 16D.

28. Peterman, "Viewing the Sports Parade," n.p.

29. Parris, "Deans Fail to Bring Luck to All-Stars," 16D.

30. Lynn Doyle, "Close-ups on the Sports Screen," *Philadelphia Evening Bulletin*, 17 October 1934, n.p.

31. John Holway, *Blackball Stars: Negro League Pioneers* (Westport, CT: Meckler Books, 1988), 200.

32. Holway, *Blackball Stars*, 201.

33. Holway, *Blackball Stars*, 201.

34. Phil Dixon, *Phil Dixon's American Baseball Chronicles: Great Teams: The 1931 Homestead Grays*, Vol. 1 (Bloomington, IN: Xlibris 2009), 296–97.

35. Frank Duncan Jr., personal interview, 15 November 1986.

36. Doyle, "Close-ups on the Sports Screen," n.p.

37. Isaminger, "Dizzy-Daffy Stars Lose Double Bill," 17.

38. Parris, "Deans Fail to Bring Luck to All-Stars," 16.

39. Holway, *Voices from the Great Black Baseball Leagues*, 83.

40. "Stan Baumgartner, "Just A Moment," *Philadelphia Inquirer*, 16 October 1934, n.p.

41. Phil Dixon, *Phil Dixon's American Baseball Chronicles: Great Teams: The 1905 Philadelphia Giants*, Vol. 2 (Booksurge: 2010), 262.

42. Doyle, "Close-ups on the Sports Screen," n.p.

Chapter 9

1. "Deans in Town for Game Tonight at Dexter Park," *New York World-Telegram*, 17 October 1934, 29.

2. Ed Hughes, "Ed Hughes's Column," *Brooklyn Daily Eagle*, 22 October 1934.

3. Frank Weitekamp, "Just Below the Majors," *Brooklyn Daily Eagle*, 23 September 1934, 13.

4. "Boland Missed as Bushwicks Lose Double," *Brooklyn Daily Eagle*, 24 September 1934, 10.

5. Harold Parrott, "Dizzy to Start 'Cashing in' at Dexter Park," *Brooklyn Daily Eagle*, 10 October 1934, 20.

6. Parrott, "Dizzy to Start 'Cashing in' at Dexter Park," 21.

7. "Dean Brothers to Fly Here for Bushwicks' Game," *New York World-Telegram*, 15 October 1934, 25.

8. "Deans to Pitch for Bushwicks," *Brooklyn Daily Eagle*, 17 October 1934, 21.

9. Ed Hughes, "Ed Hughes's Column," 20.

10. Ed Hughes, "Ed Hughes's Column," 20.

11. Ed Hughes, "Ed Hughes's Column," 20.

12. Henry McLemore, "Tired Deans," *Paterson Evening News*, 18 October 1934, 27.

13. "Deans Are Dizzy Now," *Kansas City Times*, 18 October 1934, 15.

14. "Deans Are Dizzy Now," 15.

15. Dan Daniel, "Daniel's Dope," *New York World-Telegram*, 18 October 1934, 36.

16. Daniel, "Daniel's Dope," 36.

17. C. C. Johnson Spink, *Daguerreotypes of Great Stars of Baseball* (St. Louis, MO: Sporting News, 1981).

18. Charles F. Faber, "Joe Medwick," *Society for American Baseball Research*, https://sabr.org/bioproj/person/8fed3607 (accessed June 28, 2017).

19. "The Dean Brothers Take Place among the Baseball Greats," *Kansas City Star*, 10 October 1934.

20. Letter from Robert F. Eisen, 3 December 1993.

21. "More Jews and Italians in Harlem than Negroes," *Kansas City Call*, 31 August 1934.

22. *Amsterdam News*.

23. Letter from Tom Baird to Lee MacPhail of the New York Yankees, 10 January 1949, author's collection.

24. "Black Yankees End Bushwicks Victory Streak," *Brooklyn Daily Eagle*, 27 August 1934, 7.

25. Rollo W. Wilson, "Off to Fine Start, the Yanks See Big Season," *Pittsburgh Courier*, 30 June 1934, A4.

26. Willard Brown, personal interviews, 1982.

27. Phil Dixon and Patrick J. Hannigan, *The Negro Baseball Leagues: A Photographic History* (Mattituck, NY: Amereon House, 1992), 92.

28. Dixon and Hannigan, *The Negro Baseball Leagues*, 92.

29. "Deans in Town for Game Tonight at Dexter Park," *World-Telegram*, 17 October 1934, 29.

30. Tom Reilly, "Dizzy 'n' Daffy in 'Fun in Brooklyn,'" *New York World-Telegram*, 18 October 1934, 36.

31. Reilly, "Dizzy 'n' Daffy in 'Fun in Brooklyn,'" 36

32. Reilly, "Dizzy 'n' Daffy in 'Fun in Brooklyn,'" 36.

33. John Holway, *Blackball Stars: Negro League Pioneers* (Westport, CT: Meckler Books, 1988), 94.

34. Harold Parrott, "Brooklyn Fans Yell Louder But Don't Know Baseball, Says Dizzy," *Brooklyn Daily Eagle*, 18 October 1934, 22.

35. Tom Reilly, "Escaped from a Chain Gang," *New York World-Telegram*, 18 October 1934, 36.

36. Parrott, "Brooklyn Fans Yell Louder But Don't Know Baseball," 22.

37. Robert Gregory, *Diz: The Story of Dizzy Dean and Baseball during the Great Depression* (New York: Viking, 1992), 242.

38. Parrott, "Brooklyn Fans Yell Louder But Don't Know Baseball," 22.

39. "Crawfords Smother National Leaguers," *York (PA) Dispatch*, 28 September 1932, Unknown.

40. Reilly, "Dizzy 'n' Daffy in 'Fun in Brooklyn,'" 36.

41. James P. Dawson, "15,000 See Deans Play Exhibition," *New York Times*, 18 October 1934, n.p.

42. Peter Morris, "Hank Grampp," *Society for American Baseball Research*, https://sabr.org/bioproj/person/acf72e29 (accessed July 1, 2017).

43. Parrott, "Brooklyn Fans Yell Louder But Don't Know Baseball," 22.

44. Dawson, "15,000 See Deans Play Exhibition," n.p.

45. John Kieran, "Sports of the Times," *New York Times*, 4 October, 1934, 27.

46. Holway, *Blackball Stars*, 94.

47. Reilly, "Dizzy 'n' Daffy in 'Fun in Brooklyn,'" 36.

48. "Dean Boys Flop in Exhibition Go," *Anniston Alabama Star*, 18 October 1934, 10.

49. "Dizzy's Two-Hyphen Descent," *Brooklyn Daily Eagle*, 16 October 1934, 20.

50. Parrott, "Brooklyn Fans Yell Louder But Don't Know Baseball," 22.

51. "Paul Dean Lame, Diz Tired, But Cash Rolls in So They Continue Barnstorm Travel," *Syracuse (NY) Herald*, 18 October 1934, n.p.

52. Harold Parrott, "Boro Fans Don't Know Game—Dizzy," *Brooklyn Daily Eagle*, 18 October 1934, 24.

53. Reilly, "Dizzy 'n' Daffy in 'Fun in Brooklyn,'" 36.

54. Parrott, "Boro Fans Don't Know Game—Dizzy," 24.

55. Reilly, "Dizzy 'n' Daffy in 'Fun in Brooklyn,'" 36.

56. Reilly, "Dizzy 'n' Daffy in 'Fun in Brooklyn,'" 36.

57. Parrott, "Brooklyn Fans Yell Louder But Don't Know Baseball," 22.

Chapter 10

1. "Dizzy and Paul Dean Here Tonight to Play in Oriole Park Game," *Baltimore Sun*, 18 October 1934.

2. "Dizzy Finds His Barnstorming Much Too Exciting for Fans," *Baltimore Sun*, 19 October 1934, 26.

3. Craig E. Taylor, "Dean Team Handed 4-to-0 Defeat in Night Exhibition at Oriole Park," *Baltimore Sun*, 19 October 1934, 26.

4. Taylor, "Dean Team Handed 4-to-0 Defeat in Night Exhibition at Oriole Park," 26.

5. "Deans Glad Jaunt Near the Finish," *Columbus Citizen Journal*, 22 October 1934, 17.

6. "Dizzy 'Dethrones' Ruth at Babe's Old School," *Sporting News*, 1 November 1934, 1.

7. Lewis E. Dial, "The Sports Dial," 1934.

8. "Sox Boss Tells Why No More Games Were Played in Baltimore," *Baltimore Afro-American*, 25 August 1934, 17.

9. "Dizzy 'Dethrones' Ruth at Babe's Old School," 1.

10. "Sox Boss Tells Why No More Games Were Played in Baltimore," 17.

11. "Finds His Tour Hard on Fans," *Baltimore Sun*, 19 October 1934, 16.

12. "Finds His Tour Hard on Fans," 16.

13. Tommy Holmes, "New Robin Shortstop Always Rated as Great Player in the Pinches," *Brooklyn Daily Eagle*, 14 December 1928, 6A.

14. John Holway, *Voices from the Great Black Baseball Leagues* (New York: Dodd, Mead, 1975), 81.

15. Donn Rogosin, *Invisible Men: Life in Baseball's Negro Leagues* (New York: Atheneum, 1983), 190–91.

16. "To Mr. Ruppert, Old Gold Cigarettes, and Citizens of Dayton, Ohio," *Chicago Defender*, 6 August 1938, 2.

17. "To Mr. Ruppert, Old Gold Cigarettes, and Citizens of Dayton, Ohio," 2.

18. Phil Dixon and Patrick J. Hannigan, *The Negro Baseball Leagues: A Photographic History* (Mattituck, NY: Amereon House, 1992), 253.

19. Dixon and Hannigan, *The Negro Baseball Leagues*, 254.

20. Dixon and Hannigan, *The Negro Baseball Leagues*, 254.

21. "Jake Powell Writes Dayton Police Exam," *Wisconsin State Journal*, 28 December 1942, 11.

22. "Powell, Ex-Yank Star, Is Suicide," *Cleveland Plain Dealer*, 5 November 1948, 1.

23. "Powell, Ex-Yank Star, Is Suicide," 1.

24. "Powell, Ex-Yank Star, Is Suicide," 1.

25. Taylor, "Dean Team Handed 4-to-0 Defeat in Night Exhibition at Oriole Park," 26.

26. "Ban Is Looming on Barnstorm Baseball Games," *Brooklyn Daily Eagle*, 16 October 1934, 22.

27. "Ban Is Looming on Barnstorm Baseball Games," 22.

Chapter 11

1. "Black Yankees Priming to Batter Dean Brothers Friday," *Paterson Morning Call*, 17 October 1934, 8.

2. "Deans Play in Paterson," *New York Times*, 20 October 1934, 12.

3. "Paterson Gets Peek at Dean Brothers," *Brooklyn Daily Eagle*, 20 October 1934.

4. Theon Wright, "Pitching Deans Will End Barn Storming Trip Soon," *Patterson Morning Call*, 18 October 1934, 17.

5. "Daffy Favors a Ban," *Macon Telegraph*, 19 October 1934, 8.

6. Lawrence B. Hogan, *Shades of Glory: The Negro Leagues and the Story of African American Baseball* (Washington, DC: National Geographic Society, 2006), 254–55.

7. "Barnstorming Is Still A Question," *Daily Boston Globe*, 19 October 1934, 31.

8. "Deans to Pitch Five Innings Here Tonight," *Paterson Evening News*, 17 October 1934, 21.

9. "Black Yankees Priming to Batter Dean Brothers," *Paterson Morning Call*, 17 October 1934, 8.

10. "He Plays Here Friday," *Paterson Evening News*, 15 October 1934, 18.

11. "Pitching Deans Will End Barn Storming Trip Soon," *Paterson Morning Call*, 18 October 1934, 27.

12. Theon Wright, "Pitching Deans Will End Barnstorming Trip Soon," *Paterson Morning Call*, 18 October 1934, 27.

13. Wright, "Pitching Deans Will End Barnstorming Trip Soon."

14. "Black Yankees Priming to Batter Dean Brothers Friday," *Paterson Evening News*, October 17, 1934.

15. "Black Yankees Priming to Batter Dean Brothers Friday," 8.

16. W. Rollo Wilson, "Off to Fine Start, the Yanks See Big Season," *Pittsburgh Courier*, 30 June 1934, A4.

17. "Deans Face Black Yankees Here Tonight," *Paterson Evening News*, 19 October 1934, 27.

18. Phil Dixon, *Phil Dixon's American Baseball Chronicles: Great Teams: The 1931 Homestead Grays*, Vol. 1 (Bloomington, IN: Xlibris, 2009), 158.

19. Dixon, *Phil Dixon's American Baseball Chronicles*, 158.

20. Lloyd Johnson and Miles Wolf, *The Encyclopedia of Minor League Baseball* (Durham, NC: Baseball America, 1993).

21. "Black Yankees Priming to Batter Dean Brothers," 8.

22. "Deans Aid Brooklyn Farmers in Defeating Black Yankees," *Paterson Morning Call*, 20 October 1934, page unknown;. "Deans, Farmers Triumph," *Paterson Evening News*, 20 October 1934, 24.

23. "Deans Play in Paterson," *New York Times*, 20 October 1934, 12.

24. "Deans Aid Brooklyn Farmers in Defeating Black Yankees," n.p.

25. "Dean's Farmers Triumph," *Paterson Evening News*, 20 October 1934, 24.

26. "Black Yankees Priming to Batter Dean Brothers Friday," 8.

27. "Nat C. Strong Dies Suddenly," *Queens Evening News*, 11 January 1935, n.p.

Chapter 12

1. "Great Jerome Is Scheduled to Hurl Three Innings for Rosies against Pittsburgh Crawfords," *Cleveland Plain Dealer*, 21 October 1934.

2. Bill Finger, "Dizzy Dean to Meet Satchel Paige Sunday," *Cleveland Call and Post*, 20 October 1934, 1.

3. Bill Finger, "Passing in Review," *Cleveland Call and Post*, 11 August 1934, 6.

4. "Trouble Brews as Cum Posey Takes Over Cleveland Park," *Kansas City American*, 21 March 1929, 5.

5. William F. McNeil, *The California Winter League* (Jefferson, NC: McFarland, 2002), 163.

6. Bill Finger, "Passing in Review," *Cleveland Call and Post*, 26 May 1934, 6.

7. "Schedules Unbalanced," *Cleveland Call and Post*, 15 October 1934, 6.

8. Neil Lanctot, *Fair Dealing and Clean Playing: The Hilldale Club and the Development of Black Professional Baseball, 1910–1932* (Jefferson, NC: McFarland, 1994).

9. Carlo Rotella and Michael Ezra, *The Bittersweet Science: Fifteen Writers in the Gym, in the Corner, and at Ringside* (Chicago: University of Chicago Press, 2017), 212.

10. Bill Finger. "Passing in Review," *Cleveland Call and Post*, 18 August 1934, 6.

11. James E. Doyle, "The Sport Trail," *Cleveland Plain Dealer*, 17 October 1934, 15.

12. Sam Brown, personal interviews, 1984.

13. Roelif Loveland, "Keep Dizzy Busy Hurling Ink Here," *Cleveland Plain Dealer*, 22 October 1934, 17.

14. Loveland, "Keep Dizzy Busy Hurling Ink Here," 17.

15. Bruce Anderson, "Time Worth Remembering," *Sports Illustrated*, 6 July 1981, 46.

16. Pat Gannon, "Is He Bragging?" *Milwaukee Journal Sentinel*, 14 October 1934, 21.

17. "Great Jerome Is Scheduled to Hurl Three Innings for Rosies against Pittsburgh Crawfords," 35.

18. Alex Zirin, "'Diz' and Daffy Make $3,000 in Clowning Here," *Cleveland Plain Dealer*, 22 October 1934, 17.

19. "Elden Auker Is No Admirer of the Boasting Dean Brothers," *Kansas City Star*, 21 October 1934, 4B.

20. "Elden Auker Is No Admirer of the Boasting Dean Brothers," 4B.

21. Phil Dixon, *Phil Dixon's American Baseball Chronicles: Great Teams: The 1931 Homestead Grays*, Vol. 1 (Bloomington, IN: Xlibris, 2009).

22. Dixon, *Phil Dixon's American Baseball Chronicles*.

23. Leroy "Satchel" Paige, *Maybe I'll Pitch Forever*. Edited by David Lipman (Lincoln: University of Nebraska Press, 1993), 91.

24. Bill Finger, "Deans Will Play Here," *Cleveland Call and Post*, 20 October 1934, 6.

25. "Plenty of Money for Dean Brothers on Exhibition Tour," *Cleveland Plain Dealer*, 15 October 1934, 18.

26. Chris Rainey, "Kenny Hogan," *Society for American Baseball Research*, https://sabr.org/bioproj/person/9c3ebb11 (accessed June 15, 2017).

27. Loveland, "Keep Dizzy Busy Hurling Ink Here," 17.

28. John Holway, *Black Giants* (Springfield, VA: Lord Fairfax Press, 2010), n.p.

29. Timothy M. Gay, *Satch, Dizzy, and Rapid Robert* (New York: Simon and Schuster, 2010).

30. "Negro Club Beats Deans," *Kansas City Times*, 22 October 1934.

31. Zirin, "'Diz' and Daffy Make $3,000 in Clowning Here."

32. John Holway, *Voices from the Great Black Baseball Leagues* (New York: Dodd, Mead, 1975), 97.

33. Holway, *Voices from the Great Black Baseball Leagues*, 97.

34. "Paige Strikes Out 13; Dizzy Gets a Lesson," *Kansas City Call*, 26 October 1934, n.p.

35. Bill Finger, "Satchel Paige Dominates Game," *Cleveland Call and Post*, 27 October 1934, 6.

36. Bill Finger, "Passing in Review," *Cleveland Call and Post*, 27 October 1934, 6.

37. Bill Dvorak, "Diz Gets Writer's Cramp," *Cleveland Press*, 22 October 1934, n.p.

38. Loveland, "Keep Dizzy Busy Hurling Ink Here," 17.

39. Dvorak, "Diz Gets Writer's Cramp," n.p.

40. Loveland, "Keep Dizzy Busy Hurling Ink Here," 17.

41. Finger, "Satchel Paige Dominates Game," 6.

42. "Negroes Have a Dizzy," *Milwaukee Journal Sentinel*, 16 September 1934, 21.

43. Dvorak, "Diz Gets Writer's Cramp," n.p.

44. Loveland, "Keep Dizzy Busy Hurling Ink Here," 17.

45. Dvorak, "Diz Gets Writer's Cramp."

46. "Satchel Paige Hands Beating to Dizzy Dean," *Chicago Defender*, 22 October 1934, 17.

47. Bill Finger, "Passing in Review," *Cleveland Call and Post*, 27 October 1934, 6.

Chapter 13

1. "Dizzy Dean to Be Opposed by Page," *Columbus Dispatch*, 19 October 1934, 16B.

2. "SEZ CHES," *Pittsburgh Courier*, 20 October 1934, A4.

3. "Dean Brothers to 'Teach' Baseball," *Arkansas Gazette*, 30 October 1934, 16.

4. "Dizzy Dean to Be Opposed by Page."

5. "Deans Are on Last Leg of Tour; Weary but Making Plenty Dough," *Findlay (OH) Republican*, 23 October 1934, 9.

6. "Dizzy and Daffy to Show Here Monday Night," *Columbus Dispatch*, 21 October 1934, 2C.

7. "A Bride for Paul Dean," *Kansas City Times*, 21 December 1934, 14.

8. "'Satchel' Says 'I Will' Twice," *Pittsburgh Courier*, 3 November 1934.

9. "Dizzy and Daffy to Show Here Monday Night," 2C.

10. Lloyd Johnson and Miles Wolf, *The Encyclopedia of Minor League Baseball* (Durham, NC: Baseball America, 1993), 182.

11. Johnson and Wolf, *The Encyclopedia of Minor League Baseball*, 180.

12. "Deans Glad Jaunt Near the Finish," *Columbus Citizen*, 22 October 1934, 17.

13. "Paul Doesn't Like This 'Daffy' Stuff but Says 'Dizzy' Is O.K. for His Brother," *Columbus Dispatch*, 22 October 1934, 1A.

14. "If Paul Wins 30, Deans Will Win 60," *Omaha World Herald*, 23 October 1934, 14.

15. "Deans Are on Last Leg of Tour," 9.

16. Tommy Holmes, "Dean Brothers Bubbling Over with Fame," *Brooklyn Daily Eagle*, 22 September 1934, 6.

17. "Craws–Grays Notes," *Pittsburgh Courier*, 7 July 1934, A5.

18. "Paige Hurls No-Hit, No-Run Game, 6 to 0," *Pittsburgh Post-Gazette*, 9 July 1932.

19. Johnson and Wolf, *The Encyclopedia of Minor League Baseball*.

20. "Paige, Jones to Face Dean Bros. in Columbus, Here, and in Cleveland," *Pittsburgh Courier*, 20 October 1934, A4.

21. Harry Beale, "Here's Beale's Idea of '34 Dream Team," *Pittsburgh Courier*, 20 October 1934, A4.

22. E. M. Gaynor, "Bert Gholston, Noted Umpire, Names All-Star Selection for 1934 Season," 22 September 1934.

23. Lloyd Johnson, *The Minor League Register* (Durham, NC: Baseball America, 1994).

24. Johnson, *The Minor League Register*.

25. Bill James, *The Bill James Historical Baseball Abstract* (New York: Villard, 1986), 152.

26. L. Robert Davids, "Nick Cullop: Minor League Great," *Society for American Baseball Research*, http://research.sabr.org/journals/nick-cullop (accessed April 27, 2017).

27. Johnson, *The Minor League Register*.

28. Johnson, *The Minor League Register*.

29. Bill Nowlin, "Bob Kline," *Society for American Baseball Research*, https://sabr.org/bioproj/person/af6fcb4c (accessed October 1, 2017).

30. Frank M. Colley, "Dean All-Stars Are Beaten by Crawfords," *Columbus Dispatch*, 23 October 1934, 4B.

31. "Promoter Doan Recalls Paige's Strikeout Feats," *Sporting News*, 29 September 1948, 14.

32. James "Cool Papa" Bell, personal interview, n.d.

33. Colley, "Dean All-Stars Are Beaten by Crawfords," 4B.

34. "Old-Timers Game Slated for Sunday," *New Orleans Times-Picayune*, 14 June 1968.

35. "Former Negro Pilot Is Dead," *New Orleans Times-Picayune*, 28 December 1965, 22.

36. "Paul Doesn't Like 'Daffy' Nickname," *Columbus Dispatch*, 22 October 1934, 6A.

37. Colley, "Dean All-Stars Are Beaten by Crawfords."

38. Bell, personal interview.

39. George Giles, personal interview, 1984.

40. "Dean Team Is Bumped," *Columbus Citizen*, 23 October 1934, 14.

41. Colley, "Dean All-Stars Are Beaten by Crawfords," 4B.

42. Colley, "Dean All-Stars Are Beaten by Crawfords," 4B.

43. "Fire Gives Deans Run," *Cleveland Plain Dealer*, 23 October 1934, 17.

44. "Dean Team Is Bumped," 14.

Chapter 14

1. James Doyle, *Pittsburgh Sun-Telegraph*, 24 October 1934, 35.

2. "Dizzy and Daffy Play Here Today," *Pittsburgh Post-Gazette*, 23 October 1934, 15.

3. James Doyle, "Riot Quelled as Deans Lose Final Fray," *Pittsburgh Sun-Telegraph*, 23 October 1934, 35.

4. Tommy Holmes, "Baseball Newsreel," *Brooklyn Daily Eagle*, 9 September 1934, A11.

5. Doyle, "Riot Quelled as Deans Lose Final Fray," 35.

6. Lloyd Johnson and Miles Wolf, *The Encyclopedia of Minor League Baseball* (Durham, NC: Baseball America, 1993).

7. Bill Nowlin, "Moose Solters," *Society for American Baseball Research*, https://sabr.org/bioproj/person/56581108 (accessed October 1, 2017).

8. Doyle, "Riot Quelled as Deans Lose Final Fray," 35.

9. "Deans to Gun for Pirates New Year," *Pittsburgh Sun-Telegraph*, 24 October 1934, 24.

10. "Deans to Gun for Pirates New Year," 24.

11. Volney Walsh, "Deans Go on Stage, It Should Be Good," *Pittsburgh Press*, 24 October, 1934, n.p.

12. "Dizzy Dean to Demand $25,000, Paul $15,000, for Next Season," *Sporting News*, 1 November 1934, 1.

13. Walsh, "Deans Go on Stage," n.p.

14. Phil Dixon, *Phil Dixon's American Baseball Chronicles: Great Teams: The 1931 Homestead Grays*, Vol. 1 (Bloomington, IN: Xlibris, 2009).

15. Edward Balinger, "Near Riot Marks Deans' Exhibition Here," *Pittsburgh Post-Gazette*, 24 October 1934.

16. Walsh, "Deans Go on Stage," n.p.

17. Doyle, "Riot Quelled as Deans Lose Final Fray," 35.

18. Doyle, "Riot Quelled as Deans Lose Final Fray," 35.

19. John Holway, *Blackball Tales: Rollicking, All New, True Adventures of the Negro Leagues by the Men Who Lived and Loved Them* (Springfield, VA: Scorpio Books, 2008), 66.

20. Chet Brewer, personal interview, 6 July 1987.

21. Balinger, "Near Riot Marks Deans' Exhibition Here," 15.

22. Doyle, "Riot Quelled as Deans Lose Final Fray," 35.

23. Balinger, "Near Riot Marks Deans' Exhibition Here," 15.

24. Doyle, "Riot Quelled as Deans Lose Final Fray," 35.

25. Doyle, "Riot Quelled as Deans Lose Final Fray," 35.

26. "Vic Harris to 'Bat' in Court," *Pittsburgh Courier*, 16 February 1935, 1.

27. Doyle, "Riot Quelled as Deans Lose Final Fray," 35.

28. Long.

29. "Vic Harris to 'Bat' in Court," 1.

30. Balinger, "Near Riot Marks Deans' Exhibition Here," 15.

31. "Vic Harris to 'Bat' in Court," 1.

32. "Vic Harris to 'Bat' in Court," 1.

33. Balinger, "Near Riot Marks Deans' Exhibition Here."

34. Walsh, "Deans Go on Stage," n.p.

35. John Holway, "Negro League Star Harris Dead, Club Won 134 Games in Season," *Washington Post*, 26 February 1978, M13.

36. "Players Use Fists; Deans' Exhibition Game Marred by a Free-for-All," *Kansas City Times*, 24 October 1934, 10.

37. "Fight Enlivens Deans Game at Pittsburgh Park," *Monroe (LA) News-Star*, 24 October 1934, 6.

38. "Riot Marks Game of Deans and Pittsburgh Negro Club," *Butte (MT) Standard*, 24 October 1934, 8.

39. "Police Stop Fight at Deans' Contest," *New York Times*, 24 October 1934, 28.

40. "Dizzy Almost Starts Riot as Trip Ends" *Sheboygan (WI) Press*, 24 October 1934, 10.

41. "Free-for-All Fight as Dean Boys Lose," *Hartford Courant*, 24 October 1934, 17.

42. "Fight Features Final Game of Touring Deans," *Chicago Tribune*, 24 October 1934, 19.

43. "Free-for-All Fight Marks End of Deans' Barnstorming," *Logansport (IN) Press*, 24 October 1934, 5.

44. Doyle, "Riot Quelled as Deans Lose Final Fray," 35.

45. Cumberland Posey, "Cum Posey's Pointed Paragraphs," *Pittsburgh Courier*, 23 February 1935, A4.

46. Posey, "Cum Posey's Pointed Paragraphs," A4.

47. Holway, "Negro League Star Harris Dead, Club Won 134 Games in Season," M13.

Chapter 15

1. Roger Burns, *Negro Leagues Baseball* (Santa Barbara, CA: Greenwood, 2012), 53.

2. "Old Diz Names Paige Greatest Pitcher," *Metropolitan Post*, 24 September 1938, 15.

3. "Dean Brothers to Teach Baseball," *Arkansas Gazette*, 30 October 1934, 16.

4. James Doyle, "Riot Quelled as Deans Lose Final Fray," *Pittsburgh Sun-Telegraph*, 23 October 1934, 24.

5. "Dumpsterpiece Theater #38, Dizzy and Daffy," *YouTube*, February 21, 2007, https://www.youtube.com/watch?v=CMIwFgp4lWc (accessed October 1, 2017).

6. "Dumpsterpiece Theater #38, Dizzy and Daffy."

7. "Dizzy Dean to Demand $25,000, Paul $15,000, for Next Season," *Sporting News*, 1 November 1934.

8. Robert Gregory, *Diz: The Story of Dizzy Dean and Baseball during the Great Depression* (New York: Viking, 1992).

~

Bibliography

Alpert, Rebecca T. *Out of Left Field: Jews and Black Baseball*. New York: Oxford University Press, 2011.

Auker, Elden, with Tom Keegan . *Sleeper Cars and Flannel Uniforms: A Lifetime of Memories from Striking Out the Babe to Teeing It Up with the President*. Chicago: Triumph, 2001.

Benson, Michael. *Ballparks of North America: A Comprehensive Historical Reference to Baseball Grounds, Yards, and Stadiums, 1845 to Present*. Jefferson, NC: McFarland, 1989.

Berkow, Ira. *Hank Greenberg: The Story of My Life*. New York: Times Books, 1989.

Brashler, William. *Josh Gibson: A Life in the Negro Leagues*. New York: Harper and Row, 1978.

Breslin, Jimmy. *Branch Rickey*. New York: Viking, 2011.

Bruce, Janet. *The Kansas City Monarchs: Champions of Black Baseball*. Lawrence: University of Kansas Press, 1985.

Bruns, Roger. *Negro Leagues Baseball*. Santa Barbara, CA: Greenwood, 2012.

Chadwick, Bruce. *When the Game Was Black and White: The Illustrated History of Baseball's Negro Leagues*. New York: Abbeville Press, 1992.

Chalk, Ocania. *Black College Sport*. New York: Dodd, Mead, 1976.

Craft, Jerry, with Kathleen Sullivan. *Our White Boy*. Foreword by Larry Lester. Lubbock: Texas Tech University Press, 2010.

Dixon, Phil. *Phil Dixon's American Baseball Chronicles: Great Teams: The 1905 Philadelphia Giants*, Vol. 2. BookSurge, 2010.

———. *Phil Dixon's American Baseball Chronicles: Great Teams: The 1931 Homestead Grays*, Vol. 1. Bloomington, IN: Xlibris, 2009.

Dixon, Phil, and Patrick J. Hannigan. *The Negro Baseball Leagues: A Photographic History*. Mattituck, New York: Amereon House, 1992.

Dunkel, Tom. *Color Blind: The Team That Broke Baseball's Color Line*. New York: Grove Press, 2013.

Feldman, Doug. *Dizzy and the Gashouse Gang: The 1934 St. Louis Cardinals and Depression-Era Baseball*. Jefferson, NC: McFarland, 2000.

Fink, Rob. *Playing in Shadows: Texas and Negro League Baseball*. Foreword by Cary D. Wintz. Lubbock: Texas Tech University Press, 2010.

Gay, Timothy M. *Satch, Dizzy, and Rapid Robert*. New York: Simon and Schuster, 2010.

Gregory, Robert. *Diz: The Story of Dizzy Dean and Baseball during the Great Depression*. New York: Viking, 1992.

Hardwick, Leon Herbert. *Blacks in Baseball*. Los Angeles, CA: Pilot Press, 1980.

Heapy, Leslie A., ed. *Satchel Paige and Company: Essays on the Kansas City Monarchs, Their Greatest Star, and the Negro Leagues*. Jefferson, NC: McFarland, 2007.

Heidenry, John. *The Gashouse Gang: How Dizzy Dean, Leo Durocher, Branch Rickey, Pepper Martin, and Their Colorful, Come-from-Behind Ball Club Won the World Series—and America's Heart—during the Great Depression*. New York: Public Affairs, 2007.

Hogan, Lawrence B. *Shades of Glory: The Negro Leagues and the Story of African American Baseball*. Washington, DC: National Geographic Society, 2006.

Holway, John. *Black Diamonds: Life in the Negro Leagues from the Men Who Lived It*. New York: Stadium Books, 1991.

———. *Black Giants*. Springfield, VA: Lord Fairfax Press, 2010.

———. *Blackball Stars: Negro League Pioneers*. Westport, CT: Meckler Books, 1988.

———. *Blackball Tales: Rollicking, All New, True Adventures of the Negro Leagues by the Men Who Lived and Loved Them*. Springfield, VA: Scorpio Books, 2008.

———. *Josh and Satch: The Life and Times of Josh Gibson and Satchel Paige*. New York: Carroll and Graf, 1992.

———. *Voices from the Great Black Baseball Leagues*. New York: Dodd, Mead, 1975.

———. *Voices from the Great Black Baseball Leagues*, revised ed. New York: Da Capo, 1992.

James, Bill. *The Bill James Historical Baseball Abstract*. New York: Villard, 1986.

———. *The New Bill James Historical Baseball Abstract*. New York: Free Press, 2001.

Johnson, Lloyd. *The Minor League Register*. Durham, NC: Baseball America, 1994.

Johnson, Lloyd, and Miles Wolf. *The Encyclopedia of Minor League Baseball*. Durham, NC: Baseball America, 1993.

Kountze, Mabe "Doc." *50 Sports Years Along Memory Lane*. Medford, MA: Mystic Valley Press, 1979.

Lanctot, Neil. *Fair Dealing and Clean Playing: The Hilldale Club and the Development of Black Professional Baseball, 1910–1932*. Jefferson, NC: McFarland, 1994.

Lowenfish, Lee. *Branch Rickey: Baseball's Ferocious Gentleman*. Lincoln: University of Nebraska Press, 2009.

Lowry, Philip J. *Green Cathedrals: The Ultimate Celebration of All 271 Major League and Negro League Ballparks Past and Present.* Reading, MA: Addison-Wesley, 1992.

Major League Baseball. *The Baseball Encyclopedia.* New York: Macmillan, 1969.

McNeil, William F. *The California Winter League.* Jefferson, NC: McFarland, 2002.

Nemec, David. *The Great Encyclopedia of 19th-Century Major League Baseball.* New York: Donald I. Fine Books, 1997.

Paige, Leroy "Satchel." *Maybe I'll Pitch Forever.* Edited by David Lipman. Lincoln: University of Nebraska Press, 1993.

―――. *Pitchin' Man.* Edited by Hal Lebovitz. Bronx, NY: Ishi Press International, 1948.

Peterson, Robert. *Only the Ball Was White: A History of Legendary Black Players and All-Black Professional Teams.* New York: Gramercy Books, 1999.

Ribowsky, Mark. *A Complete History of the Negro Leagues, 1884 to 1955.* New York: Carol, 1995.

―――. *Don't Look Back: Satchel Paige in the Shadows of Baseball.* New York: Da Capo, 1994.

Ritter, Lawrence S. *The Glory of Their Times: The Story of the Early Days of Baseball Told by the Men Who Played It,* new ed. New York: William Morrow, 1992.

―――. *The Image of Their Greatness: An Illustrated History of Baseball from 1900 to the Present,* 3rd ed. New York: Crown Trade Paperbacks, 1992.

Rogosin, Donn. *Invisible Men: Life in Baseball's Negro Leagues.* New York: Atheneum, 1983.

Rotella, Carlo, and Michael Ezra, eds. *The Bittersweet Science: Fifteen Writers in the Gym, in the Corner, and at Ringside.* Chicago: University of Chicago Press, 2017.

Ruck, Rob. *Sandlot Seasons: Sport in Black Pittsburgh.* Urbana: University of Illinois Press, 1987.

Rust, Jr. Art, *Get That Nigger Off the Field.* New York: Delacorte, 1976.

Smith, Curt. *America's Dizzy Dean.* St. Louis, MO: Chalice Press, 1978.

Spink, C. C. Johnson. *Daguerreotypes of Great Stars of Baseball.* St. Louis, MO: Sporting News, 1981.

Spivey, Donald. *"If You Were Only White": The Life of Leroy "Satchel" Paige.* Columbia: University of Missouri Press, 2012.

Staten, Vince. *Ol' Diz: A Biography of Dizzy Dean.* New York: HarperCollins, 1992.

Thorn, John, et al. *Total Baseball: The Official Encyclopedia of Major League Baseball.* New York: Total Sports, 1999.

Trouppe, Quincy. *Twenty Years Too Soon: Prelude to Integrated Major League Baseball.* Los Angeles, CA: S. and S. Enterprises, 1977.

Tye, Larry. *Satchel: The Life and Times of an American Legend.* New York: Random House, 2009.

Tygiel, Jules. *Baseball's Great Experiment: Jackie Robinson and His Legacy.* New York: Oxford University Press, 1983.

―――. *Past Time: Baseball as History.* New York: Oxford University Press, 2000.

Veeck, Bill, with Ed Linn. *Veeck—as in Wreck: The Autobiography of Bill Veeck.* Chicago: University of Chicago Press, 2001.
Westcott, Rich. *Philadelphia's Old Ballparks.* Philadelphia, PA: Temple University Press, 1996.

Newspapers and Reporters' Research

Daily Newspapers

Associated Press (AP), Paul Mickelson, James B. Reston
Baltimore Sun, Craig E. Taylor
Brooklyn Daily Eagle, Harold Parrott
Chicago Tribune, none listed
Cleveland News, Ed McAuley
Cleveland Plain Dealer, Alex Zirin, Roelif Loveland
Cleveland Press, Bill Dvorak
Columbus Citizen, none listed
Columbus Dispatch, Frank M. Colley
Daily Oklahoman, Bus Ham
Des Moines Register, Doyl Taylor
Des Moines Tribune, Jack North
Kansas City Journal-Post, none listed
Kansas City Star, C. E. McBride
Kansas City Times, C. E. McBride
Milwaukee Journal, Sam Levy
Milwaukee Leader, Ben Smith
Milwaukee Sentinel, Ronald McIntyre
New York Times, James P. Dawson
New York World-Telegram, Tom Reilly, Dan Daniel
Oklahoma News, Frances Corry, Meredith Williams
Paterson Morning Call, Theon Wright
Philadelphia Evening Bulletin, Lynn Doyle, Cy Peterman
Philadelphia Inquirer, none listed
Philadelphia Record, Paul Parris, Stan Baumgartner, Bill Dooly
Pittsburgh Post-Gazette, Edward F. Balinger
Pittsburgh Press, Volney Walsh
Pittsburgh Sun-Telegraph, James L. Long
Queens Evening News, none listed
United Press International (UPI), Henry McLemore, Theon Wright
Wichita Eagle, Peter Lightner
Wisconsin News, Howard Purser

Minority Newspapers

Associated Negro Press (ANP), Dan Burley, Al Monroe
Baltimore Afro-American, Bill Gibson
Chicago Defender, Julius J. Adams
Cleveland Call and Post, L. R. Williams, William Finger
Kansas City Call, L. Herbert Henegan, Fay Young
Negro Star (Wichita, Kansas), Bennie Williams
New York Age, C. Augustus Austin, Lewis E. Dial
Pittsburgh Courier, W. Rolo Wilson

Index

~

About the Author

For more than 35 years, author/historian Phil S. Dixon has recorded African American baseball with a vast array of creativity and historical accuracy. He has written numerous books on baseball and is highly regarded for his expertise on baseball history. He won the prestigious Casey Award for the Best Baseball Book of 1992 and later received the SABR (Society for American Baseball Research) MacMillan Award for his excellence as a researcher, along with a host of other honors and awards. His contributions to baseball can be found on the backs of baseball cards, in award-winning books, and in nationally recognized documentaries. He has appeared on PBS's *History Detectives*, C-SPAN, BET, Fox Sports, National Public Radio, the Canadian Broadcasting System, SiriusXM Radio, and other national broadcast media.

Dixon served as an inner-city baseball coach for more than 25 years and an advisor to Kansas City's RBI (Reviving Baseball in Inner Cities) youth baseball program. He is a cofounder and current board member for the Negro Leagues Baseball Museum in Kansas City, where he serves on its advisory board. In professional sports, Dixon formerly worked in the public relations office of the American League Kansas City Royals—he is a walking encyclopedia of baseball history, in general, and is most knowledgeable about African Americans in baseball. In addition to these activities, he is an excellent speaker who routinely give presentations at colleges, universities, civic events, corporations, and educational activities.

Dixon is a prolific speaker on the history of the Negro Leagues and Negro baseball. In January 2014, he began a tour of 200 cities and towns where the once-famous Kansas City Monarchs and other African American teams and players barnstormed. His goal was to spread goodwill and improve racial relationships through baseball history in the places where it actually occurred. The tour visited 17 states, as well as an international visit to Saskatchewan, Canada, and ended in 2018. Uniquely, Dixon refused to fly during his travels in honor of the fact that African Americans did not fly during the Negro League barnstorming. He is featured in two award-winning documentaries: *First Boys of Spring*, released in 2015, and *Kansas Town Teams, Bigger Than Baseball*, released in 2016. Dixon is a graduate of the University of Missouri at Kansas City, and lives outside of Kansas City, Missouri, with his wife, Dr. Kerry Dixon, and children.